The Complete Guide to
Edible Wild Plants, Mushrooms, Fruits, and Nuts

THE COMPLETE GUIDE TO
EDIBLE WILD PLANTS, MUSHROOMS, FRUITS, AND NUTS

Finding, Identifying, and Cooking

THIRD EDITION

KATIE LETCHER LYLE

GUILFORD, CONNECTICUT

An imprint of Rowman & Littlefield.
Falcon and FalconGuides are registered trademarks and
Make Adventure Your Story is a trademark of Rowman & Littlefield.

Distributed by NATIONAL BOOK NETWORK

Copyright © 2004, 2010, 2017 by Katie Letcher Lyle

Photos by Katie Lyle and Nick Charles unless otherwise noted.

The following poems have been reprinted by permission: "Morels," by William Jay Smith, reprinted by permission of the Johns Hopkins University Press, © 1998 by William Jay Smith, *The World Below the Window: Poems 1937–1997*; "The Hermit Picks Berries," by Maxine Kumin from *Selected Poems 1960–1990*, published by W. Norton Co., Inc., © 1972 by Maxine Kumin.

British Library Cataloguing-in-Publication Information available
The Library of Congress has catalogued a previous edition as follows:
Names: Lyle, Katie Latcher Lyle,1938- author.
Title: Complete guide to edible wild plants, mushrooms, fruits, and nuts : how to find, identify, and cook them / Katie Letcher Lyle.
Description: Guilford : FalconGuides, 2010. | Includes bibliographical references and index. | "Distributed by NATIONAL BOOK NETWORK"—T.p. verso.
Identifiers: LCCN 2010011383| ISBN 9781599218878 (paperback : alk. paper).
Subjects: LCSH: Cooking (Wild foods). | Wild plants, Edible—North America.
Classification: LCC HDTX823 | DDC 641.6–dc22 LC record available at https://lccn.loc.gov/2010011383

ISBN 978-1-4930-1864-2 (paperback)
ISBN 978-1-4930-1865-9 (e-book)

Printed in India

This book is a work of reference. Readers should always consult an expert before using any foraged item. The author, editors, and publisher of this work have checked with sources believed to be reliable in their efforts to confirm the accuracy and completeness of the information presented herein and that the information is in accordance with the standard practices accepted at the time of publication. However, neither the author, editors, and publisher, nor any other party involved in the creation and publication of this work warrant that the information is in every respect accurate and complete, and they are not responsible for errors or omissions or for any consequences from the application of the information in this book. In light of ongoing research and changes in clinical experience and in governmental regulations, readers are encouraged to confirm the information contained herein with additional sources. This book does not purport to be a complete presentation of all plants, and the genera, species, and cultivars discussed or pictured herein are but a small fraction of the plants found in the wild, in an urban or suburban landscape, or in a home. Given the global movement of plants, we would expect continual introduction of species having toxic properties to the regions discussed in this book. We have made every attempt to be botanically accurate, but regional variations in plant names, growing conditions, and availability may affect the accuracy of the information provided. A positive identification of an individual plant is most likely when a freshly collected part of the plant containing leaves and flowers or fruits is presented to a knowledgeable botanist or horticulturist. Poison Control Centers generally have relationships with the botanical community should the need for plant identification arise. We have attempted to provide accurate descriptions of plants, but there is no substitute for direct interaction with a trained botanist or horticulturist for plant identification. **In cases of exposure or ingestion, contact a Poison Control Center (800-222-1222), a medical toxicologist, another appropriate healthcare provider, or an appropriate reference resource.**

For my longtime morelling companion
Burwell Wingfield, and in memory of Janet Lembke,
whose wild crabmeat and wild essays nourish my body
and spirit, and in memory of my friend Marjorie Bendl,
who now forages in greener fields.

Whenever you see a field like this, stop and gather wonderful greens of the mustard family year-round.

Contents

Acknowledgments

My warmest thanks and love to all the friends who made this project such fun: the librarians and friends I asked questions of, those who tried out the recipes, intrepid foragers who went with me, tolerant cronies who put up with my obsessions and cheered me on. They are: Karen Bailey, LuAnn Balfry, Georgianna Brush, Carolyn Cox, Andy Johnson, Wendy Knick, Cynthia LaRue, John Letcher, Peter Letcher, Lisa McCown and C. Vaughan Stanley of the Washington and Lee University Rare Books Collection, Grace McCrowell of the Rockbridge Regional Library, my dear agent Sally Hill McMillan, Hope Mihalap, General "Jimmy" Morgan, Mario Pellicciaro, Sarah Rorrer, Edgar Shew, Tommy Spencer, Suzie Thompson, Frances Tolley, Martha Boyden Williams, Chris Wise, Maureen Worth, Rebecca Worth, and, as always, my fan club, to whom I'm most grateful—my wonderful children, Cochran and Jennie, and my deceased husband, Royster. I also want to thank my wonderful partner, George Roland (Nick) Charles, for his support of my work these last twelve years.

The author gathers watercress.

Introduction

I've been a forager all my life. My earliest foraging memory comes from San Diego, when I was only three, in 1941. We had been to the beach, my father and I, and were homeward bound in late afternoon when we crossed Mission Bay at low tide and Daddy spotted lobsters, trapped when the tide went out. All we had to collect them in was my potty, so we waded in and scooped lobsters out of the sandy pools. Three of them, and the pot was bulging. Back at the car, we found it wouldn't start, so we walked to the nearest streetcar line to wait for the next trolley (still in our bathing suits) with the potty containing the indignant lobsters. We rode the crowded trolley home, juggling the potty to keep the frantic denizens corralled, to the delight of the other commuters. At home, Mama was horrified that we had made such a scene, had been practically nude in public!

Polyporous virginiensis

But Daddy winked at me. His face was shining with pleasure, and I savored the delight of being regarded as a maverick. I loved the attention we had attracted; it was most certainly preferable to Mama standing fully dressed, hands on hips, frowning disapprovingly at her two happy, bad kids. To my mother, one of the worst sins was to make a spectacle of yourself.

So early in my life, foraging became a source of pleasure; it meant taking a walk out in some gorgeous place; it meant finding some treasure; it meant getting something for nothing. In California, there was always something ripe: We'd stop and gather windfall oranges along the road, olives out of a wild grove, garlic, figs as pink and sweet as candy, and avocados that had rolled from a lawn onto the street. Always, I felt lucky and happy to be along with Daddy on a treasure hunt.

During World War II, my father went to the Pacific, and my mother, my brother, and I moved back to Virginia and lived with my paternal grandparents, whose lives were very different from the civilized life my mother had in mind for her children. They had a black cook, primitive plumbing, and a dog, and they lived in a wonderful, dirty old house full of fusty Victorian antiques and pictures of ancestors and saints.

Andaddy, my grandfather, who called me "Little Sweetheart," took me in hand, led me down to the creek in the woods down back, and showed me how to catch crawfish and where the watercress grew. On the way home, he pointed out an immense pawpaw patch not far from the house, which would have ripe fruits like bananas later on. He handed me sour grass to eat, comparing it to clover so I could always tell the difference, and warned me not to eat buttercups (poisonous, he said). He drove me in his ancient Model T Ford, which he dubbed his "confounded machine," up into the mountains, where I found wild strawberries and my first, but not last, case of chiggers. On the way, he told me the world's biggest diamond, over fifty pounds, had been found near here, just over the border in West Virginia, so I should keep an eye out. The people who'd found it had used it as a doorstop for years before they learned it was a diamond, he told me.

Turns out, the story was, like so many others, not totally the truth. The largest diamond ever found in North America, the Punch Jones diamond, weighing almost thirty-five carats, was indeed discovered in the dirt of a horseshoe pit in 1928 near Peterstown, West Virginia, and later discovered at Virginia Tech to indeed be a diamond, and not just a quartz crystal as originally thought. It was displayed for a while at the Smithsonian and sold in 1984 at Sotheby's for about sixty thousand dollars. But it certainly wasn't used as a doorstop, being only about three-fourths of an inch across.

Why would you want to risk life and limb looking for wild food? Well, it's free, and food costs rise all the time. I once donated many (like twenty or thirty) bags of fresh watercress to our local health food store when it was having a hard time. Each bag sold for about three dollars. Only time prevented my doing twice as much, three times as much. A restaurant in Charlottesville once called me (in the days I was famous as a morel finder) and offered me forty bucks a pound for morels—but I wasn't interested, as I wanted all I found for myself. And I feel certain that wild foods add substantial vitamins and minerals to your diet. And I just love being in the woods. It's gotta be more fun than aerobics, right?

In summer, we'd fish for small bass and perch that lived in the Maury River, and I'd get a history lesson about Matthew Fontaine Maury, the Pathfinder of the Seas. Maury fascinated me for a macabre reason: He left instructions that his body be kept until the rhododendrons bloomed again in Goshen Pass and he could be carried through, presumably for one last glance at their pure beauty. His wishes were honored, and VMI (Virginia Military Institute) cadets did just as he instructed—three months after his February death. I couldn't stop wondering how they managed to do that. Still don't know.

Andaddy'd tell me about the big eels that spawned upriver all the way to Lexington until the big dams were built for electricity. In August, we'd collect the pears that grew from a wild tree in their yard, and I'd help Lizzie make pear-ginger conserve, which we'd eat all winter on ice cream. Sometimes we'd look for pawpaws. In fall, two days after the first frost, Andaddy and I would go to shake persimmons out of a tree he knew of. He taught me how to crack and pick the black walnuts that fell all over the big yard.

I loved all of it from the first. It was in my blood to forage. Later in my life, I chose my husband for his woodsy ways, and he and I chose our 1867 house at least in part because of the three gigantic hundred-year-old sugar maples in the yard, which we tapped early each spring, and the two ancient apple trees—one full of wonderful sour June apples that were too sour to eat but cooked up better applesauce and apple butter than I've ever tasted, and the other with hard little black twig October apples worthless for cooking but wonderful for eating off the tree or when smashed into cider.

In the wet summer of 1969, which culminated in the destructive killer Hurricane Camille that August, I taught myself about fungi, and I collected, cataloged, and ate, or at least tasted, over two hundred different kinds. Our children grew up knowing plants and eating wineberries, watercress, and puffballs.

Maple syrup, morels, oyster mushrooms, and watercress are all delicacies, and all of them cost dearly when you find them in stores. Yet all are free to those who go looking for them.

Foraging has got to be good for you; in our world of deadlines and noise and air pollution, the meditative calm of walking in fields or woods is restorative. The gentle exercise is healing. Emerson was right: Nature is loved by what is best in us. And the trophy of a basket of mushrooms, a bunch of pungent mint, or a bag of fragrant fresh-ground cornmeal makes you want to crow with pride. In addition, foraging is a pastime that anyone can take up at any age, and one that can last a lifetime. It's a hobby that costs nothing.

One of our children was born with cerebral palsy and mental retardation, yet Jennie has always been able to enjoy our expeditions to the woods, our long walks in search of good things to eat, our forays to a creek after watercress. I am sure she can walk better than she might have without a family committed to being often outdoors. She takes great pride in knowing her birds and being able to identify many plants.

In all, foraging is a healthy pursuit, a safe and profitable hobby, a pleasure that the entire family, any family, can enjoy, a treat for visitors, an adventure for any season. In this, the third edition of this book, I have added some questionable plants—nothing poisonous or dangerous, but plants that were left out of the first and second editions for generally good reason: I don't think they're quite as delicious as the ones already here. On the other hand, this edition includes an exciting new fungus, if the information about it is true, and even a plant that has appeared in our woods since the first edition of this book, an invasive nuisance—but absolutely delicious and beneficial—garlic mustard. It didn't grow here when this encyclopedia first appeared, over twenty years ago. It's now taken over eastern woods. It literally grows hereabouts everywhere! As do Autumn Olives.

Although foraging may be more easily within the reach of a small-town or rural population than it is for city folk, cities contain parks and vacant lots. Even if we don't own wild land, we still have access to woods in the form of national forests and national parks. And we ignore so much free food. I've personally seen unpicked ripe blackberries in New York City's Central Park, lamb's-quarters growing profusely in a vacant lot in Queens, and mulberries staining the sidewalks of a downtown Baltimore neighborhood where I lived. Just today, I ate radish greens from the store as I was contemplating my revisions of this book. They were delicious, but we don't usually eat them. I steamed them, salted them, and sprinkled them with vinegar.

Euell Gibbons, the acknowledged American authority on wild foods, has proved beyond a doubt that many wild plants are indeed edible, and even salubrious. However, Gibbons's criterion was edibility; mine has always been taste. The average, but resourceful, enthusiast can enjoy the fruits of foraging most of the year—all of the year if you own a freezer.

Wild food, of course, grows without insecticides, without human manipulation. Plants at the highway's edge may receive the residue from automobile exhaust, so pick a few feet away from roads. Always wash wild food with as much care as you would foods from the supermarket.

Gathering wild food, getting something wonderful for nothing, is one of life's greatest pleasures, and may, if we listen respectfully to the voice of "the folk," enhance health and even cure illness. In this book, I have given some attention to the folklore of the plants, including medicinal uses, as well as recipes for your delectation. Certainly, the early settlers used plants thoughtfully, believing in specific efficacies through observation and contact with aboriginal Americans, as well as relying on the knowledge and plants they brought from Europe. Folk medicine is not to be taken lightly. For instance, it was recorded often that Native Americans cured cancer by ingesting mayapple; they knew when and how to employ that poisonous plant. By taking folk claims seriously, and testing the mayapple, modern medicine has isolated a cure for testicular cancer from mayapple resin, thus saving thousands of men's lives. When remedies using wild plants are tested by sophisticated pharmaceutical companies, the results are often impressive.

Midwives in the distant past doctored other women and children and their own menfolk. But beginning in the late medieval period, male physicians trained at European universities refused to use any methods they had not been taught there, and midwifery became second-class medicine. Appalachian midwives have traditionally (but very quietly) prescribed one teaspoon of the dried seeds of Queen Anne's lace in one glass of water, drunk the morning after intercourse, as an effective post-coital method of birth control. Only recently, and by accident, an archaeologist "rediscovered" this method in an ancient Latin inscription. The two branches of medicine, folk and academic, have only recently begun to share information, and it is exciting to see folk remedies and procedures exonerated.

About Plant Names

Plants are officially known by their genus and species names, and it's not only a good mental exercise to learn the proper botanical names of the plants you gather and eat, but it will also help prevent confusion. Folk names change from one part of the country to another. Though the tendency in botanical nomenclature is toward uniformity, plant designations change all the time. Thus, species of plants are not entirely fixed either. Separating species and varieties is still an imperfect science.

The problem is not naming, but identifying. Plant identification is about three centuries old; formalized spelling is not that old. Occasionally, different spellings are both correct: *virginiana* and *virginica* are both acceptable, and *chinensis* and *sinensis* may both be applied to a plant that was first discovered in China. Standardization is slow, especially as serious botanists still disagree about how to categorize plants, arguing over minute characteristics. In nature, there is simply no finality, especially in a world where botanists believe that we have discovered and classified only about half of the plants that exist. However, when learning about plants, do learn the proper nomenclature. For instance, there are possibly twenty different berries known locally or regionally as "deerberries," since deer eat them. If you were to tell the emergency room staff you'd eaten little red berries and gotten a stomachache, they might not know how to treat you. If, on the other hand, you can tell them you accidentally ate *Solanum dulcamara*, they will know just what to do for you.

A Word about Cooking Methods

I've found "cooking by process" works best for me. This means learning a basic process, such as preparing soufflés or pizza, and then varying that process according to your own taste, available ingredients, whether you're cutting down on fat, and so on. A simple example of process cooking is rice. The process of cooking rice does not vary often. Measure your rice, then measure twice as much water. Bring that water to a boil, add the rice slowly, stir, bring it to a boil again, reduce the heat to low, cover the pan, and cook it without stirring until the rice has absorbed the water. Easy to do, easy to remember. But you can salt it or not, add a pat of butter or a little oil, some dried herbs or some chopped vegetables, or nothing.

The beauty of this process approach to cooking is that learning ten or twenty basic processes frees you to become a creative cook and to make an endless number of dishes. Once you've learned a process, many variations are possible. I often will give you imprecise amounts of ingredients, because with wild food, you can't always count on having exactly two cups. But also, in most cases, exact amounts make little difference in the final product. (It does make a difference with rice!) (This direction has been challenged, as we have access to so many more foods in our stores than we used to. For example, basmati rice wants 1¾ cups water for a cup of rice. Jasmine rice requires only 1½ cups of water to a cup of rice. So I guess I'd better change that directive to READ THE DIRECTIONS!)

A TEA BY ANY OTHER NAME

We all know what tea is, and how to make it. Often an herbal remedy will call for an infusion of dried herbs. Just so we are all clear
on the subject, a *tea* is the same as a *tisane*. An *infusion* is the same
thing, with a fancy name. And here's a thousand-dollar word for
you: a *galenical*. It's a tea, also, one such as Galen might have made.
And who was he? Galen was a first-century physician who was way
ahead of his time, ministering to wounded athletes in Greece and
Rome in the first century AD, whose astonishing medical discoveries advanced healing in the western world for the next 1,500 years.

A *weed* is, of course, any plant growing where you don't happen
to want it to grow. The implication is that it ought to be ripped up
or out.

An *herb* is any plant used for food or medicine or perfume or
flavor. I guess the sweetest herb could be a weed . . . if it dared to
grow in a "wrong" spot.

A *poultice* is a packing of an herb or herbs for an open wound.

And finally, a *potherb* is a vegetable to be steamed or boiled for
food.

In addition, basic recipes, like the one for mayonnaise, will appear
from time to time within these chapters. So come on! I invite you to the
hunt, the gathering, the folklore, the pictures, and the feast.

GEARING UP

You will find foraging an affordable hobby. One needs very little to gather wild food. Jeans or khakis, a long-sleeved shirt, hiking boots or supportive walking shoes (high-top is better than low-top for ankle support and peace of mind near snakes) with good socks, and bug repellent are the only real essentials. All your clothes should be washable. (If your jacket brushes against poison ivy, the urushiol, which is oily, will stay on the jacket until it's washed, creating a hazard for anyone who picks it up, handles it, or wears it.) You need to protect your skin not only from insects of all kinds but also from injury that can result from scraping against something thorny, so tuck your jeans into your socks and make sure your neckline is high. Wear your hair up and covered with a cap or hat, and see that your shirtsleeves protect your arms all the way down to your hands. In buggy weather, spray or slather repellent generously on all parts of your body that are still exposed.

Year-round, I carry in my car trunk several field guides to identify wild greens, wildflowers, fruits, ferns, and fungi. I also keep a supply of paper and plastic bags there, scissors, a sharp knife, a trowel, and heavy garden gloves (the last item for gathering stinging nettles, which are delicious and chock-full of vitamins), so that at any moment I am ready to pull over and gather anything good I spy by the roadside. If I walk through fields or woods, I carry necessities in a cheap, light nylon backpack to leave my hands free. And I wear a watch because time is fluid, and when I'm gathering morels or blackberries, ginseng or chanterelles, I have sometimes gone on far beyond time to go home.

A white or very light hat is good to wear because gnats go for the lightest, highest thing around, which is why they like your face instead of, say, your kneecaps. Spraying the hat with insect repellent will help keep them away from your eyes. One of those miracle fabric windbreaker/rain

Astringent: causing body tissues to shrink
Aperient: means "opening," but here implies laxative or opening of the bowel
Diaphoretic: induces perspiration
Vulnerary: enhances wound healing

jackets sold by sporting equipment companies is good to own; it adds almost no weight to your supplies, but in the event of a sudden weather change, you'll be grateful to have it. Should you sometimes feel uncomfortably hot in all this gear, remember this: If you ever step into ground hornets, as I have twice, you'll be glad you're all covered up.

In summer, it's good to shake flowers of sulfur (powdered sulfur, still available at many pharmacies) down inside your socks, and to wear long-sleeved garments tight at the neck and wrists to repel chiggers and all ticks. You can also dot yourself with oil of citronella, which smells marvelous and is safe. Bugs apparently don't like sulfur and citrusy things. Some people swear by Avon's Skin So Soft bath oil. Avon now puts out a product called Avon's Skin So Soft Moisturizing Suncare Plus, which contains the bath oil, an SPF of 15, and oil of citronella. I've found another product called T.O.P., "total outdoor protection," that includes citronella and SPF 15 by Biopharm of Bellport, New York. I could write a discourse on all the insect repellents I've tried, including the crushed leaves of a citrus geranium known as mosquito plant (never mind; it doesn't work) and a battery-operated mosquito repellent that whined until I thought I'd go mad—though the mosquitoes were unfazed by it—and crushed mint and pennyroyal leaves, plain garlic, boiled orange or lemon rinds, kerosene (my grandfather's favorite), and so on.

My husband loved to spend the night in the woods in a sleeping bag, and he never got a bite of any sort. But being a fair and tender lady, I go for Cutter, 6-12, Deep Woods Off!, or some other heavy-duty brand of commercial repellent. An insect-repelling product called Repel (Permethrine) that can be sprayed on your clothes and let to dry is also available, and it will continue to be effective through four or five washings. Whatever you do, you don't want to spend your time in the woods miserably batting at gnats, or come home covered with mosquito or spider bites (and any walk in the woods is sooner or later going to take you through a spiderweb). I once got a spider bite that took a year to heal. Now I'm more careful. And these days, a tick bite can be life threatening. So don't take chances.

I had it years ago on the somewhat questionable authority of my grandfather that snakes detest whistling because it hurts their ears (I know they don't have ears, but they do have earlike organs that are apparently very sensitive). My fellow mushroom hunter, biologist Dr. Burwell Wingfield, formerly of the Virginia Military Institute biology department, confirms that snakes "hear" vibrations, whether they be musical or "sensed" through the ground. So just to be on the safe side, I whistle and stomp my way through the woods in summer—and hardly ever encounter a snake. I am sure of this: If you give them half a chance, they will try to get out of your way.

Rabid animals are a possible threat, but an unlikely one: Most people would never get bitten if they would only remember to stay far away from any wild animal that doesn't act wild. Bands of frothing squirrels attacking and killing unwary humans is a good scenario for a horror film, but it hasn't happened yet that I know of.

BUGS, BE GONE!

In recent years, I've continued my search for an effective and sweet-smelling (and not harmful) insect repellent, and I think I've found it: 4 ounces of plain olive oil, to which has been added 20 drops of lavender oil, 20 drops of rosemary oil, 20 drops of cedar oil, and 10 drops of peppermint oil. Shake before using. It worked in Tanzania on safari for me, and it smells just great! However, without some sort of fixative, it fades pretty quickly and should be made afresh at least yearly.

There are a few rules that foragers need to bear in mind:

- *If the land you're hunting on isn't yours, first ask permission.* If a stranger came into your yard and began picking your flowers, you'd be incensed.

- *Carefully identify the things you plan to eat.* Learning to identify the wild things that grow in your area is a great pleasure, and not difficult. Peruse your local bookstore or library for field guides to wild plants and mushrooms. In the case of plants, compare not only field characteristics but also the season of growth and the locale. Learn what poisonous plants in your region look like in all seasons.

A salad of poison ivy would not sit well. Plant, mammal, insect, and bird identification increases the pleasure of walking, even if you never forage. Walking increases your joy in life. The dramatic reduction in walking since the advent of automobiles probably has as much to do with contemporary health problems as air pollution and high-fat diets. Forming a habit of walking every day may be the best possible assurance of a long and healthy life—and a long life doesn't seem desirable to me unless it is healthy.

- *Then you get to gather.* Take what you need, recalling that a lot of wild products freeze well. Treat your produce with care; a flat gathering basket keeps delicate berries, greens, and fungi from crushing those on the bottom, even if it's not as convenient to carry as plastic bags are.

- *Clean wild food well.* Nothing ruins the appetite so much as biting down on grit or finding a stinkbug crawling around in your salad. Worse than that would be getting liver flukes from polluted water. The method for cleaning watercress (see page 35) is necessary because the plants grow in running water, and running water these days is likely to be polluted. For all other greens, multiple rinses in fresh, clean tap water are sufficient. Mushrooms need to be scrupulously cleaned, as they all grow up through soil (and often manure) and may thus retain some clinging bits of bacteria and undesirable fungi. Berries need gentle washing to float out any critters, which seem to enjoy them as much as we do. Other fruits just need rinsing off.

- *When you get home, clean yourself well also,* even before you prepare your finds to eat. Search your body diligently for ticks, both the big ones (dog ticks) and those the size of poppy seeds (deer ticks). Both now carry, in addition to Rocky Mountain spotted fever, Lyme disease and a bacterial disease, HGE (human granulocytic ehrlichiosis), which may be even more deadly. Inspect your entire body, shower well, soaping thoroughly using a washcloth in case you've brushed against poison oak or ivy, and inspect your body again after bathing. Wash your clothes before wearing them again as a final precaution against poison oak or ivy. Even wash the gardening tools you've used. Remember that soap and water are not enough to remove oils; scrub with a rough cloth too.

- After you've gained permission and identified, gathered, and cleaned wild food, *use it just like tame food*.

- You might want to *keep records* of where and when you found that asparagus or the black chanterelles, so you can return next week or next year.

- Finally, *be a good neighbor*. Whenever possible, take along a trash bag and help the environment out where you see the need.

If worse comes to worst, and you find nothing on your walk, you can always stop by the store on the way home and substitute something from the produce department. Beet tops, radish tops, and turnip tops, usually discarded, are great for salads or pot greens, so if you use them, you're doing a sort of tame foraging.

A CHANGE OF HEART

Oxalis, a sour-but-pleasant-tasting toxin, occurs in many wild plants, and throughout this book, I have warned against eating too much of a food that contains it. But the consensus has changed, and nowadays, botanists believe that oxalis does not present much of a danger to the kidneys or digestive systems of healthy people, as was formerly believed.

Just a word about cooking utensils: I will assume that everyone owns a blender, a big colander, a salad spinner, kitchen scissors, a potato masher or a ricer (a heavy-duty strainer for mashing potatoes, apples, berries, etc., and separating the cooked flesh from skin, seeds, and cores), a food processor, and a big enamel or stainless steel kettle with a tight-fitting lid. (I avoid aluminum cookware, as the jury is still not in on the dangers of aluminum absorption leading to Alzheimer's disease.) All these items are helpful and in some cases necessary for cooking wild foods, not to mention anything else.

GREEN THINGS

Most of us are still related to our native fields as the navigator to undiscovered islands in the sea. We can any afternoon discover a new fruit there, which will surprise us by the beauty of its sweetness.

—HENRY DAVID THOREAU

There's an exciting and overlooked category of leafy things not as widely used as Boston lettuce, romaine, iceberg, or even mesclun. They are wild, and they include a great many greens both better tasting and more nutritious than store-bought lettuce. In addition, there are asparagus, fiddleheads, and milkweed, as useful and delicious as green beans and broccoli.

Spring is the best time for hunting wild greens, though several are also edible later in the summer, or even year-round. Any access to a field or pasture, neglected backyard, or even the edge of a country road will surely yield several delicious and healthful varieties of greens in all but the snowiest months. The ones I include here are by no means the only edible wild greens, but I believe these are the tastiest.

ASPARAGUS

Asparagus (*Asparagus officinalis*) may derive its name from the word *asper*, meaning "rough," or *aspergere*, meaning "to scatter." It has been long known throughout Appalachia as sparrowgrass, or sparrergrass, obviously through some misapprehension that made sense to the hearer: Sparrows (which name may be applied to any nondescript little birds) love the bright red seeds that ripen in mid- to late summer.

Description, Habitat, and Season

Asparagus is a light, bluish-green plant with fernlike, feathery fronds; it stands 3 to 4 feet tall, and this year's shoots grow out of and around last year's skeletal stalks. Asparagus, with its perennial roots and its annual stalks, grows wild along country roads, in old fields where fences used to run, and along present fencerows. This is because birds eat the berries, then sit resting on fences, where they excrete the undigested parts, including the seeds, which take root and grow. Asparagus also grows randomly in meadows and weedy areas. It is a plant of the Temperate Zone.

Wild asparagus is exactly the same as commercially available asparagus; sometimes the stalks may have a purplish tint and sometimes they are pure green. (The French sometimes blanch, or fade, asparagus to whiten it. This kind of blanching covers the stalks for several days prior to cutting to prevent light from hitting the plant and causing photosynthesis, the chemical process that turns plants green.) Its growing season is late spring, when the stalks appear. If the stalks are not picked, they go to seed and put out feathery fronds—but the plant shows more obviously later, in the fall, when the slender shoots have become lacy fronds and produce the red berries containing the seeds. Therefore, it's useful to identify asparagus plants in the autumn, take note of where they are, and then in the spring go looking for the tender young shoots among last year's dead stalks.

Asparagus is hardy, and it continues to put up shoots from its deep roots year after year, even if discouraged by the democratic slaughter of the highway mowers. The plant tends to grow among other long grasses in roadside ditches, making it hard to see when it's at the edible stage. When you find the stalks, snap them off a foot or so from the top. If they are less than 7 or 8 inches high, snap them off at the ground. Occasionally, if the summer is long, you can find a second growth of shoots late in that season, but it never produces as many as you find in spring.

History and Lore

Although asparagus is ubiquitous in moderate climates, it is like the legendary selkie; it was once a sea plant, growing near the ocean in sandy soil, and now lies among land plants. It is a plant included in that honorable, much sought, but mysterious group of foods known as aphrodisiacs. Me, I think it's just the shape.

{RECIPES}

From April to June, when asparagus is plentiful, save some for future use by another process called blanching. This time the word means submerging something, usually vegetables, for 1 minute in boiling water, then for 1 minute in ice water, and freezing it for future use. This blanching stops the enzyme action by which any plant continues its steady process of maturation and, finally, decline. Freezing alone is not sufficient to retard decomposition.

When you want to cook the frozen asparaguts (or any frozen vegetable), do not thaw it first. Plunge it into 1 inch of boiling water, and cook only until it is thawed.

To cook fresh asparagus, cut spears about 8 inches from the top, and steam them in ½ cup water for 1 to 2 minutes only, so they stay crisp. Eat them plain, or dribbled with melted butter, olive oil, or lemon juice, or a combination of all three. Asparagus is also fine to nibble raw, or chop raw into salads.

ASPARAGUS PIZZA

(A good way to use a few asparagus stalks. Yields 1 pizza, about 14 inches across.)
Prepare pizza dough according to the directions on pages 206–207. Bake it for 3 minutes in an oven preheated to 450°F. Remove and lightly brush the top with olive oil. Put a very light layer of tomato sauce on first, then scatter 1-inch slices of fresh raw asparagus over the

top. Scatter with 1 or 2 cloves finely minced garlic, salt and pepper, and oregano, end with a light smattering of mozzarella or provolone cheese, and bake until its color pleases you.

ASPARAGUS AND PASTA

(Serves 4 to 6)

Cook 1 pound of ziti or mostaccioli pasta (or any other pasta) until al dente ("to the tooth," or still a bit resistant). While the pasta is boiling, heat ¼ cup olive oil in a skillet, add 8 chopped garlic cloves and ¼ teaspoon, more or less, red pepper flakes. Sauté 2 minutes, stirring occasionally. Add what asparagus you have, up to 1 pound, the spears cut about the same length as the pasta, and stir-fry for 2 minutes. (This differs from sautéing in that you stir continuously.) Salt and pepper the asparagus, and toss with drained pasta. Grate 1 cup or so of Parmesan cheese over the top and serve immediately.

CHICORY

Chicory (*Cichorium intybus*) is a familiar, cheerful, intense blue jewel along country roads, and a plant generally neglected these days. "Chicory" is an anglicization of the Arabic *chicouryeh*. The Romans knew the plant as *cichorium*, which in turn was taken from the Greek.

Description, Habitat, and Season

Although this deep-rooted perennial is most easily identifiable by its profuse summer daisy-like blue flowers, chicory is best used as food for its leaves in the spring, before it flowers, or for its root in the fall. When chicory first comes out in the spring, it has oblong basal foliage that forms, at ground level, a loose head of dark green leaves that have a slightly bitter but pleasant taste. Chicory leaves are excellent salad greens. Europeans cherish this green and cultivate it, but in this country, we must gather it wild. Chicory is close kin to dandelion, as is evidenced by the upper, deeply lobed leaves. The spring leaves of the two plants can be used interchangeably, adding a slightly bitter piquancy to salads.

After flowering, in the autumn, is when to dig chicory root, which makes a very good beverage on its own, or can be added to ground coffee. But you must locate the plant by its blue summer-morning flowers, then return to dig the root after the flowers are gone.

History and Lore

Chicory was originally native to Arabic countries, from which it was introduced to Europe. Like many of our wild plants, it was first brought to North America from Europe by early colonists, then escaped to dot our fields, empty city lots, and roadsides with its cheery blue flowers.

Among the ancient Romans, chicory enjoyed a reputation as a cure not only for jaundice but also for anemia, infertility, and liver ailments. It is still said to be tonic and restorative.

Linnaeus once planted a flower bed in his native Uppsala, Sweden, to act as a reliable clock, as he had determined that different flowers blossomed at different times. In midsummer at that northern latitude, Linnaeus's chicory blooms opened at 5:00 a.m. and closed at 10:00 p.m. on sunny days. In Virginia at midsummer, it's closer to 7:00 a.m. and 7:00 p.m.

{RECIPES}

ROASTED CHICORY ROOT

Chicory roots, scrubbed clean, can be boiled and eaten and are a popular vegetable in Lebanon and other countries of Eurasia. In America, chicory roots were substituted for coffee during the Civil War. To use them this way, dig the roots out in early fall. To get the whole root out, you may have to dig as deep as 2 feet. Wash and clean each root well, and cut it with a machete or very sharp knife into chunks or thick slices. Roast the root in a medium-low oven (about 280°F) until the pieces turn from white to brown, about 1 hour. When they are cool, grind them up to the consistency of coffee grounds. Add 1 teaspoon ground root to each 1 tablespoon of coffee grounds, filtering, dripping, or perking the roots along with the coffee. Or prepare the root alone, without coffee (using 1 tablespoon for each cup), for a healthy caffeine-free hot drink. So popular was the taste that dark-roast coffee with chicory to this day remains the standard New Orleans brew.

Dandelion and chicory leaves can be blanched if you prefer. To blanch (whiten) a plant, you must either cover the plants with bushel baskets or plugged flowerpots and leave them to grow in the dark for several days, or dig up the roots and replant them in a dark cellar. The folklore is that blanching renders any plant less bitter, but if it does, it is only by a matter of a degree. And it's a lot of trouble.

DANDELIONS

Dandelions (*Taraxacum officinale*) are well known to adorn grassy areas and fields everywhere and are a bane to millions of shortsighted folks

who insist on perfectly green lawns instead of lawns dotted with yellow. The Latin name translates as "the official medical dandelion." A plant that has the word *officinale* in its name was once used officially for medicine. The English name is simply a version of the French *dent de leon*, or "tooth of the lion," from the deeply indented leaf shape, not the sunny flower.

Description, Habitat, and Season

As an edible plant, the dandelion is good only in early spring before the cheerful, bright yellow flowers bloom. The leaves, deeply lobed and bright green, are a forager's delight and have a pleasant, slightly bitter taste. (After the plant has flowered, the leaves become tough and unpleasantly bitter.) In Europe, dandelion leaves are popular in spring salads. Dandelion leaves may also be used as a potherb (that is, cooked).

History and Lore

Apothecaries of the sixteenth century called dandelions *Herba urinaria*. Even today, the plant is prized as a diuretic.

Dandelion leaf tea was drunk by Native Americans as a spring tonic, and it does have large amounts of iron and vitamins C and A, which the human body needs after months of diminished sunlight. The hollow stems exude a bitter white latex that is said to soothe bee stings, dissolve warts, and heal sores. Eating the leaves is even supposed to help ease rheumatism.

{RECIPES}

Though dandelion wines still enjoy some popularity, dandelion is best employed as a salad green. Like chicory root, which it is closely related to, dandelion root gathered in autumn may be cleaned, slow-roasted, and ground for a safe, caffeine-free hot beverage or mixed with coffee.

Thai Dandelions

(Serves about 6)

¼ cup peanut oil
9 cups dandelion leaves
½ cup coconut milk
1 package soft tofu, diced
1 tablespoon arrowroot or cornstarch
Juice of 2 limes
2 tablespoons chopped basil (there is a Thai basil, but either kind will do)
4 cloves garlic, chopped
2 teaspoons chopped fresh ginger
1 teaspoon ground cloves
1 to 2 teaspoons salt

Sauté leaves, tofu, and garlic in oil about 10 minutes. Mix all other ingredients in the blender, and blend until smooth. Add to the leaves and tofu, and simmer until heated up.

Traditional Dandelion Salad

(Serves 4)

Fry a few strips of bacon until crisp, then crumble and set aside. Drain off some of the bacon grease, leaving about 2 tablespoons. In the hot skillet, lay a great mound of fresh, washed, wet young dandelion leaves (they will spatter), and stir over the heat until the leaves are coated with the fat, just 1 minute or so. Sprinkle with salt, pepper, and vinegar, add the bacon and 1 or 2 chopped hard-boiled eggs, and serve at once. The salad should be barely wilted. (Draining off the bacon drippings, or most of them, would modernize this old recipe.)

Italian-Style Nouvelle Dandelion Salad

(Serves 4)

Heat a few tablespoons olive oil with a few cloves crushed or minced garlic, a couple inches of anchovy paste, 1 tablespoon or so of capers, and a handful of pine nuts. Mix the ingredients well, and heat and stir them together just for 1 or 2 minutes, until the pine nuts begin to brown. Then add the washed greens to the hot skillet and stir and toss for 1 minute or so, until the leaves are coated. Wilt, but don't cook, the leaves.

FIDDLEHEADS

Fiddleheads are the coiled tender tips or sprouts of several different kinds of ferns. The ones most commonly eaten in America are cinnamon fern (*Osmunda cinnamomea*), bracken fern (*Pteridium aquilinum* or "eagle feather"), and ostrich fern (*Pteretis struthiopteris* or "knotty feathered"). The second and third derive their names from the Greek *pteron*, "feather" or "wing," which describes the feathery stalks of ferns. The cinnamon fern is named for Osmunder, the Saxon war god. Ferns are among the oldest plants on earth. The common name fiddleheads comes from their resemblance to, well, the heads of fiddles, or the tops of violins, which are carved to appear coiled.

Description, Habitat, and Season

In order to enjoy these vegetables, which are commercially canned by several food-processing companies, you should identify the fern beds the year before, so that you can return in early spring and watch for the emergence of the tender young fiddleheads. This is not hard: Though ferns all look alike to the casual observer, they are not at all the same up close. So buy a good fern guide, take a trek in the woods when the leaves are out, and soon you will be an expert at spotting ferns and even identifying some of them. Then, all you need to do is remember where your ferns grow, and return in early spring before they uncurl their little heads and their feathery displays emerge.

Cinnamon fern is a large (around 3 feet high), common, coarse fern distinguished from other ferns by the late-spring gold-green leaves that turn the color of cinnamon. Cinnamon fern likes damp places and puts out fiddleheads that are large, with silvery white, fine hairs.

Bracken fern is also a very common, strong, coarse fern that grows to about 3 feet tall in colonies in fields, burned areas, sandy areas, and generally on high ground. The leaves are wavy and dark green and flatten out horizontally at the top; each stem produces three equal leaves of subleaflets. Its fiddleheads thus grow in three parts, curled tight, covered with silvery hair.

Ostrich fern is large, about 5 feet tall, and arches gracefully like ostrich feathers. Ostrich fern spreads easily and appears in dense colonies in wet habitats, by creeks and in marshy land. Ostrich fern is common in the East, but less common in other parts of the country. It is a dark blackish green, turning dark brown in winter, often matting stretches of stream banks.

History and Lore

Ferns are among our most ancient plants. Often fern fossils are discovered buried deep in rock layers. Brontosaurs and other vegetable-eating dinosaurs nibbled fiddleheads. Ferns have been employed medically for endless ailments as far-ranging as tapeworms, baldness, coughs, and dysentery.

{RECIPES}

Fiddleheads require careful cleaning of the scales or hairs, and then cooking. Once cleaned and steamed to tenderness, they are delicious hot or cold. Ostrich fern and cinnamon fern fiddleheads should be steamed only as long as it takes to tenderize them. Bracken fiddleheads require longer cooking, and some sources suggest changing the water 3 times during boiling, but I never do this. I like their distinctive flavor.

FRENCH FIDDLEHEADS

Wash fiddleheads (about ½ cup for each diner). They need to be blanched quickly (dunked in boiling water for 1 minute), then rinsed in cold water. Then gently boil them in fresh water until just tender, about as long as you'd cook string beans. Serve them with lemon butter when they are cooked but still crisp.

CHILLED FIDDLEHEADS

Wash fiddleheads (allow ½ cup for each person). Blanch them as above, boil them as above, then place them briefly in cold water to keep them from getting soggy. Drain, and marinate them in Vinaigrette Salad Dressing (see pages 204–205) overnight in the refrigerator for a wonderful addition to a salad, or a green worthy of center stage on any table. They also are great chilled with homemade Mayonnaise (see page 204).

FIDDLEHEAD SOUP

(Serves 4)

Wash and clean 1 or 2 cups fiddleheads. Beat 2 eggs with about ⅓ cup fresh lemon juice. Heat 1 quart or so seasoned stock to just boiling. You can use consommé, beef broth, chicken broth, veal broth, or vegetable broth. (See pages 203–204 for basic broth process.) First, add fiddleheads to broth and simmer 5 minutes. Remove about 1 cup simmering broth and stir into egg-lemon mix. Then turn the whole mix into the pot, stir well, and remove at once from the heat. Stir again, and serve at once, distributing the fiddleheads among the servings more or less evenly.

GARLIC MUSTARD

About five years ago, a friend casually asked me if I liked to eat garlic mustard, as she pointed it out to me on a walk. I wondered how there could be an edible plant so profuse in my area that I didn't know about. I took some home and cooked and ate it, and it was truly delicious, like mustard greens with a soupçon of garlic. It's quite delicious, but wait—there's more!

Description, Habitat, and Season
I like that this plant appears early and stays late, and it seems to have infiltrated fields, paths, and the edges of woods with its pretty, light green, scalloped round or scalloped pointed leaves that smell and taste faintly of garlic. But this green is a rapidly spreading invasive weed that

presents a severe threat to native plants—and the animals and insects that depend on them. Its habits are much the same as the white man's toward the Native American population from the beginning of our colonizing here.

Garlic mustard (*Alliaria petiolata*) is present now year-round, and indeed remains green and edible all through the winter. In some spots, it has eradicated trillium, wild ginger, trout lilies, wild orchids, Dutchman's-breeches, and other plants. Some of these plants are host to butterfly larvae, and so the garlic mustard threatens extinction of those butterflies.

In its native Europe, the plant is under control because it has numerous (almost seventy) predators—none of which are native to our continent. It is not surprising that four of those predators, which are weevils that consume only garlic mustard and are therefore called monophagous (one-eating) weevils, are being evaluated for use as possible biological controls here. The trouble is that if you introduce a new weevil, no one can be sure what else will happen to other plants or crops. In recent years, we have become a bit more cautious about those unintended results.

History and Lore

This exotic European species was first recorded in 1868 on Long Island, and in the second decade of the twentieth century, it has already appeared everywhere in Virginia and as far west as Kansas and Nebraska. Most sources say it was introduced as a medicinal as well as a food plant by Central European immigrants. It evidently loves the calcareous soil of Virginia, and it won't grow in acid soil. It is absolutely all over my big yard.

If you gather it, it's best to pull the plants up by the roots, which is the only way to keep garlic mustard from spreading. (Even that looks to me like trying to stop a hole in the dam with your finger.) The seeds of garlic mustard can survive forest fires, and they are viable for five years after being shed by the plant. You can eradicate it with strong weed killers like Roundup, but you must treat the ground for five years to destroy all the seeds.

Medicinally, the plant induces sweating and is eaten to alleviate bronchitis and asthma. A poultice of the raw leaves is reputed to help remove the sting and itch of insect bites. It's full of vitamin C and, as a member of the broccoli family, confers some of the same benefits as eating broccoli does. Mostly, it's just wonderful as a green.

Garlic mustard is simply fine in a salad, uncooked. But it's better steamed briefly, sprinkled with a little vinegar, and tossed with a pat of butter or a bit of olive oil. Like spinach, it turns slimy if overcooked. The steamed leaves are great added to a plate of pasta, then tossed.

LAMB'S-QUARTERS, AKA PIGWEED OR GOOSEFOOT

Lamb's-quarters (*Chenopodium album*) may be the greatest treasure you'll ever find. Its genus name in Latin means "goose-footed plant" (hence another nickname, goosefoot). *Album* refers to the white "bloom" or dust that looks like talcum powder on the leaf surfaces close to the stem. Pigweed, as it is dismissively called in Appalachia for the animal's preference for it, is a veritable treasure. In some places, it's known as wild spinach. Its folk name, lamb's-quarters, probably comes from its affinity for pastures, or lamb's quarters.

Description, Habitat, and Season
Chenopodium is I foot to 3 feet tall, has roughly diamond-shaped or triangular leaves, and is powdered with coarse, grainy particles of white, so

that it looks dusty. Sometimes the stalks are streaked with red. *Chenopo-dium* grows everywhere vegetables will grow, plus lots of other places. It's a grayish spire-shaped weed that likes the edges of gardens, barnyards, and unguarded parts of your backyard, as well as fields and pathways, and . . . well, once you've identified it, you'll see how ubiquitous it is. From early spring all the way to first frost, you can gather and use young leaves from plants that are between 6 and 16 inches tall. (Any taller, and the leaves may be tough. In taller plants, strip the leaves off the stalk.) In an irony of nature, lamb's-quarters loves to move into spinach patches, as well as other parts of gardens. Gardeners I know spend a lot of time trying to rid their spinach (and other) patches of it, even though it's every bit as delicious as the vegetables intentionally being grown. Euell Gibbons reports that in Hawaii and California, its cheerful willingness to take root and grow has caused farmers distress.

History and Lore

Pigweed is undaunted by the unkind treatment it receives. It's willing to grow anywhere, it's full of nutrients, and hardly anyone you ask these days has ever even heard that it's edible, much less delicious. It has exceptional amounts of vitamins A and C, only a half cup or so providing the daily needed amount of both, as well as fiber, of course, and also calcium. My vegetable-growing neighbor brings it to me with amusement, while worrying about his spinach. One time, I made spinach soup and lamb's-quarters soup with the same ingredients, only changing the greens. My neighbor agreed with me that the lamb's-quarters soup was better, but habit is so strong that he still sows, tends, and weeds his spinach carefully each year, while the lamb's quarters, without his interference, thrives exuberantly at the edge of his garden, and year after year only I eat it.

{RECIPES}

Use lamb's-quarters any way that you would spinach, but strip the leaves off the stalks. Clean the leaves well in 2 or 3 rinsings of water, to rinse off the bloom on the leaves.

LAMB'S-QUARTERS BISQUE OR SOUP

(Serves 4)

This is just about the best soup you will ever taste. Wash and rewash a big bunch of leaves stripped from their stalks. The leaves will collapse as soon as heat reaches them. To make 1 quart or so of wonderful soup, sauté or steam a bunch of the wet washed leaves the size of a basketball in 2 or 3 tablespoons butter for 1 minute or so. You can add some chopped onion too. Stir in 2 to 3 tablespoons flour to make a roux. Slowly add about 3 cups chicken or beef broth, canned or homemade (see method on pages 203–204), stir while you bring it to a boil, and add one of the following: 1 block cream cheese (you can use either a 3-ounce or an 8-ounce block, depending on how creamy you want your bisque to be), 1 cup sour cream, or 8 ounces heavy whipping cream. You can turn the bisque into plain old soup by adding milk instead, which will save calories too. Blend the mixture briefly in a blender, taste and correct seasoning, then keep hot until you are ready to serve, but do not boil again. Naturally, you could make this soup with other greens, too, including fiddleheads.

Lamb's-Quarters with Potatoes

(Serves 4)

Gather an armful of lamb's-quarters and wash well. Place in a large pot, sprinkle with salt, and steam until wilted. In a second pot, place some cubed potatoes, salt, pepper, and a spoonful of bacon drippings, oil, or a little butter. Add 1 cup water and bring to the boiling point. Pour wilted greens on top of potatoes, cover, and cook until potatoes are done. Traditionally, this is served in Missouri with pork sausage.

LAND CRESS

Land cress (*Barbarea vulgaris* or *B. verna*), a member of the mustard family, has a doubly insulting Latin name: It is "barbarous" and "vulgar," and its alternate species name implies a "spring barbarian." Some sources say it is named for St. Barbara, whose annual day is in mid-December. It grows all year if the ground is not frozen and is wet enough. This plant is known by a bewildering variety of folk names, so be sure to learn the Latin name to avoid confusion. It is also called rocket, arugula, upland cress, winter cress, creesy greens, creesies, Croesus greens (because it's worth more than gold to your body, maybe?), and (confusingly) wild mustard. (*Eruca vesicaria*, the commercial arugula, has deeply lobed leaves and a zippy flavor similar to both land cress and mustard.)

Description, Habitat, and Season

Land cress grows in full sun out from its center like a rocket, hence one of its folk names. Its shape is the best way to identify this plant. The roundish, smooth, deeply lobed, dark green, glossy leaves grow outward while staying near the ground.

It can be found from earliest spring through the summer and on into fall. Even in winter, a warm wet spell sometimes brings it out. Found everywhere in the Temperate Zone, the perennial habitats of land cress include city lots as well as country pastures, along mountain creeks, and in parks, in wet, rich, sandy, or waste soil. In early summer, it has small yellow cruciform flowers. Once past spring, land cress gets a bit tough, but it only requires a few more minutes of cooking time. The plant can be eaten until the blooms form; after that, it tastes bitter.

{RECIPES}

Barbarea is related to broccoli, and when it buds in early summer, the buds can be steamed quickly and eaten just like broccoli. It's a green that needs cooking, in my estimation, though many folks eat it raw in salads.

GREENS AND POT LIKKER

(Serves 4 to 6)

Fall greens are darker, tougher, and stronger flavored than spring greens, for the most part, and respond well to the taming effects of heat. For a wonderful feast, gather about a gallon of fall greens like land cress, wild mustard, or a combination of greens. Cut or tear them into pieces if they are big. Remove any tough stems. In a big pan, bring 1 quart water to a boil. Add 1 teaspoon or more salt. You can also cook the greens with a small amount of smoked meat for seasoning (ham skin, a ham hock, 1 or 2 slices of bacon, or a small piece of smoked ham). If you use meat, boil the meat alone for 15 to 30 minutes, covered. Add the clean greens to the pot, and boil covered until tender, about 10–15 more minutes. The tougher the greens, the longer they will take to cook. Taste them sooner rather than later: Don't overcook them. Drain. Discard the smoked meat, but save the liquid! Serve the greens alone or with sliced hard-boiled eggs and a sprinkling of malt vinegar. For a different taste, toss them with a little butter and lemon juice. The liquid they cooked in, known in Appalachia as pot likker for its sublime taste, retains any vitamins that the cooking has leached out of the greens. It is served in teacups and drunk like tea.

Traditionally, greens, pot likker, and corn bread made up the entire meal for country folks. Today they're still eaten as a hearty and satisfying supper. The corn bread was (though not in our house) dipped into the pot likker, or even crumbled into it. My mother, a Philadelphian, felt it generous to even allow us to eat corn bread and greens; dunking was way beyond her limit. (See Country Corn Bread, page 170.)

WILD ARUGULA SALAD

A large bunch of wild arugula, washed, patted dry, and roughly chopped; 1 cup olive oil; the juice of 1 large fresh lemon; sea salt; freshly ground black pepper; a nice wedge of aged Parmesan cheese—you know the drill. Shave the cheese onto the salad rather than grate it. Nice additions are a crushed clove of garlic or a handful of toasted pine nuts—or both!

MILKWEED

Milkweed (*Asclepias syriaca*) is a delicious early-summer vegetable, and it's vastly overlooked in the civilized world. Its Latin name is the same as the Roman god of medicine, *Asclepias*, and *syriaca* may suggest its origin was

Syria. It's sometimes called butter-fly weed, or butterfly milkweed, and I've heard folks call it pleurisy root. Its folk names come from the milky, sticky sap that the stem yields when cut or picked.

Description, Habitat, and Season

Milkweed is likely to inhabit any pastures and fields, waste places, and roadside ditches. It grows in full sun and is often found in enormous patches. Sometimes whole fields are full of it.

This 3-foot plant, native to North America, grows on a hardy stalk. The leaves are dark glossy green, slightly wavy, with a white midvein. They are lance shaped and 4 to 6 inches long. Milkweed flowers grow in rounded umbels and are most often whitish purple, with a greenish tinge. You can identify a patch of milkweed when its sweet purple blooms, which return each year, make it stand out in early summer. If you can find them, the youngest shoots in spring grow to 6 or 7 inches high and can be used like asparagus (blanched first for a minute in rapidly boiling water). The buds in late spring are delicious before they open; they look rather like small broccoli heads, and I think they're at least as tasty as broccoli. The buds that blossom in summer are purple and fragrant, attracting butterflies, and they, too, are a fine vegetable.

History and Lore

Milkweed traditionally was used to treat infections of the respiratory system (like pleurisy) both in North America and in Europe. Milkweed seed, when it has burst, is light and fulsome like goose down or cotton, and it once was used in Appalachia as a stuffing in vests and quilts. Milkweed seed was used in World War II as a substitute for real Indonesian kapok in life jackets before man-made fillers were invented.

{RECIPES}

Although some people eat all parts of the plant, I recommend only the shoots, unopened buds, and blossoms (avoiding the leaves and the pods).

All parts of the plant need to be washed, then parboiled for 1 minute in 3 different courses of boiling water to wash out the bitter, sticky sap. Then boil shoots, buds, or blossoms 3 or 4 minutes in a fourth pot of boiling water. When done, they can be tossed with a lump of butter and a squeeze of lemon juice, and you have a delicate vegetable that will charm your taste buds.

MUSTARD

Mustard (*Brassica* varieties) is so ubiquitous that some kind is available nearly all year even in supermarkets, and some variety of it, usually several, may be found in grasslands everywhere in this country. *Brassica* is the Latin word for "cabbage," which belongs to the same family. In the South, wild mustard grows everywhere in fields and pastures and is called simply "greens." In other places, it is called charlock, from the Old English name of the plant. One variety, *B. juncea*, was brought here by English settlers but is now wild throughout temperate America.

Description, Habitat, and Season
When mustard is in bloom, whole fields turn bright yellow with the close-growing, 4-petaled flowers. Up close, mustard blossoms look like

little gold crosses. Each blossom has six stamens, four long, two short. Although the various dozen or so mustards we have in this country differ somewhat, all mustard leaves are serrated, dark purple-green, deeply lobed, lyre shaped, and often softly prickly along the main leaf vein underneath. The stem is soft and prickly as well. The plant grows as tall as 30 inches. It's a pesky weed most of the places where it grows. There's hardly a playing field, meadow, golf course, riverbank, or roadside without its share of mustard, so it's available to almost anyone. We gather it from spring through late fall, even through the winter.

{RECIPES}

Mustard's nippy flavor enhances any salad, though it is at its best used as a pot green. It's tender in the spring, bolts early, tough in summer when it's flowering yellow, and somewhat peppery, or biting, in the fall. At our house, we eat this country relative of kale, kohlrabi, cabbage, and rape year-round.

MUSTARD GREENS

Past the tender spring growth, use mustard only as a potherb. Wash it well, and cook with only the water that clings to the leaves. Cook it slowly, covered, for 20 minutes, taste it, and cook longer if necessary. Avoid the flowers, for they're bitter. I like to add a bit of "side meat" (unsmoked bacon), a slice or two of bacon, a ham bone, or a ham hock, though it isn't necessary. Mustard is rich in calcium and vitamins A and C. Its seeds, ground to a fine flour and mixed with wine, vinegar, pepper, horseradish, and sometimes even with Jack Daniel's whiskey, are (as you know) a popular condiment, and they are often used whole in pickles. Once cooked, season mustard greens with a splash of vinegar, a bit of butter, perhaps a sliced hard-boiled egg. All these recipes work as well with garlic mustard.

POKE

Pokeweed (*Phytolacca decandra* or *P. americana*) is also known as poke, skoke, garget, and pigeonberry. Its Latin name means "crimson plant with ten stamens." Pokeberries were once the favorite food of the enormous flocks of passenger pigeons that darkened the skies over the eastern states during their seasonal migrations. (The last known member of the species, which was hunted to extinction, died in a Cincinnati zoo in 1914.)

Lovely, but don't eat poke over 7 inches high because it is poisonous. Identify in late summer, and remember or mark for the next spring.

Description, Habitat, and Season

To best locate poke for spring picking of the tender shoots, look for it in late summer when the plant is brilliantly colored and dramatically visible in the landscape.

Poke is an easily recognizable green that grows profusely in poor land, unimproved depleted soil, recent clearings, and roadsides throughout the eastern United States, from the tropics northward, throughout the Temperate Zone. It grows 6 feet or taller, with bright green alternate wavy leaves, a red-streaked or scarlet stem, white to pinkish flowers in late spring, and long loose clusters (racemes) of toxic shiny, dark purple berries that develop in late summer and stay into the winter. In late summer, the stem gets redder, and often the entire plant turns a wonderful fuchsia or sunset red. It grows also in wastelands in parts of the western United States, and even in Hawaii. Poke is a striking plant in any landscape.

The whole plant is highly toxic, containing a saponin mixture called phytolaccatoxin—except for the young tender shoots and leaves in early spring, which are often eaten as the first spring green in the southern mountains. Locate the plant in the autumn, or you may miss the shoots among the other spring greens. As they mature, the shoots (any more than 7 inches tall) develop the substances toxic to man. Many birds and other animals safely eat pokeberries.

History and Lore
Poke has been used for ink, as a dye, and in cures for cancer and arthritis by Native Americans. An arthritis cure that a ninety-year-old Missouri man told me of in one of my Elderhostel folklore classes included poke. His father, a country physician, became locally famous in Missouri and some neighboring states at the end of the last century for his arthritis potion—a formula he kept secret. It worked, according to my informant, nearly all of the time and facilitated some truly miraculous-seeming cures. It contained, as far as he can remember, only whiskey and pokeberries (well known to the doctor to be poisonous), and it was deep purple. My friend recalled as a boy seeing people walk who before had been unable to, watching his father's patients' limbs and joints straighten out. But he had no idea when the berries were gathered, whether they were crushed or added whole, if whiskey was the only other ingredient, in what proportions the brew was made, how often it was drunk, or how much per dose. Sadly, now he, too, is dead.

{RECIPES}

Poke shoots are cut at ground level when no more than 7 inches high, parboiled, drained, then cooked until tender in a second water. They are tasty and have a fair amount of vitamin C.

Old-Fashioned Appalachian Poke Sallet

Take a mess of less-than-7-inch-high poke shoots, wash them, and chop them coarsely. Boil them for 20 minutes. Meanwhile, fry some pork fatback in a skillet and remove it to drain. Keep the fatback hot. Drain the poke, salt it, and fry it for 5 minutes in the leftover grease. Serve the fried poke with the fried pork and some Country Corn Bread (see page 170). Sprinkle cider vinegar on the greens and drink buttermilk with them if you want the whole experience.

Fried Poke

Flour up the parboiled young stalks (no higher than 7 inches) and fry them in a small amount of bacon fat (or some other less sinful fat). They are said by some to taste just like asparagus. Or flour up the parboiled young leaves (just the ones on the early stalks) and fry them; they are reputed to taste like fish. To me, poke tastes only like itself, and it is delicious in its own right.

PURSLANE

Purslane, a powerhouse herb also known as "pussley," whose real name is *Portulaca oleracea*, appears in our sidewalks all over town and in abandoned clay-hard tracts of land all over the county. Folks invite it up between stepping stones in local gardens. It transplants happily from anywhere to anywhere. I have it growing between the rocks in my rock wall, and between the concrete squares on my front walk. One spot is sunny; the other shady. Purslane doesn't care. It grows all summer long, and into fall.

Description, Habitat, and Season
Purslane has reddish stems, a prostrate rocket growth pattern (out in all directions from a center, but low to the ground), fat succulent leaves, and tiny little yellow flowers early in the day, which close up as noon approaches. It must like the challenge of growing snug, wedged between bricks or behind concrete. I wonder what it might do given a nice plot of good earth. I know it can tolerate drought, poor soil, and very tight places.

History and Lore

Purslane has an honorable history of use by humans. It's known from India, ancient China, and classical Greece. It can be eaten in salad or steamed quickly. Its name, *oleracea*, seems indicative of oil; cooked, it does have a succulent, slightly oily consistency, a gently sour-salty taste, and a slightly mucilaginous quality (okra-ish, but try it before you decide to hate it). You want to remove the thick stems after collecting.

Pliny the Elder thought 2,000 years ago that purslane lowered fever-ish temperatures and advised wearing it as an amulet against evil. It was widely used against both constipation and diarrhea and for any inflammation of the urinary tract. John Gerard, the famous sixteenth-century herbalist, agreed, saying it "cools the blood." The fresh herb can draw the infection from skin wounds.

This herb is generally considered a weed, which bodes well for foragers. It's a potent source of omega-3 fatty acids, maybe the most potent of all land plants. The reddish stems and the yellow flowers and yellowish leaves are indicative of betacyanins and betaxanthins, both antimutagenic (that means they fight cell changes, or cancer).

{RECIPES}

Purslane is great in salads, dressed lightly with vinaigrette (see pages 204–205). It is also a good potherb, steamed with a little butter added.

SORREL (AKA SOUR GRASS)

Sorrel (*Rumex acetosa*) and wood sorrel (*Oxalis montana*) are two unrelated plants that grow in yards and meadows everywhere, looking like arrows (*Rumex*) and clover or trefoil (*Oxalis*). *Oxalis* is the Greek word for "wood sorrel," as *rumex* is the Latin name for "sorrel." *Acetosa* derives from the Latin *acetum*, "vinegar." Both plants are tangy to the palate, which gives them both the common nickname of sour grass. Either one adds greatly to the flavor of soups and salads. The word *sorrel* comes from an Old French word, *sur*, meaning "sour."

Description, Habitat, and Season

Both sorrels like poor soil, so they may be found in uncultivated fields, old lawns, and the edges of gardens. Both grow in temperate zones of the Northern Hemisphere. The *Oxalis* sorrel is the true shamrock, a low plant with three split leaves much like clover. It is native to the British Isles, but

like so many of our wild plants, was introduced by the early colonists. The *Rumex* sorrel is a perennial that grows to 3 feet or more, the arrow-shaped leaves about 4 inches long. In the summer, this plant flowers toward the top with small, loose, reddish-brownish flowers that last until autumn. Once the flowers bloom, the leaves are too tough to eat.

Both sorrels love to nudge your garden flowers out of the way to grow. Sorrels are found wherever and whenever grass grows, or from early spring throughout the summer and into fall, and are impressively rich in vitamin C. They also contain oxalic acid and oxalate salts, which in large quantities can be poisonous. Nonetheless, sorrel has been safely used for at least six centuries as a soup and salad green in reasonably small quantities.

{RECIPES}

Sorrel as a spring salad green should be used in combination with other greens, and probably no more than 25 percent of your salad should be sorrel. We eat it until frost, though the later the season, the tougher and stronger the plant.

SORREL SOUP, 1898

(Serves 4)

This is from page 6 of my Grandmother Letcher's handwritten cookbook, which she started as a bride in 1898. You'll need: 2 tablespoons
butter, 1 pint sorrel, 1 quart soup stock, yolks of 2 eggs, and salt and pepper to taste. Put the butter in a saucepan, set it on the fire, and as soon
as it's melted, put the sorrel in and stir 1 minute. Then add the stock,
salt, and pepper; boil 3 minutes. Beat the yolks lightly, put them into a
tureen, and pour the boiling soup over gradually, stirring all the while,
until thoroughly mixed. Serve with croutons.

STINGING NETTLES

Stinging nettles (*Urtica dioica*) are a delicious wild green, an unlikely food
in that they certainly feel poisonous, with their thousands of tiny hypo-
dermic needles on the leaves and stems that puncture your skin when you
brush against them. *Urtica* is the Latin name for the plant, from *uro*, "I
burn," and *dioica* is a Greek word meaning "of two houses." Here it means
the plant is unisexual, with male and female flowers in separate parts of
the inflorescence, or bloom.

Description, Habitat, and Season

The plants are dull green and square stemmed, with coarse-toothed, bristly, heart-shaped leaves and small clusters of greenish-yellow flowers. They stand a foot or two high on straight stalks. You find nettles along roadsides, on waste ground, in pastures, and around old house sites, from Canada to the Virginias, and also throughout the Midwest and even in California. They grow in spring, often in huge patches. You'll want to remember or record where they are so you can return next year to the same places. If in doubt, a tentative touch will assure you that you have the right plant.

Only the tender tops (stems and leaves) of nettles in the spring are good to eat; just cut the stalks off no farther down than a foot. Later in the year, even though they continue to put out new plants with apparently tender tops, they are full of tiny crystals that make them gritty and unpleasant. Thus, only one picking a year, in any one patch, early to late spring, is my rule. Gather them carefully, with heavy gloves and scissors or a sharp knife.

History and Lore

The Romans cultivated nettles, as they proved to be one of the most effective plants for alleviating the miseries of rheumatism. In past times, arthritis and rheumatism sufferers underwent applications of stinging nettles for relief. Today, that treatment of one pain to mask another (lotions with capsaicin, the hot stuff of peppers, is one) is called counterirritant. In addition, the fresh stinging leaves are said to stanch bleeding quickly.

A folk adage has it that nettles brewed into tea will "melt fat" from corpulent people. It's worth a try, and even if you don't get thin, you might derive other general health benefits from "taking" nettles.

{RECIPES}

Not only are nettles delicious, they are also extremely high in vitamins A and C. Cooking them quickly converts the formic acid into a digestible protein. Wash them with rubber gloves on, by dousing them up and down in a sinkful of water.

STEAMED NETTLES

Gather and wash a large bunch of nettles—they cook down—then place them directly into a pot with ¼ cup steaming water in the bottom. Nettles only need about 15 minutes of steaming in a covered kettle, and like magic, the sting has vanished, and they are ready to eat. The greens are delicious with a bit of melted butter and a burst of lemon juice. Drink the pot likker (the water left when they are done) for its wonderful taste and for the benefit from the minerals that have leached into it. It's better for you than a vitamin pill.

Creamed Nettles

Gather, wash, and steam a large bunch of nettles. Drain well. Make a medium or heavy cream sauce (see page 210), and season it with onion and grated nutmeg. Mix it with the hot greens, and serve as a first course.

TAKING THE STING OUT OF NETTLES

I once ran heedless into a large patch of nettles, in pursuit of a neighbor's child's ball. I was barefoot and stuck in the middle of the patch before I became aware of them. I had to turn around and retreat the same way I'd come, adding insult to injury. Their formic acid sting (the same thing that ants sting with) was painful for several hours, finally cooling down to a severe itch, then going away. Though painful, nettles are not dangerous.

After that episode, I learned what to do the next time. If you ever get stung, look for the tall, hairy, yellow-flowered mullein to crush and rub on the sting. Mullein is a popular folk antidote for bee stings, which also contain formic acid. Or soothe the sting with aloe vera. Or use a paste of meat tenderizer and water, or even douse the affected skin with vinegar. The most recent thing I've read prescribed is vitamin C in water applied directly to bites and stings. Although it may not work for nettles (I haven't had occasion to try it), it is miraculous on scalds. Crush a 1,000-milligram ascorbic acid pill with a hammer in a plastic bag, stir it into ½ cup water until it's dissolved, and apply the liquid directly to burns. It stops pain instantly, and there is no blistering or scarring.

WATERCRESS

Watercress (*Nasturtium officinale*) is one of our most delicious and popular wild greens. The name of the genus comes from *nasus*, "nose," and *torqus*, "twist." It seems to be a comic description of what one does when confronted with the smell of nasturtiums. The species name, *officinale*, always designates a plant that was once thought to be medically useful, or "officially" recognized.

Description, Habitat, and Season

Watercress is a succulent perennial with round compound leaves and tiny white flowers that grows in running water: Creeks and rivers, stream-fed ponds, brooks, and even ditches throughout the country. Watercress is tenderest and most flavorful in early spring, but available in all but the coldest weather. In the summer, its stems get leggy and its leaves get hot, but it may prevail in streams in autumn, and sometimes (though of course more rarely) throughout the winter—at least in the mid-Atlantic states. There are several varieties, some emerald green and some with a dark red tinge to both the stems and leaves. Anytime you find it, make a watercress and cream cheese sandwich with mayonnaise—my all-time favorite lunch. Heaven on earth.

Watercress is antiscorbutic and diuretic and has a good dose of several vital minerals, including potassium, calcium, and iron. It is edible year-round, and even if it grows in a stream flowing through pastures used by cows and deer, bears and raccoons, it is safe to eat if you take the precautions described in the "Cleaning Watercress" sidebar.

History and Lore

The Romans fed watercress to the mentally ill as a cure. It is interesting that what the Romans may have figured out is that people who are well nourished are healthier mentally as well as physically. Hildegard von Bingen, a twelfth-century mystic, wrote that anyone with jaundice or fever should steam watercress in a bowl, eat it warm, and drink the water. Its energy, she claimed, comes from water, so she believed watercress tea was a good food for someone so sick he could take only liquids. Native Americans used it as a treatment for kidney disorders, and as a cure for constipation. Early African Americans used watercress as an abortifacient, and it was also believed to cause temporary sterility. On the other hand, watercress had among the Native Americans and early settlers a reputation as an aphrodisiac; a song by blues singer Josh White tells the story of a man who goes to court a lady. Three times she hands him "a bunch of watercresses" and rejects his suit. Is she telling him to eat watercress to improve his sexiness? Again, it is only speculation, but the high iodine content of watercress may help stimulate the thyroid gland, which, if underactive, leaves one generally sluggish.

CLEANING WATERCRESS

Cut watercress stems just above the waterline. I use a sharp, long knife to skim along under the leaves at water level. This helps keep mud out of your takings. Once home, wash the leaves carefully in a large sinkful of cold water. Drain that off and run another sinkful, adding about ¼ cup chlorine bleach to that sinkful (or about I tablespoon per gallon). Stir to mix the bleach in the water, then put the cress in it, dunk it under, and let it sit for five minutes or more. This will kill anything undesirable on the cress. Rinse two or three times to take away all traces of the disinfectant, and you'll have the best salad green you'll ever taste or the most delicate soup green. The several rinsings also ensure that the cress (or other greens) will be clear of dirt. Nothing ruins a salad like grit.

{RECIPES}

Spring Salad

Anytime from early spring until hot weather, collect any tender greens, such as watercress, mustard, chicory, or dandelion. Add violet leaves

and/or violet flowers. (Nasturtium flowers and leaves, later in the summer, are close kin to watercress and are also delicious; see pages 148–
149.) Remove any tough stems, and tear into bite-size pieces. Wash the
greens very carefully. Salad ingredients can vary endlessly, according to
what's available, and what you like. A spring salad with wild greens is not
only delicious, but worth a hundred vitamin pills. You can also blend
wild greens with the more familiar romaine, endive, butter or Boston
lettuce, red lettuce, radicchio, and so on. And of course, wherever dandelions grow, you can add their slightly bitter leaves to your salad in
the spring and early summer. Later, dandelion greens are distinctly bitter and tough, and not recommended. Search creatively at any grocery
store, as well as in the fields. Most wild greens have lots more food value
than lettuce, as well as more taste. Many vegetables sold as pot greens are
also good in salads, such as mustard, kale, and chard. Dress lightly with
Vinaigrette Salad Dressing (see pages 204–205).

WATERCRESS BISQUE

(Serves 4 or 5)

This is popular in upscale restaurants both here and in continental
Europe. The less you cook the watercress, the better the soup will be.
Chop a big bunch of washed watercress coarsely, and set aside. Sauté 1
small chopped onion in 2 tablespoons butter until soft. Stir in 2 tablespoons flour to make a roux. Stir for 2 minutes over medium heat, but
do not let the roux brown. Slowly add about 1 quart chicken or beef
broth (see pages 203–204). Reserve 1 cup of the watercress for garnish.
Add the rest of the watercress and cook 1 minute. Add one of the following to the soup: a 3-ounce block of cream cheese, warmed to room temperature; 1 cup heavy cream; or 1 cup sour cream. When the mixture just
begins to boil, take it off the heat, stir in the reserved, uncooked cress,
and serve the soup at once.

WATERCRESS SANDWICHES

Collect a bunch of watercress about the size of a basketball, or gather a
gallon-size plastic bag full. Wash the cress well, strip off the leaves from
the tough center stems, and chop it up fairly well. By then you'll have
about 1 quart. Cream a large package of cream cheese (you can use Neuf-
châtel or fat-free) with 2 tablespoons good mayonnaise or butter. To this
mixture add 1 small crushed clove garlic and about 1 tablespoon shaved

onion. A little grated cucumber is good, too. Add the chopped watercress and beat until blended. Add pepper to taste. Stand a loaf of soft white sandwich bread upright on the counter, out of its wrap, and gently shave off the crusts on all sides with a serrated knife, sawing slowly down from top to bottom. Then, smear each square with some of the mixture, and gently roll each into a cylinder. Pack them close together to prevent unrolling, or secure each with a toothpick. Or just make crustless tea sandwiches, and slice them gently crosswise into triangles. Cover the sandwiches with a soaked and wrung-out clean cloth and refrigerate until serving time. If possible, arrange on a bed of more fresh dewy watercress (or other very clean greens) to serve. As everyone knows, these are the epitome of elegance for English teas and lawn parties.

Mustard or land cress leaves substituted in this recipe also make great sandwiches, though not as great as watercress.

If you don't have mayonnaise on hand, see page 204 for how to make a superior mayonnaise yourself.

WILD ONIONS AND GARLIC

The *Allium* (Latin for "garlic") genus is a large one, and includes at least a dozen pungent herbs of the Northern Hemisphere. All are oniony or garlicky in odor and flavor. *Allium canadense*, *A. sativum*, and *A. vineale* are some of the most common wild garlics that grow throughout Canada and pretty much all over the forty-eight states below. *A. cernuum*, *A. stellatum*, and *A. textile* are common onions. *A. tricoccum* is the wild leek, or ramp; it is ubiquitous throughout the United States and Canada. *A. schoenoprasum* is the wild chive. Use them interchangeably.

Description, Habitat, and Season
Onions and garlic, chives and leeks, all grow from base bulbs and bear flowers of purple or white on a leafless stalk that often turns into a little bulb itself. All have green stalks, either flat like onion leaves or round and hollow like chive or scallion leaves, above bulbs that smell distinctly oniony or garlicky. But beware: Onion and garlic belong to the lily family, and some similar-looking (but not similar-smelling) flat-leaved, bulbous plants are poisonous. A case in point is lily of the valley (which can look a lot like ramp). If a bulbed plant looking like a wild onion does not smell garlicky or oniony, let it alone.

In Virginia, there is not a month of the year that some wild onion or garlic can't be found, though some species are early, some late, and they

are certainly more common in spring. They flourish in woods, lawns, gardens, and parks, in sun or shade. In the wild, I find it sometimes difficult to distinguish between the two odors (so that I'm not sure if I have onion or garlic). But never mind; they are all good to eat, bulb and stalks, though you may find that some are too tough to use.

History and Lore

In times when plague rampaged throughout cities in Europe, a garlic clove carried in the mouth was believed to protect the bearer. Garlic was supposed to be effective against vampires too. One wonders if it was that garlic so isolated the taker that no one, vampire or otherwise, would come near. I personally love the scent and flavor of all the alliums, but I gather a lot of people don't.

West Virginia has made famous *A. tricoccum*, the ramp, rampson, or wild leek, which tastes of onion and garlic, and sponsors a spring ramp festival when these flat-leaved, light green onions are ready to eat. Folklore has it that a ramp eater can coexist only with another ramp eater for several days after eating the plants, until the body has rid itself of the sulfur compounds caused by eating the strong-flavored vegetable. But I have eaten ramps on many occasions when people I live with have not, and nobody has shunned me. In my opinion, ramps do you no more

harm, fragrantly speaking, than garlic does.

Ramps grow from Nova Scotia to Georgia, from the Atlantic to the Midwest. All the alliums are high in vitamin C, which is often missing in traditional winter diets. Our ancestors probably instinctively craved these greens when they appeared in the spring, which was the body's way of stocking up. Use both the bulbs and the leaves of ramps. They grow in rich hardwood forests, especially maple, beech, and hemlock. They start in early spring, with rolled-up, quill-like foliage that flattens to long green leaves about 1½ inches wide and 8 inches or so high. Your nose

Ramps look like several poisonous plants, for example lily of the valley, but the onion smell gives it away.

will tell you when you've found them. Ramps grow in large patches that return year after year. Digging them up doesn't hurt them at all. They disappear as soon as the summer foliage overtakes them.

When I was a kid, spring milk often tasted of onion and garlic when the cows ate them along with the new grass in the fields. Nowadays, I learn, the reason we don't have oniony milk in the spring is that dairy farmers don't graze cattle the way they used to, but rather give them prepackaged feed. Even those farmers who graze their cows on fresh grass make sure in the spring (when there might be wild onions in the grass) that the cows are not let out of the barns until they are full, so that they are unlikely to munch onions, or even grass. They just want to lie down and chew their cud.

Garlic and onion are both mildly antiseptic, and in recent years, garlic has been raised from obnoxious insignificance to a place of honor: Both onions and garlic appear from some clinical studies to be effective in lowering cholesterol, as a first-line defense against colds, and even might be useful in preventing cancer.

Finally, the mighty city of Chicago may have been named for ramps. The Menominee Indians called ramps "skunk plants," and a place where they grew abundantly near Lake Michigan, where Chicago is now located, was called *shikako*, or "skunk place."

{RECIPES}

RAMPS WITH EGGS

Carefully clean a mess of ramps (or any wild onions), removing the roots, and chopping the bulbs and stems coarsely. Heat a small amount of butter, oil, or bacon grease in a frying pan, and cook the ramps covered until limp and beginning to brown. Beat some eggs with milk or cream and a little salt. Pour the eggs over the ramps and scramble quickly, not overcooking. This is a typical ramp dish, though ramps are also eaten fried or made into ramp pies, which in places other than West Virginia might be called quiches.

RAMPS AND POTATOES

(Serves 4)

Fry 4 strips of bacon to render the grease. Chop the bacon and set aside. Fry 4 potatoes, thinly sliced, in the bacon grease until done. Add 16 chopped ramps and cook until wilted, just about 2 minutes, then pour in 8 beaten eggs. Gently stir until the egg is lightly set. Sprinkle chopped bacon on top.

RAMPS AND SAUSAGE

(Serves 8 or more)

Fry and separate 1 pound of pork sausage until no red remains. Beat together 4 eggs and 2 cups milk. In a big casserole, layer 8 large potatoes, thinly sliced, and the cooked sausage with 2 dozen chopped ramps, bulbs and greens. Pour the egg-milk mixture over the potatoes and ramps, and top with 2 or 3 cups of grated cheddar cheese. Bake in a 350°F oven for 1 hour or more, or until the potatoes are tender.

ONIONS WITH PASTA

(Serves 4 to 6)

When you put the water on to boil for the pasta, melt a stick of unsalted butter, and sauté as many (up to a whole gallon-size plastic bag full) wild onions, garlic, or ramps as you want, tops and bulbs together.

Sprinkle with 2 teaspoon sugar, reduce heat, and cook slowly for ½ hour, which allows the sugar to begin to caramelize and the butter taste to thoroughly permeate the onions. Cook 1 pound of pasta al dente. When the pasta is ready, add ½ cup white wine or dry sherry to the onions, stir in and cook for just 1 or 2 minutes, and toss with the freshly cooked pasta. Taste, then salt and pepper lightly if needed. Serve with freshly grated Parmesan, pecorino, or Romano cheese for a meal of great delicacy. Note: Olive oil might be substituted in this recipe, but it will taste quite different. The slow cooking and caramelizing in the butter give this dish its unusual taste. Red onions or yellow may also be substituted if you haven't got any wild onions.

CHICKWEED

Chickweed is also called by its botanical name *Stellaria* (presumably for its flowers' starlike shape). It is a good wild plant to know and to eat.

Description, Habitat, and Season
Chickweed rockets out in a starburst from the ground, and in the spring rises up from the ground like a—uh, weed. It grows anytime it's not freezing. In spring, it has a small white flower at the tip of the plant. It has only five petals, but they are double so that they appear to be ten. You gather it in May and June as soon as flowers appear. I have noticed it most thickly near rocks and rock walls in my garden, and I presume it's benefitting from the sun's warmth on stone. There are literally thousands of similar species, and these fill a need for spring tonic plants; they're palatable and very healthy, and have lots of ascorbic acid, magnesium, niacin, selenium, and potassium. My paternal grandparents had some notions about spring green plants being "tonic" and thinning the blood after winter. This is one they ate.

The whole plant is crisp, juicy, with laxative and antihistamine traits. In my yard, it's everywhere, and word is that's true in most temperate places in the world. This plant supposedly combats obesity. You can eat it alone or in salads in spring. It makes a great sandwich, reminding one of sprouts (and maybe corn) in both flavor and consistency. It grows about 2 feet tall and has oval leaves with pointed tips. Steaming it is certainly possible, but it's stringy. I like the fresh "green" taste. I don't recommend cooking chickweed.

MILK THISTLE

Milk thistle (*Silybum marianum*), also called Scotch thistle, is all over Virginia in the spring. I've heard it called Mary's thistle, and mostly just called "thistle." Goats and donkeys eat it eagerly.

Description, Habitat, and Season
This plant is easy to find, and to identify, as it grows its purple or pink spiky flowers to about 3 feet in sunny fields and rocky pastures pretty much everywhere. It's found in early summer. The prickly leaves, when cut, bleed a milky sap that, according to myth, is Virgin Mary's milk. I add it here as it is reputed to protect and strengthen the liver. The leaves are a nice addition to salads, and liver healing when eaten with carrot and dandelion leaves.

History and Lore
All parts of the milk thistle are edible: stalks, leaves (remove the prickly parts), roots, and yes, those purple flowers. It can be eaten raw or cooked, but in my opinion, it's only really good if cooked like spinach, which taste it's closer to than any other. Add salt and butter. You can also make a tea out of crushed seeds and leaves, which doesn't taste exactly great in my opinion, but isn't unpleasant either. (And if it cures the

liver, after a little too much booze, well—isn't that worth suffering for?) Botanist James Duke comments that there is such a great abuse of alcohol in our society today that we should all be using milk thistle. Sources warn against eating too much milk thistle, but you probably won't be tempted to. I have used it in a dried pill form.

CLEAVERS, OR GOOSEGRASS, ALSO CALLED BEDSTRAW

Description, Habitat, and Season
Cleavers (*Galium aparium*) will find you, and cling to you like a needy cat. In spring, they grow maybe 24 inches high in Virginia, in woods, or in the shady parts of my backyard, and in "moist thickets." The early sprouts are tenderest, but I just like to eat them by themselves. They get a bit stringy as they grow higher.

History and Lore
Cleavers have long been a favorite spring green in Appalachia. I actually like the taste of cleavers, and I actually believe the folklore—namely, that they can help you lose a few pounds of winter weight. Grown every-

where but in arctic zones and the desert, you don't have to even identify them. They will find you—and cleave onto you. They stick by little hairs to your clothing. They appear in early spring, can be eaten out of hand or cooked, and are said (scarily) to be many good things to many folks: astringent, diaphoretic, vulnerary, and aperient. If examined closely, they show a natural precedent for Velcro-like closures: hook-like hairs. I put them in this edition because I'm for anything natural that might help folks lose weight. Since we all create our own realities, if you believe it, it just might work.

LEMON BALM

This delightful herb probably grows wild somewhere near you, maybe even in your yard. Lemon balm (*Melissa officionalis*) is a strongly smelling citrusy herb.

Description, Habitat, and Season
Lemon balm has scallopy leaves that smell strongly of lemon. It grows in profusion in the vicinity where once a single plant grew. *Melissa* is

quite strongly sedative, so use half a dozen fresh leaves only for a cup of tea that tastes heavenly. It induces sleep, and so would be useful at bedtime. It is also a useful stress-reliever. It can be crushed and dried for winter use, in which case don't use too much for a cup of tea, only about a teaspoon. It is used mainly for flavoring, but James Duke claims its antifungal activity can relieve Chronic Stress Syndrome. He, possibly America's foremost herbologist, advises ginseng and melissa tea to alleviate distress or depression.

JEWELWEED

Jewelweed (*Impatiens capensis*) is one of many similar species, with orange, yellow, or reddish spotted flowers. It's also called Touch Me Not. This lovely plant grows all summer by streams and rivers in shady woods. It has water-holding properties and becomes very liquid when crushed. And that liquid is very useful in scrubbing off the oily substance called urushiol that poison ivy can spread to your skin merely as you brush by it. I include jewelweed as antidote for itching. It's fun, beautiful, and useful for the skin, but can also be used as a food. It's also said to be good for stomach upsets, and it doesn't taste bad.

History and Lore

Fun game: When you walk by jewelweed in summer, the seeds violently explode onto anyone who brushes against them. You can encourage this bursting by touching them with your hands. The tickly sensation has led friends of mine to call it the sex plant. Of course, you are helping the seeds to scatter and make new plants.

It's beautiful, a gorgeous scene in summer woods. The leaves are grayish; upon them, water balls into jewel-like droplets after rain, creating, along with the colorful flowers, a scene of diamonds sparkling in the sun.

I, for all my love of the woods, have all my life been a magnet for anything that might cause a body to itch: mosquitoes, poison ivy, ticks, etcetera. If you know or suspect you've got a bite or been in poison ivy, just grab a handful of jewelweed, which is usually somewhere nearby, crush it and rub it all over what might have been exposed. It's very soothing and does halt itching.

{RECIPES}

I know a useful recipe for a very good bug repellent—I've experimented with insect repellents all my life, not being as fond of insects as they are of me. Collect as much jewelweed as you can crush and stuff into a quart jar. Fill the jar with about 2 cups apple cider vinegar. Store for two weeks, covered, then strain. You probably know that cider vinegar alone, with no herbs added, is reputed to be useful to settle the stomach. But this is repellent we're talking about: add 10 to 20 drops of each of the following herbal oils: lavender, peppermint, cedar, and rosemary. Shake before using. It stays strong and potent, and lovely smelling, for about a year. Insects just hate it!

KUDZU

My take is that you need no pictures. Everyone knows by now what the green carpet or blanket of kudzu (*Pueraria lobata*) looks like as it's taken over roadside fencerows, hillsides of cedar scrubs, and low bushes everywhere in the southern states; the vines, as they drape over trees, create fantastical shapes, leading to nicknames for the cheerful vine such as Green Giant and Green Godzilla. Kudzu was brought to this country to grow feed for cattle, with unintended consequences—each branch and shoot can grow a foot a day, and a plant can sprout millions of shoots a season. As we know, the plant has quickly grown out of hand. The good news is that it is indeed great fodder food for animals, and for us the news is that leaves, flowers, and root are not only edible but quite tasty. The steamed downy tips of shoots taste a bit like snow peas, or cinnamon fern—and there's plenty of it! Use only those tender shoots that break off readily. The purple, grape-scented flowers are edible, but not especially good. I have not tried the roots as, so far, I haven't found any.

As kudzu is a 3-leaved plant, carefully compare the photos with those of poison ivy. They don't really look much alike, but they might to a beginner. As poison ivy could well grow amongst kudzu, you might make a mistake, and you don't want to do that.

Poison ivy.

BEWARE!

There are some plants you don't want to fool with any more than you'd want to pet a rattlesnake.

Woodland plants to be avoided include the lovely Jack-in-the-pulpit, mayapple, jimson weed, poison ivy and poison oak, and, surprisingly, buttercups.

If you forage for wild cherries, beware of the leaves and twigs. They contain cyanide. As do peach pits. If you collect elderberries (and, in my opinion, you should), don't ever put the leaves, twigs, or bark in your mouth. Don't eat acorns. Even if the Indians did. They knew how to get the kidney-compromising compounds out before making acorn bread.

[3]
FUNGI: MUSHROOMS

It is not those far-fetched fruits which the speculator imports that concern us chiefly, but rather those which you have fetched yourself in the hold of a basket, from some far hill or swamp, journeying all the long afternoon, the first of the season, consigned to your friends at home.

—Henry David Thoreau

Mushrooms are among the most mysterious plants on earth. The word *mushroom* is thought to derive from an Old French word, *mousseron*, meaning "moss grower." They spring up apparently out of nowhere overnight, and disappear nearly as quickly. Their growth habits were not well understood until recently. Some gleam at night with a green phosphorescence. Many grow in ever-widening circles. Some toxic mushrooms have long been part of certain secret rituals, providing mind-altering substances. Thus, mushrooms have been revered as doorways to other dimensions that only the users are privileged to visit.

One theologian, John Allegro, in *The Sacred Mushroom and the Cross*, states that the Egyptian mushroom hieroglyph, long believed to represent a kind of parasol, really represents the toxic *Amanita muscaria* mushroom, which in its early stages of poisoning causes bright hallucinations. The mushroom is phallic in appearance and is "born" from a volva that looks like an egg. Allegro thinks that there has existed throughout the ages a mushroom cult—and that the Christ figure actually evolved from this primitive fertility cult.

The word *toadstool*, though colorfully evocative, refers usually to any mushroom that is poisonous. To forage for mushrooms, you will need good mushroom field guides. Choose one with drawings or tinted lithographs and another with good photographs of the mushrooms, for poisonous mushrooms can kill you. But my philosophy about that is similar to my philosophy about poisonous snakes and Lyme-disease-carrying ticks: You don't stay out of the woods because there are things in there that might hurt you; you just proceed with caution and awareness. In the case of fungi, stay with the safe ones.

Fungi like wet weather, wet wood, wet woods. They lack chlorophyll, which is the green-making chemical found in plants, and they flourish in heat and dampness. There are thousands of different kinds of mushrooms, and thousands more fungi, a huge group without which we could not live, including everything from the yeast that raises our bread to the beast that gives you athlete's foot.

If you want to test mushrooms that are not described herein for safety, a step further is to make a spore print, a simple process that I often use to identify new fungi. All you need is a pack of black construction paper and regular white paper. To make a spore print, lay a piece of black paper slightly overlapping a white one. Then lay an open mushroom, gills down, over the line where the black paper and white paper meet, so that its spores will fall half on white paper and half on black. Cover the mushroom with an upside-down bowl, and leave it for two to eight hours. Then examine the spores. Compare them with what your books say; all mushroom books identify the color of the spore print. The spores will deposit on the two colors of paper, and the contrast will allow you to see the subtlety of the spore color.

A flat-bottomed basket for gathering keeps mushrooms in good shape, though a grocery bag or plastic bag will do. You can pretty much tell from your specimens which ones need special pampering and which are all right to toss into a plastic sack.

Morels

Mushrooms sometimes get a bad rap because of the harmful varieties. But good mushrooms, if you stay with those easy to identify, are nearly calorie free, taste like the woodland air smells after rain, are easy to find, and make delicious meatless gourmet dishes. In all the mushroom recipes, any mushroom can really be substituted for any other. And once again, amounts of the mushroom are not crucial. Mushrooms (and eggplant) are the worst culprits for soaking up oil and butter. Try brushing them lightly with oil or melted butter and roasting them in the oven for the same effect.

I offer here only easily identifiable fungi. For heaven's sake, never taste a mushroom you can't identify. Do not try to identify any mushroom by my description only. You need to check with at least one other reference, and possibly a third. The best guides, in my estimation, are Alexander H. Smith and Nancy Smith Weber's *The Mushroom Hunter's Field Guide*, University of Michigan Press, 1980; and Orson K. Miller's *Mushrooms of North America*, Dutton, 1972.

MORELS

Morels (*Morchella appalachiensis, M. esculenta, M. angusticeps, M. deliciosa, M. crassipes*) are possibly the most delicious of the wild mushrooms, and once identified, they are impossible to confuse with any others. *Morchella* is

Golden morels emerge later than the dark ones in Appalachia.

simply the Latin term for "mushroom," and *esculenta* and *deliciosa* mean that one is "edible" and the other "delicious." *Angusticeps* means "narrow," and *appalachiensis* is the name of the subspecies that grows in the Appalachian Mountains from Newfoundland to Georgia; mycologists differ on whether it is a different subspecies from *angusticeps*.

Morels, popular throughout the Temperate Zone here and in Europe, go by various folk names. They are called land fish or upland fish (perhaps from their shape, perhaps from their elusive flavor, which I would call earthy but which some might call fishy); marls (surely a corruption of the name, but also maybe after the kind of soft, crumbly rock geologists call marl, which is full of holes and pits like the fungi); merkles, which is a corruption of "miracles"; smokies (the dark ones); honeycomb mushrooms; sponge mushrooms; musharoons, which one assumes comes from a folksy mishearing; and *morchellas*, from the Latin name. There is a dark morel, ranging in color from gray to tan to rusty brown, a pale golden one, and a grayish white one. All are fine to eat.

Description, Habitat, and Season
Though the dark ones (*M. angusticeps* and *M. appalachiensis*) appear a couple of weeks earlier than the lighter ones, they overlap, and most "messes" will have specimens of two or three kinds, including one that may or may not be a true morel, but looks like the others, *M. semilibra*, or the half-free morel (so called because the cap attaches to the stalk halfway down the

cap). It is also edible. Morels pop up in hardwood forests in the middle of spring "when the oak leaves are the size of mouse ears," and are said to be especially numerous in years and places following a forest fire. Where you find Jack-in-the-pulpits and trillium, look for morels. Some variety grows everywhere north of the tropics all the way to the Arctic Circle.

All morels have the characteristic appearance variously described as pitted, ridged, spongelike, cone shaped, or wrinkled; all are between 3 and 6 inches high; all have hollow stems and hollow interiors; and all are shaped vaguely like trees. They have no gills. None of them is easy to see on the woodland floor. The flavor is absolutely gorgeous: smoky, earthy, elusive, echt mushroom!

A flat basket is probably the best thing to take picking, for it keeps the delicate morels intact better than grocery bags or plastic bags. But a flat basket is unwieldy, and I opt rather for the convenience of a red plastic tote. (Red can be seen from a distance, and you can use it to mark a hunting boundary while you are circling looking for mushrooms.)

History and Lore
Morels are so wonderful that even poets have eulogized them. Among the best descriptions of morels is that of my friend the poet William Jay Smith:

> Not ringed but rare, not gilled but polyp-like, having sprung up overnight—
> These mushrooms of the gods, resembling human organs uprooted, rooted only on the air,
> Looking like lungs wrenched from the human body, lungs reversed, not breathing internally
> But being the externalization of breath itself, these spicy, twisted cones,
> These perforated brown-white asparagus tips—these morels, smelling of wet graham crackers mixed with maple leaves;
> . . . Tasting of the sweet damp woods and of the rain one inch above the meadow:

> It was like feasting upon air.

{RECIPES}

As morels are hollow, they need special cleaning treatment. Slice each in half from top to bottom to determine if it houses any insalubrious creatures: I've found stones, centipedes, and slugs inside morels, so be warned. Then jostle them in warm, heavily salted water for about 5 minutes (this dislodges any dirt fragments that may be caught in the wrinkled surface) before draining the halves on paper towels. The salt will force out the tiny wood fleas that also call these mushrooms home.

There are several ways to keep morels. Of course they are best used fresh, as most things are. But once cooked, they can be frozen. Some folks dry morels by sewing them onto a string and putting them in a warm, dry oven or attic until they are totally dry or by using a dehydrator.

MORELS AND WILD RICE CASSEROLE

(For a crowd, to celebrate spring)

Preheat the oven to 350°F. Assemble a basketful of morels, butter, onion, celery, wild rice, 2 cups chicken or beef broth, 1 can smoked almonds, white rice, dry sherry, and fresh parsley.

Sauté at least 2 dozen morels in a little or a lot of butter, stirring occasionally, for 5 to 10 minutes. Set aside. In 4 tablespoons butter, sauté 1 cup chopped onion and a few finely chopped center stalks of celery, with leaves (about 1 cup). Add to this 1 cup washed, uncooked wild rice and 2 cups salted chicken or beef broth. Cover and simmer on low heat for 35 minutes. While the rice is simmering, chop the cup of almonds. Set them aside.

To the half-cooked wild rice, add 1 cup plain uncooked rice and 1 cup each salted water or water with a bouillon cube dissolved in it and dry sherry. Stir, turn the rice immediately into a greased casserole, add the morels and almonds, stir again, and bake, covered, in the oven for about 1 hour, or until the liquid is all absorbed. You may want to sprinkle chopped parsley on the finished product. You can leave out the almonds or substitute roasted pecans. The best accompaniment for this is briefly steamed fresh wild asparagus.

MOREL OR OTHER MUSHROOM SOUFFLÉ

(Serves 4)

Chop 20 to 30 morels finely, and sauté them in 2 tablespoons butter, margarine, or bacon fat. For this recipe, olive oil isn't recommended. Sprinkle them with 1 tablespoon flour, stir over heat to make a roux, add about 2 tablespoons heavy cream, stir until thick, and dust with nutmeg. This will make about 1 cup. Cool slightly.

After, follow the soufflé instructions (see pages 205–206) using a straight-sided soufflé dish and 5 eggs plus 1 extra egg white. Don't forget to preheat your oven. Beat the yolks until smooth. Beat the whites until glossy, add a little of the mushroom mix to the yolks, then add the yolks back into the mushroom mix. Add a big spoonful of the whites to "lighten" the mushrooms, then fold it all into the rest of the whites carefully. Bake until the center is just firm, and serve at once.

PUFFBALLS

Puffball, like so many folk names for wild foods, describes this fungus well: a puffy ball. This fungus belongs to several related species. Its most common genus name, *Calvatia*, comes from the Latin word *calva*, meaning "scalp," "bald head," or even "skull," which aptly describes this round, whitish fungus. The western puffball, *Calbovista subsculpta*, has *bovis* in the name, perhaps suggesting its propensity to grow in cow fields; *subsculpta* describes the peculiar carved effect of the surface.

Description, Habitat, and Season
Puffballs grow all over the world in temperate zones, in the spring or in wet summer weather, but most often they pop up overnight in the early fall, after rain, in fields. They like golf courses, lawns, and pastures, and they return to the same locales year after year. Puffballs vary enormously in size, at their smallest like round white golf balls, and at their largest like round lightly browned loaves of bread, 6 to 8 inches across. They are pure white throughout, with no gill structure, and are firm and foamlike inside, something like dense angel food cake in both weight and consistency.

One western species has flattish, cone-like scales covering the surface. Throw out any that are not pure white throughout, that smell like wet dog, or that have soft spots, worm holes, or insects in them.

Puffballs can be safely collected in baskets or bags. Once home, they need a quick rinse to get any dirt off the outer surfaces. Always slice small puffballs through from top to bottom to make sure they are white throughout. Since *Amanita*, deadly poisonous white-gilled mushrooms, do often grow among other mushrooms, be sure you haven't accidentally picked up the button form of an *Amanita*. If you have, you will clearly see the outline of the gill structure, stalk, veil, and cap. Of course, you must discard that specimen and wash your knife well before going on to the next mushroom.

{RECIPES}

If the mushrooms are a firm, solid white "sponge" throughout, then they can be sliced, diced, or chopped, and sautéed slowly, or sliced and brushed with oil or melted butter and baked until brown. They can be frozen after cooking for later use if there are too many to eat right away. I have never heard of anyone trying to dry puffballs, though in theory it ought to be possible, if you slice them thin.

PUFFBALL SLICES SAUTÉ

Cut the puffballs into ¾-inch slices, and sauté them in pure butter, or half butter and half cooking oil, until nicely browned. Sprinkle lightly with lemon juice and salt for a wonderful side dish.

Puffballs can be used in any other recipe that calls for mushrooms. They have a nice earthy "mushroomy" taste, and remind some of tofu. Like tofu, they're adaptable.

CHANTERELLES

Chanterelles (*Cantharellus cibarius*) are midsummer, wet-weather mushrooms that can be seen from afar. The Latin name of the genus, *Cantharellus*, comes from *cantharus*, "a drinking goblet," and thus defines the shape perfectly. The black chanterelle is indeed reminiscent in shape of a cornucopia, whose name derives from the word for horn in Latin. All types are wonderful.

Description, Habitat, and Season

Chanterelles have fluted edges, are shaped like flared wineglasses or vases, and in place of gills underneath have veins. Chanterelles come in many colors. The easiest to see, *C. cibarius*, are egg-yolk yellow and look like flowers blooming on the forest floor. There are also white chanterelles in New England woods called *C. subalbidus*, or "almost white," and black or gray chanterelles called *Craterellus cornucopioides*, which describes the fungi as both "crated" and "cornucopia shaped." These are called also death trumpets, though they are delicious and safe. There is a gray-purple-brown chanterelle called *Cantharellus clavatus* (which means "club shaped," from the Latin *clavus*), and tiny red-orange, or cinnabar, chanterelles called *Cantharellus cinnabarinus*. These mushrooms, like most others, spread by underground mycelia (tiny white threads you sometimes see hanging off the bottoms), so look year after year in the same locality where you found them once. I have found chanterelles most often in coniferous, especially pine, woods, a day to three days after a good soaking rain in midsummer.

Again, a basket with a wide bottom would be best, but a flat-bottomed bag, or even a plastic bag, will do.

{RECIPES}

Collect only the young mushrooms. Insects also find chanterelles delicious, and since you don't want to ruin your batch with one bug-infested specimen, check for insect infestation by cutting the stem off halfway between the veins and the soil and checking the stem. If it has bug tunnels, discard the specimen.

Stewed Chanterelles

(For pasta, rice, steak, or toast)

Melt a small amount of butter over medium-low heat, add clean chanterelles, sliced if they are big, and sauté, stirring occasionally to coat mushrooms evenly. Add a splash of dry wine, cover, stew for about 20 minutes, and salt lightly. Chanterelles need slow, relatively long cooking, as they can be tough. Add a squeeze of lemon juice, and serve them at once on pasta, rice or wild rice, steak or roast beef, or toast.

LION'S MANE

This delicious autumn mushroom (*Hericium erinaceus*) is fairly rare, but I add it here, confident that no mistakes can be made with this one—it is so easily recognizable. It grows throughout the country, on hardwood, and looks most like a big white beard. It should be eaten only if pure white; yellowing of a specimen indicates spoilage. It can be small or large, and it tends to be tough, so cook it slowly to tenderize it. It is really good if fresh and white. The specimen in the photo, brought to me by a friend, weighed over fifteen pounds. I cook lion's mane slowly in butter and white wine.

BEEFSTEAK MUSHROOM S

This is one of my favorite late-summer mushrooms. Beefsteak mushrooms (*Fistulina hepatica*) look on the top rather like raw liver (which its Latin name reflects) or a piece of steak, and it grows shelflike out from old logs or stumps, especially dead oak and chestnut.

Description, Habitat, and Season
Beefsteak mushrooms sometimes even "bleed" when cut. It looks whitish or pinkish underneath, but if you look at it with a magnifying glass, you will see that the underside is made up of crowded fistulas, or tiny separate tubes. Most pieces will be about the size of a hand. Beefsteak mushrooms have a sourish meaty taste and a nice chewy consistency, and it grows throughout the summer if it's wet. Hold out one hand, then run your other hand over the top, noticing how the skin seems loose. Beefsteak mushrooms have a similar feel, caused by a gelatinous layer just under the surface. Use them the way you'd use any other mushroom.

{RECIPES}

I found a great recipe for this fungus in a British magazine.

HERB-CRUSTED BEEFSTEAK FUNGUS

(Serves 4)

Marinate about 1 pound sliced beefsteak mushrooms in white wine, salt, pepper, and chopped parsley for half an hour. Dip mushrooms in an egg-flour batter, then sprinkle with chopped parsley, along with other herbs if you like. Dip in bread crumbs and fry in olive oil or bland vegetable oil. Serve on a bed of salad greens with vinegar on the side. I have been unable to try this one, as I haven't found beefsteak recently.

SULFUR SHELF (OR CHICKEN MUSHROOM)

The name *Polyporus sulphureus* tells anyone with even a smattering of Latin that this is a many-pored mushroom of a yellow hue. The common name, sulfur shelf mushroom, describes its growth pattern, out from the trunk of a tree like a pile of shelves, as well as its sulfur-yellow color. This is sometimes called the chicken mushroom: The flesh is fairly dry and dense, and it tastes much like chicken breast.

Description, Habitat, and Season

Polyporus sulphureus are easy to identify: They grow in midsummer on the sides of hardwood trees or on rotting logs and are sunset-orange colored on top, with fluted edges and yellow, porous bottoms instead of gills. Sulfur shelf fungi sometimes grow to enormous size, with brackets climbing many feet up on a tree. However, if the ones you find are big, take only the smallest, freshest brackets, or the outer edges, for the older part closer to the tree can be tough and strong-flavored, not to mention full of bugs. These fungi aren't as fragile as most, so they needn't be treated with as much delicacy. Merely take them home, carefully brush and rinse off all dirt, and drain until dry on paper towels.

{RECIPES}

Sulfur shelf mushrooms are best, I think, creamed. They need thin slicing and slow cooking or sautéing, as they are tougher than most mushrooms. But they have a wonderful flavor.

CREAMED SULFUR SHELF

Slice about 1 quart sulfur shelf fungi thinly, and sauté in butter and a bit of mashed garlic for 10 minutes. Make a Cream Sauce (see page 210) using 2 tablespoons flour, 2 tablespoons butter, and 2 tablespoons cream, and enough dry sherry or milk (or a combination) for the consistency you like. Add salt and pepper to taste. These are great served on toast, rice, or pasta, or alone.

FUNGHI ITALIANO

Slice the sulfur shelf mushrooms thinly, and sauté in olive oil, not too much, with chopped garlic added. Stir frequently, salt and pepper to taste, finish with fresh lemon juice sprinkled over the whole, and stir one last time. Sprinkle with chopped parsley before serving. Serve alone or tossed with hot pasta.

OYSTER MUSHROOMS

Oyster mushrooms (*Pleurotus ostreatus*)

The botanical name of this mushroom, *Pleurotus ostreatus* or *P. sapidus*, comes from the word for the lining of the thorax that covers the lungs, *pleura*, and is kin to our word for the inflammation of that lining, pleurisy. It is likely that the shape of the mushroom suggested this name. *Ostreatus* is Latin for "oyster," and *sapidus* means "flavorful" or "sapid."

Description, Habitat, and Season
Oyster mushrooms grow from spring to fall on the sides of dying hardwood trees or from the tops or sides of dead stumps, and they are rounded down at the margins, with off-center, thick, tough stalks and white gills, caps of unequal size, and a delicate odor like oysters. *Pleurotus* is often available in grocery stores, as it is now grown commercially.

{RECIPES}

When you find oyster mushrooms, slice off only the fresh ends of the mushroom tops or the small young growth. The old part closest to the stalks may be tough. *Pleurotus* need scrupulous cleaning to remove the little hard black beetles that like to live in the gills. Soak them in warm salted water for a few minutes, jostle them up and down in the water, and drain and pat them dry before using. Sliced, sautéed, and made into soup or a casserole, they are especially wonderful, and they taste much like scalloped oysters.

FAUX OYSTER STEW

For this elegant soup, you might want to keep the mushrooms as whole as possible (to be suggestive of the shapes of oysters), though you can also slice or chop them.

Sauté in a large saucepan with about 4 tablespoons butter about 1 pound, or 25 to 50, oyster mushrooms (and a bit of diced onion and celery if you like). As they begin to brown a bit, add a splash of dry sherry. Cover and cook 5 minutes. Sprinkle with 4 tablespoons flour and a half of a nutmeg, grated, and stir until smooth. Slowly add 1 quart milk, and a little salt and pepper, stirring constantly. Simmer gently just until bubbles begin to form around the edge of the pan. Take the soup off the heat before it boils, and serve at once. You can also use half chicken broth and half cream, or milk and half-and-half, or even evaporated skim milk. (The process for this rich soup works equally well with any mushroom.)

BOLETUS

Boletes (*Boletus castaneus*) are great favorites in Europe and gaining popularity in America. In Italy, these beloved fungi are called porcini ("pig food"), in France, cèpes (this word derives from an Old French word for onion, *caepa*), and in Germany, Steinpilz, or "stone mushrooms." (They may in fact appear from a distance like stones.) The genus name *Boletus* comes from *bolo*, the word for "ball," and the species name, *castaneus*, Latin for "chestnut," probably refers to their toasty brown color. They are also called *B. edulis*, the "edible boletus."

Description, Habitat, and Season
Boletes are large autumn mushrooms, 3 inches to a foot across, and grow in coniferous forests in America and Europe. They have brown, dry, rounded tops with creamy pores underneath instead of gills and fat reticulated (crisscrossed like netting) stalks. Having tested probably two dozen different boletes, the chestnut, or edible, boletus is the only one I would

recommend. Some are poisonous: Avoid any that are red or that stain blue when a piece of the flesh is broken off. The American chestnut boletus has a look-alike that is benign, but bitter tasting. The ones you want are toasty brown and have firm ivory flesh, a mild earthy odor, and a pleasant taste.

History and Lore

Boletes are marvelous, and safe if you identify them carefully. They apparently dry well, and that is how they are sold in Italy, although the ones I've tried in Virginia have molded before I could dry them out.

Boletes are often the "toadstools" you see in illustrations for fairy tales; elves are rumored to use the big boletes for resting places.

{RECIPES}

PORCINI IN PUFF PASTRY

(Serves 4 to 6)

Preheat the oven to 400°F. Thaw I sheet commercial puff pastry for 20 minutes, and roll it into a 12 × 14-inch rectangle. Sauté I cup or so sliced boletus (or other) mushrooms in 2 tablespoons butter with I or 2 crushed or minced cloves garlic, and season to taste with salt, pepper, a squeeze of lemon juice, and a scattering of nutmeg. Sprinkle the lightly browned fungi with 2 tablespoons flour, and stir until a roux is formed. Add 2 to 4 tablespoons heavy cream to the mix, stirring well. The sauce should be thick. Spoon the mix down the center of the rolled-out dough, fold both sides over the middle, and press a fork along both ends to seal the puff. Quickly brush the top with cream before putting it in the oven, to enhance browning. Bake 15 to 20 minutes, or until puffed and golden. Let cool about 10 minutes. Slice for a sublime first course.

I sauté all my wild mushrooms in a little butter, then freeze them for further use in labeled ziplock sandwich bags. The cooking stops the natural enzyme action that causes them to spoil, as well as reducing them in volume.

GRILLED PORCINI

(Serves 4)

Slice 2 large boletus (or 4 smaller specimens) thickly. Brush them with 2 tablespoons melted butter and 2 tablespoons olive oil with a mashed clove of garlic added. Salt them lightly, and lay them on a hot grill. Turn them after 5 minutes, sprinkle them with ½ cup hearty dry red wine, such as Chianti, watch them carefully, and cook 5 more minutes. Remove to a plate and keep warm. Arrange slices on four plates with parsley garnishes for a delicate first course. Serve with crusty Italian bread. This recipe also works well with the large portobello mushrooms now available in stores.

COPRINUS

Coprinopsis atramentarius and *Coprinellus micaceus*, both called inky caps, humble in the world of fungi. The genus name comes from the word *koprus*, meaning "excrement." They often grow where deadwood, or in fields frequented by cows. The *C. micaceus* ules much like the tops of sugar cookies (*mica* in Latin is "grain"), while *C. atramentarius* (meaning only "edible") do erwise they are similar.

The largest of this autodigestive genus, *Coprinus comatus*, mane mushroom, has scales that become curly or shaggy become inky with age. *Coma* is the Latin word for "hair." can be found along paved roadways, driveways, and in fields and lawns.

Description, Habitat, and Season

The coprini are bell-shaped mushrooms usually on thin, brittle stalks, most often found in urban settings, especially around the stumps or bases of old rotting trees, and sometimes they are as dense as a carpet. You can find them in spring, summer, and autumn, in muggy weather after rain. They are grayish brown, deeply striated, packed together, and distinguishable because they are autodigestive. That means that the old specimens have a wet, black, melted appearance at the margins, caused by the process of self-digestion. They range in size from under an inch to nearly 2 inches in diameter.

Coprini may be ignored by some because many of them are small and difficult to clean: They push dirt up with them, on top of them, and are packed so densely that it's sometimes hard to get them to part company with their clods of dirt. They are also thin fleshed and break easily. But all the coprini are absolutely delicious and, to my mind, worth the trouble. Also, you don't have to go far to find them. They probably grow somewhere on your street, or in your yard, or near your woodpile. They love the mulched ground underneath our azaleas. I've seen them come up through concrete driveways and, once, beside a bathroom toilet, during a rainy summer.

I have recently read that the coprini's autodigestive principle keeps your liver from processing alcohol; thus you ought not to drink alcohol within several hours of eating coprini, nor eat them within several hours of drinking alcohol.

{RECIPES}

SAUTÉED COPRINI

(For rice, pizza, or pasta)

Wash coprini carefully, discarding any old, deteriorating specimens. Drain them thoroughly on plenty of paper towels or kitchen towels. Melt 3 or 4 tablespoons butter or olive oil over medium heat, and add the drained mushrooms. Season with a little salt and pepper, some garlic if you like, and a squeeze of lemon juice. Being thin fleshed, the coprini cook down quickly and release a dark, rich gravy. At this point, you can dry them out by keeping them over the heat until the liquid is evaporated and use them to scatter on pizza. Or you can add a little cream to the mushrooms before they dry out and serve them on rice or pasta.

Mushroom Pizza

Make a pizza crust according to the process in the recipe on pages 206–207. Lightly oil the pizza by drizzling with 1 teaspoon olive oil. Scatter the top with sliced fresh coprinus, morel, or field mushrooms sautéed lightly in olive oil. Sprinkle with chopped garlic, salt, pepper, parsley, and a bit of fresh basil. Add a light layer of grated Parmesan cheese, and bake quickly (about 10 minutes) until it begins to brown, for the best pizza you ever tasted.

FIELD MUSHROOMS

The field mushroom, *Agaricus campestris*, is America's most popular mushroom. Its close relative, *A. bisporus*, or the double-spored *Agaricus*, is the button mushroom available fresh in grocery stores and the mushroom found in commercially canned mushroom soup. A large relative is the portobello, found fresh these days in grocery stores. They are the fungi most widely used in America and are called, simply, mushrooms. *Agaricus* comes from a word in Latin, *ager*, related to "acre" and "agriculture," meaning "productive field" or "pasture." *Campestris* is related to "campus" in English, and in Latin it, too, means "plain," "open level spot," or "field." Both names tell clearly where this mushroom is to be found. The French name, *champignon* (champs plus pignon), means "field nut."

Description, Habitat, and Season
The favorite habitats of field mushrooms are golf courses, fields where cattle graze, parks, and wide lawns. They like wet weather and grow in late summer or early fall, sometimes in prodigious quantities, often in small or large circles, from white buttons about an inch in diameter to big specimens 5 inches across. Their color is whitish to pale beige. The way to identify them is to pick a young, an old, and an in-between specimen. The young buttons have tender, pale pink or flesh-colored gills, sometimes still folded into themselves; in time the young gills darken to a chocolatey brown, and the old, larger specimens have very dark reddish brown or blackish brown gills. Avoid any field mushrooms with white gills.

Take along a flat-bottomed basket to gather field mushrooms, for they are a bit brittle and have a slight tendency to break. Also take along a knife, with which to cut the caps off just beneath the caps. This avoids most of the dirt that so often clings to the stems, which are stringy and tough anyway.

{RECIPES}

Try to brush the dirt off field mushrooms, then rinse them off with water instead of soaking them, for they blot up water like sponges and you might end up with a watery mess of spore-stained mushrooms. If you have to dunk them, then drain them thoroughly on paper towels or kitchen towels before you cook them.

In the early fall, field mushrooms are often so numerous you can gather a year's supply in an hour. After sautéing them in butter, you can freeze them in small containers for year-round use.

MUSHROOM-STUFFED CHICKEN WITH GRAVY

(Serves 2 to 4)
Preheat the oven to 350°F. Wash a raw young frying chicken well, and rub it inside and outside with crushed garlic and salt. Stuff it full with fresh, raw, salted field mushrooms or morels. Let them overflow the cavity and fall around the chicken. Bake the bird for 1½ hours. Rice and gravy is the perfect accompaniment. Cook the rice on top of the stove. When the chicken is done, with a basting syringe suck up about 1 cup of the cooking liquid, which will be dark, rich, and delicious. To a small pan, add 2 or 3 tablespoons flour, then add the chicken-mushroom

liquid slowly, stirring the whole time, until you have an unbelievably delicious gravy. If it gets too thick, add a little water and keep stirring. Add 1 tablespoon soy sauce at the end for the richest flavor. This will serve four in a pinch, or three, but it's delicious enough that two people can devour it with ease.

Mushrooms, once cleaned, can be cooked whole, chopped, or sliced. The best way to cook them is in a scant amount of butter, bacon fat, or vegetable oil brought to medium-high heat, the mushrooms stirred in quickly, and a top put on the pan. Cook only a few minutes. Mushrooms are about 99 percent water, so no extra water is needed when you cook them. You can add a smashed clove of garlic to 1 stick butter and use part of that for a bunch of mushrooms—but be careful not to use too much garlic. Or you can add a scant spoonful of bacon fat to a big pan of the fungi to enhance the natural smokiness. In my part of Appalachia, many folks cook morels in plain bacon grease, but that would overwhelm their delicate flavor in my opinion. They can also be prepared by steaming for 1 or 2 minutes with no more than 1 tablespoon water. I've steamed them in ½ cup dry sherry, and that's better. One or two tablespoons brandy might be sprinkled over a ready panful, lit, and the blue flame savored by the eye before the dish is savored on the tongue. But go easy; mostly you want to taste the mushrooms.

Mushroom Catsup

This condiment was more popular in England in the nineteenth century than tomato catsup, and it reminds the taste buds of Worcestershire sauce, steak sauce, and catsup. If you get a bumper crop of field mushrooms and have extras, give this a try.

In an earthenware dish, pack freshly gathered and cleaned mushrooms in layers, with salt in between. Let sit covered for a day in a cool spot. Mash and strain through several layers of cheesecloth. To every quart liquid, add 1 ounce peppercorns, a fat slice of ginger, 12 cloves, and 1 cracked nutmeg (or 3 blades mace). Boil gently for 15 minutes, and allow to cool. Strain again through fresh cheesecloth, and bottle. Dip the closed bottles in paraffin to seal, or refrigerate and use quickly.

Mushroom Quiche

(See basic quiche directions, page 207.) Set the oven at 350°F. Into a raw pie shell (see pages 207–208) lay ¼ pound Swiss cheese. Add a custard made of 3 raw eggs, 1½ cups half-and-half or whole milk, a little salt, and nutmeg, stirred with about 3 cups wild mushrooms sautéed in sparing amounts of butter and oil or brushed with butter or oil and roasted. Lay on the top ¼ pound sharp cheddar or, if you prefer, a mild cheese, and bake about 1 hour, or until the center doesn't jiggle.

ESCALLOPED MUSHROOMS

(From my grandmother's cookbook, 1898)
Put the honeycomb mushrooms (undoubtedly she meant morels) in a buttered baking dish with alternate layers of breadcrumbs, seasoning each layer plentifully with butter; add salt, pepper, and ½ cup cream. Bake 20 minutes, keeping covered while in the oven.

SHIITAKE

I had never heard of the shiitake mushroom (*Lentinula edodes*) when this book first appeared in the nineties. There's a reason for that: These popular fungi are fairly recent arrivals to this country.

My friend Ann Tutwiler Rogers Carman tells me that shiitake means "oak mushroom" in Japanese (*shii* is "oak tree"; *tak-e* means "mushroom").

These fungi grow wild on various species of oak (and sometimes other) trees in their native Asian forests, but only rarely can be found in the wild in this country, though their incidence grows with every passing year. They are a decomposing fungus (which says their raison d'être is to decompose oak wood). Their silvery spores float around in Asian forests and land on oak branches. (Or a shiitake is placed upon an oak branch.) The spores "eat" the wood until the branch rots enough to fall to the ground. The jolt of the fall "wakes up" the dormant mushrooms, forcing them to fruit. So shiitake growers, who infect oak logs with spores, often drop their logs to the ground in an effort to shock them into growing. They also often soak the logs in water to saturate them and make them fruit. Shiitake are believed to love thunderstorms, and some growers actually play sounds of thunder to their crops and flash light around them to imitate lightning.

Description, Habitat, and Season
Shiitake are brown with whitish gills, 2 to 10 inches across, with a leathery texture and woody stems. They grow gregariously on oak logs. Shiitake (singular and plural are the same) are mushrooms that are not only deliciously edible, but also medically very useful, as they are antiviral and antibacterial. They are useful in suppressing herpes outbreaks, and tests have found them promising as treatments for allergies, arthritis, and even melanomas. This makes them nutritional powerhouses. They're also supposed to be powerfully aphrodisiac, especially the ones with cracked tops. They grow throughout the warm months, and sometimes, after a good soaking, on warm days in the winter.

History and Lore
Shiitake are charmingly anthropomorphic. They are said to die if left by themselves, but to thrive in the company of their fellow shiitake and in the company of human beings. In Asia, they are regarded as a symbol of long life and health. But, in this country, the shiitake was confused with another Asian mushroom, and it was long believed that shiitake would colonize on and destroy all the bridges and railroad ties made of chestnut oak (*Quercus prinus*) or white oak (*Quercus alba*), its favorite host plants. Thus, it was outlawed in this country until the 1970s when the facts got straightened out.

In the intervening years, the shiitake has been grown domestically in warm climates everywhere, with some attendant wilding. I have a modest shiitake farm in my garden behind some box bushes, and I put firewood logs nearby several years ago to see if the shiitake would send some spores to my fire logs. Mine did not produce mushrooms, but my friend Milt McGrady dumped a load of firewood near his shiitake logs, and two years later, shiitake grew there, thus proving that wild shiitake exist. The spores, he says, must fall on perfect substrate to produce fungi—usually only certain oaks, but perhaps occasionally, he thinks, on other oak trees too.

{RECIPES}

Shiitake are used fresh and dried, and are delicious sautéed in butter and served over wild rice. The stems are woody, so they should be removed. If the fungi are dried, they must be reconstituted in warm water before cooking. Once reconstituted, they may be used as any other mushroom. Shiitake have a nice chewy consistency and a smoky, meaty flavor, and they do well with slow cooking.

CREAMED SHIITAKE MUSHROOMS

(Makes about a quart)
Sauté 2 cups sliced shiitake (or other mushrooms) in 2 tablespoons butter until tender. Add 2 tablespoons flour, and cook and stir until browned. Slowly add 2 cups or so of milk, stirring all the while. Season with salt, pepper, nutmeg, and garlic powder or fresh crushed garlic, and cook until smooth. Good for toast, rice, or pasta.

CHAGA

I am going to add here a recent discovery among fungi, which I myself have been unable to locate: chaga (*Inonotus obliquus*). It's apparently something of a miracle plant for health, but, until recently, I had never heard of it. It is claimed to be anti-inflammatory, anti-oxidant, anti-fungal (though it is a fungus)—in fact, it is claimed to have the highest antioxidant component of any plant in the world! If the qualities attributed to it are even a little bit true, we could all live to be 150. At least. Chaga is a broad-spectrum healing mushroom found on birch trees in cold climates around the world. Birch trees are easily recognizable by their vertical- or horizontal-peeling barks—of many colors, from white through creamy to dark brown.

The list of virtues of the fungus chaga is so long and so complicated, I can only send you to do your own research on the Internet. Is that cheating? Okay, I'm cheating. But this fungus has a long history in other parts of the world than ours, yet is reportedly available growing wild in the northern parts of North America. And therefore, I reason, it cannot possibly be left out of this book. Chaga is a birch tree parasite (yellow birch, white birch, silver birch, and other birches). The energy of the birch trees is said to be concentrated in the chaga. It's found on live birches as well as dead birches. It's all over Canada and Alaska (and at the same latitudes around the globe). It's been used for at least five hundred years in Asia and northern Europe to treat cancer, heart trouble, liver ailments, aging, and almost any other illness you can name, but it's been a secret in America until recently. It's also been reported in the mountains of western North Carolina, apparently above 3,000 feet. My hunch is, if it grows there, it ought to grow here in the mountains of Virginia where I live. (However, the Shenandoah Valley is not even 2,000 feet above sea level, so perhaps not.) But, if so, I can't find it. So I ordered some, and find it perfectly palatable without any taste I can identify. It reportedly has no negative side effects. I don't notice any difference since taking it, but I'm essentially very healthy. I have back pain from stenosis, which did not change during the ninety days I took chaga.

What it looks like is an ugly black burnt-looking cancerous growth on the trunks of birch trees. It can be large: say, a foot high, a foot across, and bulging out of the birch tree trunk 8 to 10 inches. You knock it off the tree with a tool or a rock, and inside is a sterile, brownish, corky fungus. Since Fukushima's nuclear disaster, Oriental chaga is not safe (say my sources), as the fungus absorbs radioactivity.

It breaks up easily into a crumbly texture, from which tea can be made.

I have searched fruitlessly (so to speak) for a year to find a birch tree with chaga. Modern science has allowed the study of the components of many plants that was not possible before the end of the twentieth century. Thus, I can report on at least one Russian study (of fifty folks) proving the ability of chaga in neutralizing auto-immune diseases such as psoriasis. All fifty had a lessening or disappearance of symptoms. Studies are ongoing.

[4]
FRUITS

The value of these wild fruits is not in the mere possession or eating of them, but in the sight and enjoyment of them. The very derivation of the word "fruit" would suggest this. It is from the Latin fructus, meaning "that which is used or enjoyed."
—HENRY DAVID THOREAU

The saga of Erik the Red, who visited North America five hundred years before Columbus, mentions salmon larger than any that had ever been seen in Norway and other wonders of the western land. Tales in Norway shortly after AD 1000 told of a land to the west so full of growing things that a man could go there and never have to work another day in his life. "Beer as sweet as Munchener springs from the ground and flows away, the cows all love to milk themselves, and hens lay eggs ten times a day," goes one verse to the old Norwegian folk song "Oleanna." So promising did the newfound land seem that "the poorest knave in Norway becomes a king in a year or so."

Perhaps Erik also is the guy who really gave America its name. Though by default, we think these western continents were named for Amerigo Vespucci, an old-world mapmaker, Norwegian scholars have recently opined otherwise, noting that in Old Norse, Am-eric-a means "land of Erik." So perhaps there is another etymology for the name of our country.

Wild fruits were a whole category meriting praise. Fruit has been important food for humans as far back as we can trace. In general, fruits provide vitamins, especially vitamin C. Some nutritionists have opined that fruits are the least consumed of any of the major food groups; difficulty of preparation seems to be the reason. Americans habitually eat a vegetable with the evening meal, but where in our diets is fruit consumed? Further, wild fruit may, ironically, be the one thing that there is more of now than there was when our forebears first came to this continent, since hardly anyone forages anymore.

Native Americans knew and used everything edible in the plant kingdom. Many native fruits were used medicinally, as well as for food. The first settlers clung for a while to English medicine, then slowly adopted Native American cures. After the American Revolution, native drugs were, for a time, the only drugs available, and around 1800, the Shakers developed a brisk trade growing and selling American herbs when there was a national resistance to buying medicines from England.

In the late nineteenth century, patent medicines became the rage, made mostly of plant distillations in alcohol. Christian ladies who wouldn't touch a drop of the devil's firewater stayed tipsy all day sipping on their herbal remedies, prescribed by doctors who hadn't a clue about what was wrong with most of them. Any cures may have been attributable to the alcohol rather than the plants. Many of the fruits discussed here were important in folk remedies.

Some excellent fruits are omitted here. Wild gooseberries, for example, are subject on this continent to certain molds, and this makes finding good ones a rarity. Peaches grow wonderfully in America tended in orchards, but a peach untended (in the wild) reverts very quickly to small, inedible fruit useful only "to fatten hogs," according to one disgruntled source. I found two years ago a tree of wild peaches in a clearing in the woods. The tree appeared to have been hit by lightning. The peaches were ripe and wonderful, and I went back a second day with a big basket to gather all I could, and I made frozen peaches, peach preserves, and brandied peaches.

BRANDIED PEACHES

I am sure there are more reliable modern recipes, but I bet none as exciting as this one. Lizzie, my grandparents' maid, made these every summer. She'd dip ripe peaches into boiling water for a minute, then slip off the skins but leave the peaches whole. She'd pack Ball mason jars with the peaches, then add as much sugar as the jars would hold. Then at the end, she'd add about four tablespoons of the best brandy and screw on the lids. They'd go to a dark corner of the basement then to "work." On Sundays, we'd open one up and eat the peaches and syrup on vanilla ice cream.

Every now and then, we'd be treated to a loud explosion in the basement, as one of the jars would burst, spreading sticky fruit and glass shards everywhere. Those peaches were so alcoholic that I spent many childhood Sunday afternoons dozing in the study, drunk out of my mind. My friends all loved coming to Sunday dinner.

APPLES

Pyrus (Latin for "pear") is the genus apples, crab apples, pears, and (according to some botanists) quinces belong to. Apples, known to be one of the earliest fruits cultivated by humans, are placed in a subgenus, *Malus* (Latin for "apple").

Description, Habitat, and Season
There are literally thousands of apple varieties, some of which bear fruit in every season. They grow on long-lived small trees with gnarled, hard, short branchlets, with serrated oblong-ovate leaves and white to pink fragrant blossoms in the spring. All apples have a cartilage-like covering that protects the seeds. Apples are highly variable in flavor, texture, size, sweetness, and color. The only things they have in common are white or whitish flesh that browns on exposure to air and that elusive, delightful "appley" odor and flavor.

Though wild apples are apt to be wormy or partially eaten by birds, often these old-fashioned apples have more flavor and sweetness than any of the modern cultivars, so large and symmetrical that they hardly look real. (Cultivated varieties of any fruit, bred selectively by man, cannot perpetuate themselves sexually through seeds, and thus do not exist in the wild.) If you can locate two or three good wild trees, they will reward your annual wait with more apples than you can possibly use.

History and Lore

Apple trees can live a hundred years, and apples have been eaten by humans for eons. Swiss prehistoric lake dwellers ate crab apples and larger apples, and carbonized remains show that they were sometimes cut in half, as if to be dried for future use.

One of America's favorite legends recounts the journey by John Chapman (born in Boston around 1774), better known as Johnny Appleseed, who set out on his charming and peculiar mission to plant all America with apple trees grown directly from seeds. After 1800, it was rare to find any homestead between the East Coast and the Mississippi without several apple trees. It is clear to any forager that folks used to tend apple trees of different varieties, often quite near to one another. This is because different varieties mature at different times and are good for different things. Our legacy is that we often have a wide variety of apples to choose from within a fairly small area. Those old-fashioned apples were abandoned when newer, more disease-resistant strains were developed, or when farms just fell into ruin. Apples are deeply American: Regional cookery gives us New England apple cobblers, Pennsylvania German apple pancakes, Virginia apple candy, Appalachian cider, and southern fried pies. Apple pie is probably the most American dessert there is.

But for every benefit, there is a cost. Though some of the new cultivars like Gala and Braeburn are wonderful, and I buy them at the grocery store, personally, I'd rather pare away the wormy parts of those intense, hard, strong Black Stem Stayman or Winesap apples left over from another time than eat a perfectly formed, perfectly tame Golden Delicious from the supermarket.

Although apples have no specific medical uses, they are rich in vitamins and fiber, pectin and minerals, and must be listed among the most famous medicines in the world: Everyone grows up knowing that "an apple a day keeps the doctor away."

{RECIPES}

To find out if a wild apple is good for cooking, just steam a few chunks or slices of it and try it for flavor and consistency. For the forager, trial and error is the method. For instance, after years of looking and testing, we now keep an eye on three wild trees: The first, which ripens and drops its streaky reddish fruit near the end of June, is full of hard apples that taste sour when bitten into but are absolutely without peer as cooking apples, as they stay firm, have a good strong flavor and tartness, and can be sweetened with sugar, maple sugar, or honey. This means that in June, I make our year's supply of applesauce, apple butter, apple jelly, and fried apples. We have an August tree along a country road near town, with crisp, hard yellow apples that never blush but are full of rural integrity. The tree we gather from in October and even later is full of dark, black-red apples that are wonderful to eat and make cider out of—so crisp they almost cut your mouth, so juicy and tart-sweet they drip down your chin—but they cook up pappy, mushy, and tasteless. We eat the biggest ones and make cider out of the rest of them.

FRIED APPLES

Carefully chop cooking apples. I leave the skins on, for flavor and consistency. If discoloration bothers you, sprinkle the cut apples from time to time with lemon juice. Heat a little butter or margarine, just enough to coat the bottom of the skillet. Add the apples, and sprinkle with sugar, ground cinnamon, and allspice. Stir to distribute the sugar, spice, and fat, cover the pan, and cook over low heat, stirring occasionally, until the apples are tender. Naturally, the amount of sugar can vary enormously, and other spices can be used as well. Scandinavian apple dishes are often seasoned with cardamom, and some people like to add a bit of ground cloves, nutmeg, or ginger. I use brown sugar sometimes in place of white.

APPLE CIDER

Cider is nothing but chopped or ground apples pressed to force out the liquid, which turns brown immediately upon exposure to air.

For cider, you need some kind of press. A real cider press (now available only in specialty or antiques shops) has gears for grinding up the apples. The pieces fall into a straight-sided wooden bucket with slightly separated slats on the sides and bottom. When the bucket is full, a weight is placed atop the apples, and pressure mechanically applied. The cider is expressed through the slats in the bucket into a trough that carries it to the receiving bucket. The mash is thrown out when no more liquid can be forced from it, and the process is repeated.

Today, an electric juicer can be used to make cider. You could even try a ricer. Grind up the apples, cores and all, and press the pulp in some way to expel the juice. It won't be as efficient as using the real item, but you can make great fresh cider, or use the liquid for apple jelly (instructions for which are found in any box of commercial pectin).

Apple Chutney

This is an elegant condiment for curries or roast meats. Gather enough tart cooking apples to yield about 3 pounds of small chunks, and put them into an enamel cooking pot. Add the following: 1 huge onion, cut into small chunks; 2 to 4 cloves garlic, chopped fine; 1 cup raisins; 1 teaspoon salt; 2 teaspoons ground cinnamon; 1 teaspoon ground ginger; 1 teaspoon ground cloves; 1 teaspoon dry mustard; 1 cup brown sugar and 1 cup white; and 1 cup cider vinegar. Cook this mixture slowly for about 1 hour, or until it is thick, stirring frequently with a wooden spoon. Refrigerated, this keeps well for many months.

Curried Apple Soup

(Serves 4 to 6)

Melt 2 tablespoons butter and sauté 2 cups chopped tart windfall apples (5 or 6 apples), 1 chopped apple-size onion, and ½ cup chopped celery over medium-high heat, stirring occasionally, for 5 minutes. Add 1 tablespoon curry powder and 1 teaspoon chili powder, stir well, and sauté another minute or two. Add 1 cup apple cider or apple juice and 2 cups salted chicken broth (made with cubes or from scratch) and bring to boil, then reduce heat, cover, and simmer for 15 minutes.

In a measuring cup, place 1 egg yolk and fill to 1 cup mark with heavy cream (about ⅞ cup), and beat well with a fork or beater. At the end of the cooking time, blend the soup to smoothness, add the cream/yolk at the end of the blending, reheat without boiling, and serve at once.

CRAB APPLES

Crab apples are varieties of apples with what botanists refer to as "inferior fruit" (fruit that is sour, like a crabby person is sour). They are often planted as ornamental trees today, for they have lovely shapes, fragrant blossoms, and beautiful foliage. They are native to America, while apples were introduced by the English.

Or maybe Johnny Appleseed.

Description, Habitat, and Season

Crab apples are small, slender trees with showy blossoms of reddish pink or white in the spring. Later in the year, they produce oval, sunset-hued fruits with no depression at the stem end, anywhere from ⅓ inch in diameter to about 1½ inches. None that I know of is palatable raw.

History and Lore

In England in the past, the sour juice of crab apples was sold under the name verjuice and believed to be a great health enhancer. It must have tasted bad enough to feel like medicine.

{RECIPES}

Use crab apples just as you would use any other sour apples. The fruit of some ornamental crab apples I found planted at the law school near our house was perfect for my experiment. Nobody ever picked them. I'd seen recipes for crab apple jelly everywhere, so I brought home a big basketful of the apples. They sat on the dining room table and scented the whole house with apple. I cooked a handful up, tasted some of the flesh cautiously, decided it was fine if I added sugar, cooked some more up, made crab apple sauce, then crab apple jelly, then pickled crab apples using a method I usually use for Watermelon Rind Pickles.

PICKLED CRABS

(See recipe for Watermelon Rind Pickles, pages 195–196)
Just leave out the lime water soak, and substitute whole crab apples for the rind. It was so successful that I plan on doing tons of them next year. The pickled crab apples are beautiful, deep red, and a tasty and pretty garnish for dinner plates.

Apple/Crab Apple Sauce

First scrub clean apples, or crab apples, and pare them into chunks without worms or beak holes. Do not peel them, but if you prefer, you can remove the cores of the apples. Leave crab apples whole or you'll never finish! Then add just the smallest amount of water, say ½ cup for a big pot of apple chunks or crab apples, and steam them quickly, just until they are tender. Watch them, stir them often, and add water if necessary to prevent scorching. Force the cooked apples or crab apples through a potato masher or a ricer, and add sugar to taste. That's basic applesauce. Serve it hot, cold, or at room temperature. Add cinnamon, nutmeg, allspice, or a combination if you like it spicy.

Apple/Crab Apple Butter

Begin with basic applesauce. You need to add approximately half as much sugar as you have fruit sauce. But taste, and add to your liking. Then, the spices. Start with 1 teaspoon each ground cinnamon and ground nutmeg, ½ teaspoon each ground cloves and ground ginger, and 1 split vanilla bean (optional). Adding the spices and sugar slowly is a good idea, for you can add more but you can't take them out. You'll probably need a little more of the spices. When you have it tasting and smelling wonderful, cook this mixture slowly, in a pan with a lot of surface (wide and shallow is best), stirring it often to keep it from scorching, tasting it until it's just right (you can add spice or sugar at any time), simmering until it is reduced and thickened to suit you. This shouldn't take very long: 20 minutes to about 1 hour. Taste is the determinant here; as apple butter is a condiment, it should be spicy and sweet. The grown-ups I watched cook as a child had a way to test the readiness: On a clean saucer, spoon about 1 tablespoon of the hot butter. If it retains its integrity as a puddle, it's ready. If it leaks at the edges, it's not. Try for yourself.

When it is done, take out the vanilla bean if you used one, jar the butter in boiled (sterilized) jars, cap them, and, if you like, dip the tops in melted paraffin to seal. Don't forget to date and label each jar.

Crab Apple Jelly

This is something you just can't miss. Find a place with ornamental crab apple trees, and watch for the fruit to ripen. Gather 5 pounds ripe (they'll still be hard) crab apples. Wash, but do not peel or core. Place in a large saucepan, stainless steel or enamel. Add 5 cups water, bring to a boil, cover, and boil until the crab apples split and are soft. Make a double cheesecloth bag by sewing two layers to two more layers on a machine, so that you have a square sewn on three sides. Put the bag in a big bowl, pour the cooked apples and juice into the bag, and hang the bag up higher than the bowl. Let it drip, or when it is cool enough, press and knead the bag to release more liquid. When you have 7 cups juice, stop. Discard the bag and its contents, or put the pulp on your mulch pile. Measure 9 cups sugar into a separate dry bowl. Stir 1 box fruit pectin into the juice, and bring to a boil, stirring continuously. When it is boiling furiously, threatening to climb to the top of the pot, add the sugar all at once. Return to that furious boil, and boil exactly 1 minute, stirring the whole time. Remove from the stove, skim any foam, and pour quickly into sterilized jars. This makes about 10 cups. To me, it's the best jelly of all.

I made 30 cups of absolutely wonderful crab apple jelly last June when the ornamental crabs fruited and ripened at the law school near our house. The caretaker assured me the fruit was just something else she had to rake up, so I collected a huge basket, I took her a jar of the jelly, and everybody was happy.

BLACKBERRIES, RASPBERRIES, AND THEIR KIN

And the running blackberry
would adorn the parlors of heaven
—WALT WHITMAN, SONG OF MYSELF: 31

Rubus means "red" in Latin, and is kin, of course, to our word ruby. The Rubus genus includes perhaps as many as 600 species, subspecies, and cultivars of berries, all of which look like the native blackberries (*Rubus allegheniensis*), or blackberries of the Allegheny Mountains, and have solid centers, or like raspberries (*R. idaeus*), which have hollow centers.

Description, Habitat, and Season

The *Rubus* berries all look more like a bunch of tiny fruits glued together than a single fruit, and in fact, each tiny segment of each berry does contain a single tiny seed. They all have serrated gray-green leaves, usually three, five, or seven, and nearly all of them have prickly stems. Often the leaves are lighter underneath than on top. Out of season, the old canes, or stalks, reddish, gray, or greenish blue, show where the berries will be in harvest time. *Rubus* ripen from the early summer through early fall, depending on the species. In the mountains of Virginia, I grew up with a berry calendar in my head: June 20, black raspberries, or blackcaps; July 3, wineberries; July 20, blackberries; dewberries, or ground blackberries, from mid-June to mid-August. The seasons never vary more than a few days either way, though of course the crops vary with rain and sunshine. And now, with global warming, I've been seeing berries arrive early for several years. But I've also seen them arrive later. The seasons for berries in general seem "wider."

Rubus berries are a lot like starlings: They have learned to live anywhere. The edges of woods, the back lots of city buildings, farm pastures, creek- and riverbanks, fields, vacant city lots, the perimeters of in-town gardens. All can and do support some kind of *Rubus* berry. Birds eat the berries, then distribute the seeds widely, and the seeds take hold and grow with tenacity.

All of the *Rubus* are edible, wherever they grow, whenever you find them ripe. Though they differ in sweetness, tenderness, and juiciness, all share the characteristic berry flavor. Whether they grow trailing along the ground, on upright stalks, or on arching canes, gather them and remember where you found them so you can come back year after year. With blackberries, note their incurving thorns—you can reach far in to get distant berries, but then you are badly scratched trying to get your arm out. Therefore, when blackberrying, long sleeves are necessary.

History and Lore

Throughout history, blackberries have not only fed people, but also tinted their garments, soothed their illnesses, even served them as ink. People have long appreciated the high vitamin C content of blackberries and their kin, even if they didn't know what it was. They probably noticed that people who ate berries fresh and dried didn't get sick a lot, and that was all they needed to know. The berries of *Rubus* varieties, as well as blueberries, were used to dye the popular mauve ribbons so beloved of girls of the seventeenth century. Blackberries (and blueberries) were sold to navy-blue merchants into the nineteenth century for the dying of sailors' uniforms. A dark gray dye has been made from boiling the branches and roots. Blackberry juice has been used in this century to stamp the appropriate grades on inspected US Department of Agriculture meats.

Rubus berries hold an honorable and consistent place in folk medicine. Roman use dates from around AD 600, when Apuleius published his herbal, in which can be found the drawing of a blackberry, *Rubus fruticosus*. Blackberry was believed by Herodotus to cure gout (from the French word for taste). One of its folk monikers is goutberry—perhaps because eating the high-fiber, low-calorie blackberries may ease a digestive system too long marinated in the rich fatty foods that caused gout in the first place; blackberries are not known to actually inhibit purine formations in the joints, which is the crystal that causes the pain of gout.

The dried bark of the rhizome and roots of *Rubus* plants was in the official United States Pharmaceutical list from 1820 until 1916 as an astringent and tonic. Teas made from *Rubus* leaves or roots are astringent and have been used by many primitive peoples. John Gerard's 1597 *English Herball* lists both leaf and fruit as astringent.

In this country, the salmonberry was used by the Indians of the Pacific Northwest as a diuretic in the form of a tea made from the canes. It is said to taste better cooked than raw.

In early American medicine, blackberry leaves were believed to counter diabetes, and blackberry root extract was the major ingredient in a seventeenth-century Virginia cholera cure. As the leaves are astringent, tea made from most species' leaves has been used for ages to staunch things that need contracting, closing up, shrinking, stopping. These include diarrhea, dysentery, uterine hemorrhage (miscarriage or abortion), and sometimes even runny noses. Rappahannock Indians in Virginia used the roots and berries in steeped tea to allay diarrhea. Crusoe's 1771 *Treasury of Easy Medicine* advises soaking blackberry leaves in hot wine and placing them on (skin) ulcers morning and evening. The fruits have been eaten to cool fevers. Many of the early settlers believed that the *Rubus* species had special efficacy against "summer complaint," a diarrhea brought on, it was believed, by heat, but more probably by spoiled food in an era before refrigeration. On August 4, 1804, one James Anderson wrote a testimonial that was printed in the *Philadelphia Medical and Surgical Journal*, Volume I, Pt. I, in 1805:

> Last summer, when I was near the settlement of the Oneida Indians [in the state of New York], the dysentery prevailed much, and carried off some of the white inhabitants, who applied to the Indians for a remedy. They directed them to drink a decoction of the roots of Blackberry-bushes which they did, after which not one died. All who used it agreed, that it is a safe, sure, and speedy cure.

Ripe blackberries

It has been reported that blackberry leaf juice will fasten loose teeth back into the jaw. Perhaps this is because the juice seemed to "pull" at the flesh of the mouth, to "tighten" it. Some Indian tribes used blackberry root steeped in water as an eyewash; others favored an eyewash made of a tincture of red raspberry leaves. (Tincture means an alcohol solution, so I doubt if that is correct; still I am loathe to change folk wording. My impression is that tincture can also mean a weak mixture of something.)

The doctrine of signatures suggests that the color and/or shape of anything in nature dictates its use to man. Consequently, yellow plants are useful for kidney problems, and walnuts are beneficial for the brain. By this reasoning, the black-red blackberry juice might darken "pale," or anemic, blood. A nineteenth-century commercial gargle for sore throats, Blackberry Glycerite, combined glycerin and blackberry vinegar. One contemporary midwestern writer described watching her mother dry fresh blackberries in a low oven and grind them to a powder to be used as a diarrhea remedy in this century. The powder was to be taken, she wrote, a teaspoon at a time, stirred into hot water. A medicine named Blackberry

Unripe blackberries

Balsam was marketed in this country as a diarrhea remedy from 1846 until well into the twentieth century.

Most recently, blackberries have been the subject of much cross-breeding, in modern science's endless search for the perfect berry: one that will resist mold, ripen slowly, "hold up" in transport, grow big, be tender and juicy, and of course taste like ambrosia.

A BERRY BOVINE ENCOUNTER

It was June 1959 when I graduated from Hollins, a college in Virginia. That summer, I invested a large percentage of my salary from my first paid teaching job on my first car, a wrecked-but-still-mobile 1940 Plymouth. Nothing on the car ever worked very well. My memory of that summer is of many suitors, interested chiefly in Gerontion, for that was what I named the car, from T. S. Eliot's poem about an old tired man. Each beau of that summer yearned to solve its mysteries, to be the one who would finally make it run. While Harry, Sam, Scotty, Ralph, or Rick performed surgery under the hood, I brush-painted it a wonderful metallic 1959 turquoise-blue color, and it shone burnished, bumpy, and streaky. I hammered out its dented fender, which gave its contours the pocked appearance of a turquoise-blue orange. When I had finished, I made flowered seat covers for it, to cover the burn holes from the first owner's dropped cigarettes.

But one day in midsummer, Gerontion stopped, sighed, and sat down on the job somewhere on a country road. My friend Jeanne and I had been swimming at Goshen Pass; we had no clothes but the bathing suits and tennis shoes we were wearing. We started walking toward town to find a telephone, calmly because by then such behavior on the car's part had become standard operating procedure, and who knew what wild game we might be able to flush out to come rescue us?

Suddenly, around a curve, there appeared a lush patch of ripe black raspberries just beyond the fence at the edge of the road. We looked around, and in the roadside honeysuckle, we found an old chrome hubcap. So in we plunged, holding the barbed wires apart for each other, determined to pick as many berries as we could eat there and carry home. Gingerly, we made our way through the patch, the laden wickets springing together like a magic forest behind us. We were well away from the road and surrounded by the dense bushes, when a bellow caused us to look up. Coming at us, fast, in hide considerably thicker than ours, was one mad cow, with horns.

We arrived safely back on the road, mostly just shaken and a bit scratched up and stained. We walked on to find a farmhouse and called up some boys who gladly came out to fetch us and make the car run again and deliver us to the doctor's office.

As we were getting tetanus shots some hours later and having our brier-and-barbed-wire wounds scoured clean by a grumpy nurse, we tried to figure out what had been wrong with that cow. It was not a bull. We were country girls and knew the difference. Bovine hormones? A calf hidden nearby? All we could ever conclude was that it must have been her berry patch. She liked black raspberries as well as we did, and we hadn't asked permission.

Most recently, a substance in the leaves of red raspberries called framamine, or fragrine, or fragerine, isolated in the 1940s, has been shown to strengthen, relax, and tone the uterus, thus exonerating the old wives' advice that raspberry leaf tea be taken throughout pregnancy, during labor, and post-parturition. The leaves, according to modern analysis, are high in magnesium, which is still in use to prevent miscarriage.

Another tea, which is antiscorbutic, a tonic for the uterus, and febrifuge, is made by crushing the dried root (gathered in the fall). One tablespoon of the crushed dried root is added to a pint of boiling water. When it is cool, it is ready to use, though folk sources are not in agreement on how much and how often.

{RECIPES}

BLACKBERRY JELLY

Gather at least 2 quarts of ripe (mostly), underripe, and green blackberries, cover with a little water, and simmer until soft. Squeeze or drip through a jelly bag to make 4 cups juice. Measure 4 cups sugar, and stir it into the juice until dissolved. Bring to a full boil, add a pea-size lump of butter, and boil until jellied, which will only take a bit of time. This is really superior to any other berry jelly I have ever tasted. But you do need about a quarter of your berries to be green or underripe.

BERRY MOUSSE

Sprinkle 1 envelope gelatin in ¼ cup water and set aside. Boil 1 cup water and 1 cup sugar together for 5 minutes. Add the gelatin and stir until dissolved. Add 1 quart or more berries, picked over and washed, and cook just until soft, under 5 minutes. While still hot, strain the berries and syrup through a sturdy sieve, ricer, or cheesecloth to remove seeds. Add the juice of 1 lemon, stir thoroughly, and set aside. When the mix is warm-cool, beat 4 egg whites until stiff and fold into the berries. Then beat until stiff and fold in 1 cup whipping cream with 1 teaspoon vanilla and 1 tablespoon sugar. Pour into a fancy dish and refrigerate several hours, until it's jellied. A variation on this is to use flavored gelatin, 1 small box, low-calorie or regular. Lemon is always a good choice, but you could use strawberries with strawberry gelatin, or raspberries with raspberry gelatin, or raspberries with lemon gelatin, or blackberries with raspberry gelatin—your choice. And great news for calorie watchers: The sugar-free gelatin desserts taste just as good in this mousse as the sugared.

BLACKBERRY JAM CAKE

This is taken from my great-grandmother Mrs. Governor John Letcher's recipe book, written in her own hand circa 1870. Beat ½ cup butter to a cream, then beat in ⅔ cup sugar. When very light, beat 1 cup blackberry jam in, then 1 small grated nutmeg and ½ teaspoon ginger. Dissolve ½ teaspoon baking soda in 1 tablespoon cold water and add it to 2 tablespoons sour cream. Add this and 2 eggs well-beaten to the other ingredients. Now add 1 cup flour and beat for half a minute. Sprinkle 1 tablespoon flour over ⅔ cup stoned (seedless) raisins and stir them in. Pour the batter into a well-buttered loaf pan and bake at 350°F for 50 minutes. The yield is 1 small loaf, and I think it's almost as good as plum pudding.

RUBUS LIQUEUR

A quart of any *Rubus* berries, a quart sugar, a quart vodka. Mix these together and store in a dark place for about a month.

Seventeenth-Century Blackberry Wine

Take one Bushell of Blackburys, nine quarts of water, six pounds of sugar; boyle your water and suger together; then bruize your blackburys in a marble mortar; when they be cold put them together and let them stand 24 hours; then put it into a vessell that will fill and let it stand one month, and then if it be clear bottle it off.—*F.F.V. Receipt Book*, Richmond, Virginia, 1794

Blackberry Wine #2

Squeeze berries in cheesecloth to extract juice and pulp. Add an equal amount of water to the juice, pouring it over the seeds and skins. Stir daily, let set a week, and strain. Add 1 pound sugar to each gallon of liquid. Put in bottles loosely topped, and leave until fermentation stops, which will take three to six weeks. To tell when bottles are ready to cork, listen. If you can hear bubbles, don't tighten or stopper the bottles yet. Wait until they are silent.

Blackberry Wine #3

In Appalachia, the receipt for blackberry wine, a traditional Christmas treat for both the recipient and the maker, is simple: a gallon of ripe blackberries in season is mixed with two pounds of sugar and a quart of boiling water. They are stirred together, left overnight, put through cheesecloth, and bottled. They will, say the mountain dwellers, be ready by Christmas.

Berry Vinegar

Pick over 2 pints of the fruit you are going to use to flavor the vinegar: raspberries, blackberries, strawberries, elder berries, gooseberries, etc. Place them in a crockery jug or jar, and pour over them 2 quarts of good cider vinegar. After a day, pour the whole thing into a cheesecloth bag and let it drip until no more juice comes out. Save and refrigerate the liquid, throw away the fruit pulp, clean the earthen jug or jar thoroughly with hot water and soap to prevent any airborne mold. Repeat the process, using the refrigerated liquid over more pints of the same fruit. Do this three or four times over three or four days for a strong-flavored vinegar, being careful to wash out the crock thoroughly between each day's new fruit.

Raspberry Charlotte

Butter a pudding dish and cover the bottom with dry breadcrumbs. Put over this a layer of ripe raspberries, sprinkle with sugar, and then add another layer of crumbs; proceed in this way until the dish is full, having the last layer crumbs. Put bits of butter over the top and bake, with a plate over it, half an hour. Remove the plate and let it brown just before serving. Use only half the quantity of crumbs that you do of the fruit. Eat with cream. —*The Book of Forty Puddings*, 1882

Shrub

Shrub is a summer drink of yore and is usually made of blackberries or raspberries. One gallon berries, 1 quart cider vinegar, 2 cups sugar, 2 sticks cinnamon, and 20 cloves. Let the flavors marry for 24 hours, then bring the mixture to a gentle boil, cool, and bottle. To serve, add water and ice to taste.

Berry Flip

This warm drink of sixteenth-century England was made of "one quart of beer, ale, or cider and one of berries" to which was added molasses and cloves, ginger, and cinnamon, and sometimes milk and eggs. The whole was then heated up by inserting into it a red-hot poker.

RED RASPBERRIES

Description, Habitat, and Season
Raspberries are "rare," in that they mold within two or three days after being picked ripe (and of course are not good if picked green), which makes the marketing of them rather expensive.

History and Lore
Rubus idaeus was named for Mount Ida on Crete, renowned playground for immoral immortal lovers.

Some Indian tribes found the soft leaves of some *Rubus* species useful as toilet paper.

Reputed Medical Virtues

The red raspberry was used medicinally by ancient Greeks. They believed that red raspberries, along with strawberries, would whiten teeth.

In addition, many varieties of *Rubus* are used in wines, cordials, vinegars, and brandies—for uses medicinal and otherwise.

Moistened leaves of any *Rubus* plant have been used as poultices to draw bad blood from wounds and pustulence from festering sores.

Folklore has it that raspberry leaf tea eases labor. I'm not sure if that's true or not, because, though I dried the summer leaves while I was pregnant the first time, and had the tea ready to go, I forgot it in the excitement of breaking water, and so had to go without. The second time, I remembered to take the tea, but my labor was so short that I had no chance to have someone make me some, so I failed at that experiment.

{RECIPES}

ICED RASPBERRY VINEGAR

This was a popular summer drink at the end of the nineteenth century. It's worth a try, and you may even like it. Mix water, sugar or honey, and raspberry (or blackberry) vinegar to taste (see the Berry Vinegar recipe, page 90), and serve over ice for a refreshing summer ade. It's a sort of forerunner of Gatorade.

RASPBERRY (OR CURRANT, OR STRAWBERRY) SYRUP

One gallon berries, ½ gallon sugar, and 1 cup water. Mash together and let stand overnight. Bring slowly to a boil, and boil thirty minutes. Force through cheesecloth and let cool to room temperature. This syrup can be used to soothe sore throats, pour over ice cream, waffles, or pancakes, or even as a base for ice cream.

BLACK RASPBERRIES

Description, Habitat, and Season

Black raspberries, *Rubus occidentalis*, create thickets of wickets in their growing, dipping down to touch the ground, and sending out their sturdy roots and shoots from their tips. The briar patch that Br'er Rabbit begged not to be thrown into was almost certainly a black raspberry patch. They are native and have hooked prickles should you care to look. Black raspberry first-year stalks don't produce and are greenish bluish in hue. The second-year stalks are reddish and waxy. In winter, the habitat of the black raspberry is recognizable as a tangle of arches made of thorny canes, or stems, which grow to be 6 to 8 feet long, bend gracefully over from their own weight, and, where they touch the ground, put down new roots. The plants spread quickly, creating huge, nearly impenetrable, patches of blackcaps and making the picking of the ripe berries fairly treacherous. The berries are dark purple instead of red, and seedier than red raspberries.

If you are not inclined to brave the tangles of wickety thorns, you can buy black raspberries in roadside stands or at farmers' markets. If you were intent on taming them, you might plant in a field several small patches instead of one big one, so as to be able to pick around the edges.

THIMBLEBERRIES

One day in midsummer while climbing the nearby Peaks of Otter in Bedford, Virginia, I came upon a *Rubus* berry I'd never seen before. It was different in several ways from the *Rubus* I knew. First, no thorns! Second, the fruit was flatter than a raspberry, but obviously a relative. It was bloomy (sort of a powdered look) and hollow, like black raspberries and wineberries, but softer. Maybe a bit tarter than a raspberry or blackberry. The berries tended to break apart when I picked them. I've not found them anywhere else, but they grow, I have learned, all over this continent. They must be called thimbleberries (*Rubus parviflorus*) because at least theoretically, you could fit one on a finger like a thimble.

History and Lore

Black raspberries, called also blackcaps and thimbleberries (possibly because they are hollow, like caps—or like thimbles—and would fit over the fingertip of a child) ripen one month earlier in any given area than blackberries.

When pioneer John Lewis with his sons, William, Thomas, Andrew, and Charles, explored the wilderness at the western range of the Valley of Virginia in the mid-eighteenth century, they noted the profusion of these wild black raspberries. A western variety of the thimbleberry

(*R. nutkanus*) has a soft velvety juicy texture, is bright red, and is common throughout the Pacific Northwest, as black raspberries are common throughout the mid-Atlantic states.

The French monks who make Chambord, the rich black raspberry cordial, and Framboise, the dry fruity eau-de-vie, reportedly distill 20 to 40 pounds of berries for each liter of precious liqueur.

Reputed Medical Virtues

Ojibwas used black raspberry root tea, as well as the berries, for stomach aches. Black raspberries were used interchangeably with red raspberries.

{RECIPES}

Black raspberries are the best flavored of all the berries, by many accounts. They are wonderfully aromatic, delicious on cereal, over ice cream, or in pies, and make a dark, perfumy jelly.

BLACK RASPBERRY MOUSSE

Syrup of 1 cup water and 1 cup sugar, boiled 5 minutes
1 quart black raspberries, cleaned and picked over
Juice of 1 lemon
1 envelope gelatin softened in ½ cup hot water
4 egg whites, beaten stiff
1 cup whipping cream, whipped with 1 teaspoon vanilla and 1 tablespoon sugar

Add raspberries to syrup and cook until soft, just a few minutes. Strain through cheesecloth. Add lemon juice. Add gelatin, and stir thoroughly. Cool, fold in egg whites and then whipped cream. Chill in a pretty mold or a soufflé dish. Garnish with whole raspberries.

FLUMMERY

(My father used to make this fruit pudding with wineberries, black raspberries, or blackberries.)

¼ cup cornstarch
1 cup sugar
¼ cup water
Few grains salt
2 cups juice extracted from berries

Mix first four ingredients together, and stir until smooth. Gradually add juice. Heat to boiling and boil gently for 1 minute, stirring constantly until the mixture thickens and clarifies. Remove from heat. Pour into four individual serving dishes and chill thoroughly. Serve with whipped, sweetened, vanilla-scented cream.

BLACK RASPBERRY ICE

(Much better than those made with more cholesterol-modest substitutes)
1 quart ripe black raspberries
1 cup sugar
1 quart whipping cream (do not substitute fake whipped cream)
¼ teaspoon salt
Mash the berries and sugar together. If you object to the seeds, then squeeze the sweet juice through cheesecloth. Mix with the cream, and churn-freeze. If you must still-freeze it, as it begins to harden at the edges, remove and beat until smooth. Repeat this operation three times, to ensure smoothness, before allowing it to freeze completely.

KATIE'S HOMEMADE BERRY JELLIES

I am an advocate of the pectin method for the reason that the less cooking of any berries you do, the closer to the natural flavor you get. The powdered pectins include raspberry, blueberry, and blackberry recipes, but less frequently one for black raspberries. Follow a raspberry method if none is available for blackcaps or wineberries. Follow it precisely.

WINEBERRIES

Description, Habitat, and Season
Wineberries (*Rubus phoenicolasius*, which means "brambles with purple hair") grow wild, at least in the northeast quarter of the continental United States. The shiny, slightly waxy, or sticky berries of brightest red, with three serrated leaflets, grow on vigorous arching canes. The fruit falls intact from a dry center receptacle, leaving the berry hollow. They fruit in between the black raspberry and blackberry seasons.

History and Lore
Wineberries are a favorite berry where I live. They resemble raspberries, but with a much tarter flavor. Where raspberries are dry, with a

Wineberries, still slightly underripe

bloomy finish, wineberries are shiny, with a sticky or tacky surface. Euell Gibbons, one of the few naturalists treating the wineberry, claims that it is "a recent immigrant from Asia," but that is not what I grew up hearing. Though they have now spread to all the middle Atlantic states, according to local legend they were introduced east of the Blue Ridge, to his estate near Charlottesville, around the turn of the nineteenth century, by none other than that greatest of all American horticulturists, Thomas Jefferson.

In 1771, Jefferson planted a vineyard at Monticello, reasoning that he had roughly the same climate and conditions as the Bordeaux region of France, which he so admired. The enterprise failed, so Jefferson, frustrated by root louse and late frosts, imported a wild member of the raspberry family from the south of France, introducing the plant to Virginia, where it grew exuberantly but still produced only inferior wine. The story goes on that he also persuaded an Italian family named Shifletti to immigrate to the area and turn the berries into good wine—the enterprise, alas, also failed.

Today, we have locally a berry that is neither raspberry nor blackberry, but certainly kin to both. In addition, the Americanized name Shiflett abounds in and around Charlottesville. And finally, it is certain that wineberries, though delicious fruit, make miserable wine. They make a clear red jelly that is tart and delicate, similar to currant jelly, and they make wonderful desserts with whipped cream or ice cream.

If it is true that raspberries were named after an already existent French wine, Jefferson might have reasoned that any member of the family would be a good bet for good wine.

Seeking the truth, one finds this story to be a charming fiction, but typical of our mountain folklore: a good story, convincingly told, with names and proofs to convince the listener. But according to the botanical research department at Monticello, there are no Shiflettis mentioned in Jefferson's writings, and no wineberries, despite the fact that they grow wild now on Little Mountain.

And as far as I have been able to determine, there are absolutely no wines made from anything but grapes in France.

{RECIPES}

Wineberries are tart, becoming sweet only when overripe, and have little of the berry taste, yet are considered by some their favorite berry of all. Those who love them say they are of "delicate flavor."

DANISH BERRY PUDDING

(Serves 6 to 8)

1 heaping cup blackberries, red raspberries, or wineberries, and 1 cup red currants

3 tablespoons cornstarch

1 cup white wine

¾ cup purple grape juice

1 cup sugar

1 cup sour cream

Reserve a few perfect berries for garnish. Stir the cornstarch and the wine together until smooth. Mix fruit, wine and cornstarch, and grape juice thoroughly, and add ½ cup sugar. Stirring constantly, bring the mixture to a gentle boil and boil until the cloudiness clarifies. Taste, and add more sugar if you need to. Chill the pudding thoroughly, and serve with a dollop of sour cream on top of each serving.

A Simple Dessert

(Nothing better in the universe!)

1 quart fresh cleaned blackberries, wineberries, red raspberries, dewberries, etc.

1 cup heavy cream

A few grains salt

1 teaspoon real vanilla

¼ to ½ cup sugar, depending on the sweetness of your berries

Whip the cream until stiff with the salt, vanilla, and sugar. Fold in the berries gently, and serve immediately. Don't make this ahead.

BLUEBERRIES AND HUCKLEBERRIES

Blueberry

Blueberries, many different species of them, belong to the *Vaccinium* genus. The genus name, kin to our word *vaccination* comes from the Latin word for *cows*, *vacca*, and probably designates the location of many of the berries: pastures. The way we get from cow to vaccination is that during the time people were dying of smallpox, dairymaids, who worked around cows, often got a milder pox called cowpox. In 1796, Edward Jenner, an observant physician, noticed that they never got smallpox afterward. He reasoned that if everyone could get a case of cowpox, they'd wipe out smallpox. He invented vaccinations, made of serum from the blood of victims of the lesser cowpox, and eventually the world was freed of the great disfiguring and devastating scourge of smallpox. The huckleberry, dangleberry, sunberry, or wonderberry is technically one of several varieties of the *Gaylussacia* genus, named for its discoverer, a nineteenth-century French chemist named Gay-Lussac.

Huckleberries

Description, Habitat, and Season

Huckleberry plants grow 2 to 5 feet high and frequent swamps, woodlands, roadsides, and especially burned-over ground. The *Gaylussacia* are close kin to the *Vaccinium*, and to the untutored eye look the same. However, having said that, it is a fact that blueberries and huckleberries are generally indistinguishable to the foraging eye as well.

Many plant books show one of several *Vaccinium* and call it huckleberry; in fact the word *huckleberry* is a corruption of *whortleberry*, a name for the blueberry. Confused? Don't worry. They're all good to eat. Botanically, the difference lies in how many teensy seeds are in each berry (ten in *Gaylussacia*, four or five in *Vaccinium*). But as the seeds are virtually too small to count, it really isn't necessary to distinguish between the berries.

A friend, a New Hampshire Pulitzer Prize–winning poet, describes the ripening of blueberries in "The Hermit Picks Berries."

> . . . At this hour a goodly number
> of blueberries decide to ripen.
> Once they were wax white.
> Then came the green of small bruises.
> After that, the red of bad welts.
> All this time they enlarged themselves.
> Now they are true blue. . . .
>
> —Maxine Kumin

Blueberries are larger, lighter in color, and "dustier" than huckleberries, which are by contrast smaller, darker, shinier, and more purple than blueberries.

Blueberries and huckleberries, which grow throughout temperate North America, and ripen in mid- to late summer, are small (¼ to ½ inch), blue to deep purple to black, on insignificant little shrubs with small, oval, dark green leaves. Euell Gibbons claims to have picked swamp huckleberries in New Jersey on bushes 15 feet high, and my friend from New Hampshire says her blueberry bushes stand about 5 feet tall. In Virginia, where they are sometimes called buckberries, I've never seen a blueberry or huckleberry bush higher than 3 feet, and they're usually closer to 18 inches.

The highbush blueberry, *Vaccinium corymbosum*, is the most common blueberry of our New England states, the berry dark blue with a bloom (a dusty or powdery look).

Huckleberries grow sparsely, on spare bushes 12 to 18 inches high, in sandy soil and scraggly woods, ripening on or about the first of August. In general, the places to look for blueberries and huckleberries are open fields, any area that has recently been burned over, along country roads, and on sandy paths at the edge of sparse woods, for they will only grow in wide-open scrubby areas, and they like light soil and sunshine all day long.

Go out with a bucket in late summer and pick whatever looks like a blueberry or huckleberry. If you find a laden bush, lay a sheet under it and shake it for a clean, fast harvest.

History and Lore

Although they are similar and interchangeable, there are semantic differences between blueberries and huckleberries. Blueberries are usually associated with New England and the Midwest, while huckleberries are considered southern. Blueberries provided the dye for the navy-blue garments of New England whalers. Huckleberry Finn, one of America's most-loved literary characters, is wild and southern. Remember, too, how Robert McClosky's Sal gathered blueberries in Maine, while Br'er Rabbit, from the southern briar patch, stole Br'er Fox's huckleberry jam.

{RECIPES}

BLUEBERRY BUCKLE

Preheat oven to 375°F. Assemble 1 stick butter, 1¼ cups sugar, 1 egg, 2⅓ cups self-rising flour (or 2⅓ cups flour with 2 teaspoon baking powder and ½ teaspoon salt stirred in thoroughly), ½ cup milk, 2 cups blueberries, and ½ teaspoon cinnamon. Cream half the stick of butter with ¾ cup sugar. Beat in the egg. Add 2 cups self-rising flour (or flour mix) alternately with ½ cup milk. Fold in the washed blueberries. Pour the batter into a greased 9 × 9-inch pan. Sprinkle the top with crumb topping made by fork-blending the remaining 4 tablespoons butter, ½ cup sugar, ⅓ cup flour, and ½ teaspoon cinnamon. Bake for 35 minutes. You will see how the top "buckles" and understand its name.

BLUEBERRY COFFEE CAKE

Preheat oven to 350°F. Assemble 2 cups biscuit mix, ½ cup sugar, ⅓ cup safflower oil or melted butter or margarine, 2 eggs, and 1 cup milk. Mix

the dry ingredients thoroughly. Mix the liquids well. Mix the two lightly, and pour into a square 9-inch pan. Over this, place the topping, which is 2 cups blueberries, ½ cup sugar, ½ teaspoon cinnamon, ½ teaspoon allspice, and 4 tablespoons melted butter, tossed together. Bake until done, about 45 minutes.

HUCKLEBERRY CAKE WITH HARD SAUCE

(My favorite summer recipe of my childhood)

Turn on the oven to 375°F. Cream ¾ stick butter, I teaspoon vanilla, and I cup sugar. Add 2 big eggs, well beaten, and beat mixture well. Mix and sift 1¾ cups flour, ½ teaspoon salt, and 2 teaspoons baking powder. Measure ½ cup milk. Alternately add flour mixture and milk to the creamed ingredients, beating until the batter is smooth and thoroughly mixed. Flour 2 cups berries by tossing them in 2 or 3 tablespoons flour until all are coated. Pour into a sieve and shake gently to remove extra flour. Fold into the yellow cake batter. Bake in a buttered loaf pan for about 45 minutes, while dinner is being eaten. Serve the cake hot, in slices, with a generous dollop of cold Hard Sauce (recipe follows). A yellow cake mix works fine too. Add the floured berries at the end of the mixing time.

HARD SAUCE

With an electric beater, cream ¾ stick room-temperature butter, and slowly add 2 tablespoons cream, I tablespoon each brandy, rum, and sherry, and ½ teaspoon vanilla until smooth. Little by little, add I pound of confectioners' sugar, more or less, until the mixture is rich and smooth and homogenized. It should hold a shape. You can do this quickly in a blender or food processor. Mound the sauce in a dish, grate half a fresh nutmeg over the top, and chill until serving time. Top each hot slice of cake generously with hard sauce.

PEACH-BLUEBERRY COBBLER

Turn on the oven to 350°F. Mix together 8 peaches, peeled, pitted, and sliced, with I pint blueberries or huckleberries, 2 tablespoons lemon juice, 3 tablespoons cornstarch, and I cup sugar. Pour into a shallow casserole to make a bottom layer. Make the crumbly topping and crumble it over the fruit: 6 tablespoons margarine, I cup sugar, 2 teaspoon vanilla, ½ cup flour, I cup old-fashioned rolled oats, and I teaspoon ground cinnamon. Bake the dessert until the top is nicely browned, about I hour. Serve it hot with vanilla ice cream or frozen yogurt on top.

AUTUMN OLIVE

They are those recent immigrant, highly invasive, hedgerow plants growing 10 to 15 feet high, the leaves in the wind dark green atop, sil-

ver underneath, berries red and juicy, maturing in late summer–autumn olive (*Elaeagnus umbellata*). Despite its bold spread, it is a beautiful plant, providing a ruby-red jelly and abundant ascorbic acid–rich speckled berries you can strip off quickly. The flowers in spring are a light yellow. Birds and deer love the berries, and so might you. They provide vitamins A, C, and E, as well as lesser amounts of many minerals. Some sources say they have seventeen times more lycopene than ripe tomatoes. Russian olives, of the same family, have dry useless berries. That is the way to tell the difference between the plants.

CHERRIES

Pin cherry, wild cherry, bird cherry, choke cherry, fireberry, and choke-berry are some of the folk names of various small berrylike drupes of the *Prunus* genus, which is that genus of fruits with a single stone. *Prunus* is kin to our word *prune*, which is of course a dried plum.

Description, Habitat, and Season
Cherry trees are small trees or shrubs; they have erect or trailing branches, opposite long, thin, shiny, single, serrated leaves, and lovely 5-petaled white or pink blossoms in the spring. They are a Temperate Zone fruit and ripen in late summer. All cherries, red, black, purple, or yellow, have a round, globular, single seed in the middle, and grow on stems. They vary in size from blueberry- or pea-size to an inch in diameter.

There are many wild cherries, and they all yield fruit, some better than others, some sweet and some bitter. The ripe fruit of all cherry trees is safe. Let taste be your guide.

Some folks are fond of the almond flavor in fruit seeds that warns of the presence of cyanide. In my childhood, many housewives added a peach pit seed, which looks just like an almond, as flavoring to each jar of peach preserves they made, and a few cherry seeds to each jar of cherry preserves. A family I knew ate several seeds from each apple they ate, believing that the seeds were somehow protective against disease. In fact, laetrile, also known as vitamin B17, made of the seed of a cherry-almond-peach-apricot relative, the bitter almond, contains cyanide—a known poison—and yet many believe it is effective as a cancer cure.

History and Lore

Grocery store cherries are cultivars from *Prunus cerasus* (Latin for "cherry"), brought to America from Europe, brought to Europe from Asia in ancient times. (This is why you don't find cherry trees in the wild with fruits that look like cherries you'd find in the grocery store.)

Lucullus, remembered today for the splendor of his banquets, is believed to have introduced cherries to Italy. Perhaps this is why cherries have always been an elite fruit to man.

Cherries are all technically poisonous, for the leaves, pits, bark, and twigs are all loaded with cyanide. But the flesh of the drupe, which has no poison, is one of man's favorite fruits, and cherry is an extremely popular aroma in candies, wines, liqueurs, preserves, cough drops, and pies, as well as in perfumes and room deodorants. The roots were sought by Native Americans, scraped and boiled, to make a soothing wash for abrasions, and a tea for stomach troubles. Wild cherry bark is an ingredient in many cough syrups even today. Indeed, my own grandmother made such a remedy, with a teaspoon of the inner bark shaved into a cup of boiling water, adding honey as a sweetener. But this is not recommended, as the amateur forager has no way of knowing how much bark is too much.

Wild cherry wine is used in Appalachia as a diarrhea cure, as well as a popular homemade beverage. The Italian liqueur amaretto has crushed cherry seeds as an ingredient.

Because wild cherries are more seed than flesh, they are mostly fun to just eat out of hand while spitting out the seeds. (Swallowing a single cherry seed will not harm anyone, or we would all be dead; it's large amounts that do damage. Besides, the cyanide-containing seed is enclosed in its hard shell covering.) But if you manage to bring home a lot of cherries, you can make a delicious wild cherry sauce for pancakes or ice cream. If you want to enhance the flavor of peaches or cherries, I suggest using a little almond extract from the supermarket.

{RECIPES}

CHERRY SAUCE

Cook whole, washed cherries until tender in a little water. Once they are soft, to remove the pits, put them in a ricer or potato masher and mash them. The flesh will be pressed through the ricer, coming out sort of like cranberry sauce, leaving the pits and skins in the ricer. Heat this sauce with sugar to taste, and you have cherry sauce. You can make a jam out of this cherry flesh by adding an equal amount of sugar and the juice of 1 lemon and slowly cooking it to an agreeable thickness, stirring often to prevent scorching.

CHERRY BOUNCE

The grandfather of one of my friends made this, and we stole it as kids and drank it and got giggly.

Stem and pick over 1 gallon wild cherries, any type. Mash them in a crock with some of the shattered seeds included (about 12 to 20). Add 3 pounds sugar, 1 gallon good whiskey, and 1 pint brandy. Cover tightly and let stand for two weeks or so in a dark closet. Strain and bottle. As I recall, this was outstanding.

CORNEL CHERRIES

The cornel cherry (*Cornus mas*), or cornelian cherry, is a member of the dogwood family. *Cornus* means "horn," and it is so named for the sturdy resilient wood of the species. The cornel cherry tree is shaped much like other dogwoods and has yellow lacy blossoms. In the fall, the leaves turn red, like other dogwoods. *Cornus mas* bears (profusely in some cases) dark red oval astringent fruits an inch long that mellow as they ripen in late fall and taste somewhat plummy. The wood is hard, and one of its folk names, arrowwood, suggests one of its uses.

Description, Habitat, and Season

The cornel cherry, a small, rounded tree, has profuse rounded flower buds, yellow flowers in spring, red half-inch fruits shaped like olives, and dark green glossy foliage. Though some folks like to have these trees as ornamentals, the fruit can make a mess and stain sidewalks.

Cornel cherry trees are popular in eastern Europe, where the fruit is used in candies, compotes, and preserves. Genetic engineering has led to bigger and sweeter varieties of the berrylike fruit sometimes called "pudding berry."

History and Lore

The common family name of "dogwood" is said to have originated when someone remarked that the fruit was not fit for the dogs. (You need a ricer to get the seeds out of the tiny berries, but it's worth the game, I think.) Don't try to pick the fruit off the tree; it won't be ripe until it falls to the ground. Then you have to pick the berries up before the squirrels and birds get them. The cornel cherry is an old plant, a native of southern Europe, and mentioned by no less a figure than Homer: "Ulysses shook his cornel spear to rouse the savage battle."

{RECIPES}

CORNEL CHERRY SAUCE

The cornel cherry is mostly used for making jam, or a sauce rather like cranberry. To prepare, put whole berries in a stainless steel pot. Add a little water, just enough to create steam for a while. Cover and steam for 15 minutes. When the berries are soft, mash them, then strain the juice through cheesecloth or a ricer. Add an equal amount of sugar to the juice you get, and cook until the sugar dissolves. Either use as a syrup for pancakes or make into jelly. One source suggests adding water and ice for a great cornel cherryade.

CORNEL CHERRY PIE

Make a double piecrust (see pages 207–208). Peel and slice 5 cups apples. Add 1 cup pitted cornel cherries, 1 cup sugar, 1 tablespoon cornstarch, a dash of salt, and 2 teaspoons cinnamon. Mix and pour into one shell, cover the contents with another, and bake for 50 minutes at 325°F.

CRANBERRIES

Vaccinium vitis-idaea or *V. macrocarpon*, bog cranberries, are familiar to Americans. The wild fruits taste identical to the cultivated variety we eat at Thanksgiving, which is to say, sour. They are part of the same genus as blueberries, and their names describe them: *Vaccinium vitis-idaea* suggest that the fruit is of the cow pasture and looks like grapes (*vitis*) of Mount Ida, which is on Crete. The name of the second variety tells us that they have "great fruit," or *macro carpon*. They are still not as big as the commercial cranberries we can buy, but are well worth the effort to gather them.

Description, Habitat, and Season

Cranberry plants are evergreen, and have tiny leaves. They have skinny branches, with the fruit-bearing branches erect but still low (½ foot to 1 foot). In *V. macrocarpon*, the spring-to-summer flowers are white to pinkish and bell shaped, and the plant usually occurs with water within reach of the root. Cranberries prefer a cool to cold climate, sandy soil, and protected locations, and grow most abundantly from Cape Cod south to New Jersey and across to Wisconsin. The most likely place to find them is

on the borders of ponds, down low where they can find protection from freezing, with the red berries ripening from fall through winter by the water's edge. In *V. vitis-idaea*, the red berries grow on a low, creeping evergreen trailing shrub, generally no more than 3 inches high, and both the leaves and the berries tend to be small, the fruit somewhat smaller than the cranberries found in markets, which have been pampered and protected and fed vitamins.

When Ponce de León and his sailors, long at sea without fresh produce and suffering the aches and stiffness, the loose teeth and enervation of scurvy, disembarked in Florida, the first thing they did was to gorge themselves on fresh fruits and green plants. The second thing may have been to jump in some of those glorious springs that dot Florida, to get clean after months at sea. The antiscorbutic effects went to work at once, and they began to feel much better quickly. They'd had fruit before, but they'd never seen springs like those. They attributed their restored youths to the clear, crystal waters and believed they had found the Fountain of Youth.

History and Lore
The Native Americans gave the scurvy-wracked English the tart red berries to eat after their long ocean voyage to New England. The Native Americans' ibimi, as they called the berries, literally saved the English

adventurers' lives, and must have seemed like a miracle food. We know now that cranberries, fruiting after most fresh foods are past harvest, are rich in ascorbic acid, vitamin C, the only vitamin humans cannot store, and thus need daily for bountiful health. The effects of scurvy are reversed quickly with the addition of vitamin C to the diet.

The Native Americans drank cranberry juice and cranberry tea and made cranberry bread. They showed white men how to make cranberry sauce or jam (sweetened with maple sugar) to accompany venison. The East Coast Algonquians made an aboriginal fast food out of cranberries, called pemmican, as traveling fare for their seasonal migrations. The Native Americans' use of cranberries included poulticing wounds with the roasted berries. Cranberries were believed to be effective against poison arrow wounds, and perhaps they were, as the berries are astringent, especially when raw. Cranberries have been praised for easing cramps and childbirth, as well as convulsions, "hysteria," and "fits." Other early American chroniclers noted that cranberry tea overcomes nausea.

Soon, cultivated varieties provided bigger and better berries.

My Maine nieces, Lucy and Susan Letcher (famous for hiking the Appalachian Trail in both directions in only a few months—Jackrabbit and Isis are their trail names), tell me they know how to tell a ripe cranberry from either an unripe one or an overripe one. They bounce them: The green ones bound away at once, and the soft, or overripe, ones more or less just lie there. The good cranberries bounce lightly right into their hands. Thus, they collect only the good cranberries for their sauce or juice.

{RECIPES}

CRANBERRY SAUCE

We still make it about the same way today as the Native Americans did. Cranberries pop as they cook, which signals that they are done.

Bring to a boil 4 cups cranberries, 2 cups sugar, and 1 cup water. Boil for 10 minutes, or until the bursting of the berries stops, stirring occasionally (once a minute). Pour at once into a mold and refrigerate until it is jelled. The ample amount of pectin in the berries causes the jelly to gently set.

Assemble I large orange, 4 cups uncooked cranberries, and 2 cups sugar. Cut the orange into chunks, removing all the seeds carefully, but leaving half the skin on. Grind the orange or quickly chop it in a food processor. Quickly chop the cranberries. Stir both together, and add the sugar, stirring thoroughly. Refrigerate for at least I day, preferably 2, to let the sugar dissolve before serving.

ELDERBERRIES

The elderberry, *Sambucus canadensis, S. nigra, S. racemosa*, is a delicious drupe, black when ripe, and the size of a small pea. The name is a Latin word derived from the Greek word for a harp or other musical instrument. The Native Americans, half a world away, called elderberries music trees, because the hollow stems made wonderful flutes.

Description, Habitat, and Season
Elderberry species are shrubs that grow in wet woods and near creeks and rivers throughout all fifty of the United States and are members of the honeysuckle family. The annual branches die down to the ground

each winter. This characteristic helps identify the plant. Elderberry is a stoloniferous plant, which means the roots send out new shoots near the original plant, making thick stands of the plant. Thus, elderberry grows in dense thickets of 5- to 10-foot-high bushes of many branches. The leaves are compound, opposite, with five to eleven leaflets, pointed and serrated. Elderberry stems are so pulpy they were hollowed out not only for flutes and whistles but also as blowguns and syringes in past times. The bark, as well, grows in easily detachable tubes.

In spring, the off-white, sweet-smelling flowers are borne in a flat bunch rather like Queen Anne's lace. The shrubs yield small, flat clusters of blue-black, three-seeded drupes in late summer. Avoid the red-fruited elderberry (*S. pubens*) with the berries in dome-shaped clusters; that one is poisonous.

History and Lore
Folklore credits the elderberry plant with magical properties, among them the ability to confer invisibility and second sight and to cure the bites of mad dogs. Elder is said in Celtic mythology to be the tree of compassion. Elderberries were believed by Culpeper and Gerard to restore youth; perhaps this is because gray hair can be restored to black by a dye made from the dwarf elder bush.

{RECIPES}

Though the stems, roots, and leaves of elderberries are poisonous, the spring flowers and the ripe fruit are delicious and safe. Elderberries and their flowers are still made into wine today by country folks here and in Europe; an Italian liqueur, sambuca, is flavored with the ripe berries; elderberry pie and elderberry wine are common in Appalachia.

While ripe elderberries are an excellent fruit when cooked—personally, I think they have the best flavor for pie of any berry—eating unripe or uncooked elderberries can cause vomiting and diarrhea. Ripe elderberries are high in vitamins A and C, potassium, iron, and plant protein.

The spring flower heads are popularly dipped into pancake batter and deep-fried into fritters—hence the folk name fritter tree. The flowers can be dried for a mild, pleasant herbal tea; and in the early fall, when you find the berries turned from green to red to black, they make a wonderfully flavorful pie, with a rich, spicy, grapy flavor.

ELDER-FLOWER FRITTERS

Mix a thin pancake batter. Heat I quart vegetable oil to 380°F, dip a branch of the flower heads into the batter, drip or shake off excess batter, and fry quickly. Repeat. I use I small packet of biscuit or pancake mix stirred with one egg and as much milk as it takes to make a thin batter.

ELDERBERRY PIE

Preheat oven to 350°F. Make a double piecrust according to the directions on pages 207–208. Mix I quart ripe picked elderberries thoroughly with I heaping cup sugar, I tablespoon cornstarch, I tablespoon lemon juice or cider vinegar, and 3 tablespoons melted butter. Pour them in the bottom crust. Cover with the top crust. Press the top and bottom crusts together, make some slits in the top to let steam escape, and bake the pie until golden.

FIGS

Figs (*Ficus carica*) have escaped into the wild and spread southward from the mid-Atlantic states to the extreme southern parts of this country, but because a single dip to thirty-two degrees will kill a fig, the trees

are somewhat rare farther north than the Carolinas. For the last ten or fifteen years, I've been able to grow figs here in Virginia if I mulch them heavily and burlap the trunks all winter. The fig bushes appear to die, losing all leaves and leaving dead-looking stalks. But in the spring, they resurrect and, in some cases, branch out into large bushes.

Ficus means "fig" in Latin; *Caria* in Asia Minor was its habitat in ancient times. The Carian method of preserving figs for export gives us the dried figs we buy in markets today. Fresh figs are infrequently found in markets because they are extremely delicate, and no way has yet been found to ship them fresh safely.

My father, whose favorite fruit was figs, decided he would grow them in Virginia, although he knew that was virtually impossible. (It's warmed so that now I have four fig bushes in my yard, and there are others around. Either they've developed cold-hardy figs, or global warming has allowed figs to survive in the mountains of Virginia.) He used to treat his single fig tree better than he treated the rest of us.

He built a stone terrace for it and planted it in a protected southwest-facing ell of our Shenandoah Valley house (which I suspect he planned with that fig tree in mind). On winter nights, he'd haul out mountains of old quilts, parkas, and tarps and wrap blankets over and around its low, spreading limbs. He'd make charcoal fires and set them in buckets near it, and go out in the night to worry over the shrub. If you looked out an upper window, you could see his breath in great puffs in the air, and his bare feet sticking out from under his overcoat as he patted and pushed and tucked that tree around. Most years, he succeeded in getting a pretty good crop of figs, which he kept count of and did not share except most grudgingly. But one hard frost would ruin the crop for the next season.

Description, Habitat, and Season
Ficus carica is a large spreading shrub or a small tree, with 3- to 5-lobed, large leaves; a sweet, soft, fleshy fruit that is brown or deep purple, striped on the outside and pink on the inside; and soft, edible seeds throughout the flesh. Fig trees do flower, but the blossom, from which the fruit develops, is so insignificant as to go unnoticed. If frost kills a fig tree, stolons (root sprouts) arise from the ground to begin anew their climb toward the sun. Thus, figs in the wild may be found in tight patches. (This low growth also helps protect them from frost.) Figs ripen in late summer or early autumn. Ours this year began to ripen on September 1, and by September 24, they were all gone. An ancient practice still used by fig growers as a ripening aid is to touch the end, or "eye," of the fig with oil. I declare it works!

History and Lore
This plant of warm locations appears often in ancient manuscripts, and is most common in Asia and eastern and southern Europe. The Bible mentions figs often, and we know the Greeks and the Romans cultivated these sweet, pulpy fruits, as their descendants today still do. Figs were once so common that they became objects of contempt: I don't give a fig, people say, even today. The Romans ate and used them extensively, and Pliny, who is our authority on what the Romans ate, mentioned thirty varieties.

Today, figs are more often than not relegated to the category of a laxative, and so they were employed from ancient times, but to label them thus does figs a disservice, for they truly are a delicious fruit, one that many people never have the chance to taste fresh. The only way most people eat figs is in the popular confection called Fig Newtons.

When I was a child living in San Diego, we had a fig tree out back of our house, and the figs, pink and seedy and sweet as honey inside, were the best fruit I ever ate. They can be grown in hothouses, and even in the mountains of Virginia, but it's difficult.

FIG ICE CREAM

(Daddy's idea of heaven)

Combine 1 quart ripe figs, chopped, 1 cup honey, 1 quart heavy cream, and 1 tablespoon vanilla. Mix and freeze. Three times during the freezing, take out as the sides begin to freeze, pour back into the bowl, and beat with a wooden spoon or an electric beater until smooth.

FIGGY PUDDING

This is a favorite holiday dessert in Great Britain, made the old-fashioned way. This recipe is from an 1888 cookbook. I used dried figs (Carian figs), as I suspect they have always had to do in England. It's a dessert you ought to try once.

Assemble ½ cup brown sugar, ½ cup finely chopped beef suet, 1 cup chopped apple, 1 cup chopped figs, ½ cup milk, ½ cup dry bread crumbs, 2 separated eggs, ¾ cup flour, and a bottle of brandy. Add the sugar to the suet, apple, and figs. Pour the milk over the bread crumbs, and add the yolks, well beaten. Combine mixtures, add the flour, then the whites beaten stiff. Turn into a greased pudding mold, and steam in a covered steamer for 4 hours. (I did this by placing the pudding casserole into my pasta pot, adding water halfway up the casserole, and covering with the lid. I continued to add boiling water during the cooking time, to keep it about level.) Finally, this steamed pudding is soaked with as much brandy as it will hold, for several hours before serving, then set on fire to be brought to the table. You can substitute margarine or butter for the beef suet, though that will change the taste. I do like the addition of 1 teaspoon each of cinnamon, allspice, and ginger, though they are not in the original.

GRAPES

Grapes are one of earth's most ubiquitous plants. The genus name, *Vitis*, is from the Latin word for *life*, and kin to our words *vital* and *vitality*. All grapes, whether gold, pale green, purple, brown, or red, grow in clusters on vines, and have the edible characteristic grape leaves. Some few

are seedless, but most have seeds in the center of each fruit. The grapes themselves range in size, depending on the variety, from less than ½ inch in diameter to over 1 inch in diameter. They range from tasteless to extremely sweet, fragrant, and tasty. Grapes grow worldwide; there are more than one hundred varieties, and there are thousands of subvarieties. On our side of the Atlantic, wild grapes, including *Vitis labrusca*, which means "wild vine," *V. riparia*, or "riverbank vine," *V. vulpina*, the fox grape, and *V. aestivalis*, the summer grape, flourished all along the Atlantic coast when the white man sighted land in the 1600s.

> *Always eat grapes downward—that is, always eat the best grapes first; in this way there will be none better left on the bunch, and each grape will seem good down to the last. If you eat the other way, you will not have a good grape in the lot.*
> —SAMUEL BUTLER

If a wild grape tastes all right, it is all right. Look for tendrils. All grapes have them. Grapes are famous for escaping from cultivars and wilding. There is one poisonous look-alike: the unpalatable Canada moonvine, with bitter berries that at first glance might look like a grapevine, but it has no tendrils. Further, if you taste one of the acrid, bitter berries, you will not be tempted to eat them. Finally, moonvine berries contain one sickle-shaped seed; grape seeds are always tear shaped.

Description, Habitat, and Season

So familiar are the leaves, the coiling tendrils, the sinuous forked vines, and the grapes themselves that any description seems excessive. The heart-shaped leaves are 4 to 6 inches in diameter, not serrated, but are often deeply indented to form three lobes.

The best grapes are those that get full sun, so the vines may climb high in trees, thus putting the grapes tantalizingly out of reach. Grapes ripen in late summer or early autumn. Grapevines can be identified in winter by their irregular ropy stems, and the little coiled tendrils that cling even when the plant is dormant.

In the *Aeneid*, the hero Aeneas received a typical puzzling oracular message that said, in effect, that he and his wandering sailors would know their new native land by this sign: that they would consume their plates along with their food. One night on the shores of Latium (Italy), Aeneas glanced up and saw that his men were eating the vine leaves that they had used to hold the roasted meat from the fire, by which he realized that they had indeed arrived at their new home.

History and Lore

In AD 986, Viking sailors returning to Scandinavia reported that there lay a land far to the west, beyond the land they called Greenland, whose splendors were such that, a hundred miles at sea, the scent of the ripening grapes could be detected by the weary sailors. This story gave rise to the name they gave to the western continent: Vinland, or vine-land.

Grapes are generally believed to be among the earliest of all cultivated fruits. Their country of origin is unknown but suspected to be the fertile crescent between the Tigris and Euphrates. Grapes have been blessed and cursed throughout history, for their devilish ability to addle human reason (as wine, of course) while at the same time providing so much pleasure. Grapes average a life span nearly the same as the people who enjoy them, and there is one vine seven hundred years old at Hampton Court Palace outside of London, claimed to be the oldest living grapevine in the world.

Grapes are mentioned more frequently in the Bible than any other fruit. Among the ancient Romans, Bacchus, the god of wine, was reputed to have discovered wine by accident and was rewarded by the Etruscans with god status. Cato the Censor wrote that the custom of kissing as greeting between kinfolk began with men attempting to discover if their wives had been drinking in their absence.

Grapes were believed in both ancient Europe and pre-English America to be "eye clearing." Hildegard von Bingen in the twelfth century said that anyone with blurry eyes should lubricate the eyelids daily with the drops that come from the vine after cutting. Grapes were believed to be antiscorbutic (preventing scurvy) and refrigerant (cooling to fevers). Dark grapes like the Concord provided early on, and still do, a purple dye for wool.

Being in a constant state of inebriation helped buffer the miserable colonists against the rigors of frontier life: cold, boredom, too much salted meat, and too little in the way of medical services. However, Thomas Jefferson, a moderate drinker, was concerned with the widespread drunkenness of Virginians during his time and the easy availability of hard liquors. It was always Jefferson's belief that a healthy wine industry would prove an antidote to the drunkenness that plagued American colonial life. From the beginning, brandies were made from wild fruits, liquor from corn, but wines made in this land were notoriously bad.

{RECIPES}

In the cuisine of eastern Europe and throughout the Middle East are certain dishes that use the large, tender leaves of grapevines (picked in the spring) to enclose meat or rice mixtures. The Native Americans ate wild grapes and also used them for medicine. The Seminole stuffed fish with grapes before cooking them; the Iroquois stuffed ducks and other game birds with grapes and roasted them.

Jefferson introduced a serious wine industry to America. Recent research gives us the go-ahead on moderate wine drinking, especially red wine (which is red because the grape skins are used in its making). A substance in wine called resveratrol helps to reduce cholesterol and lower blood pressure. Of interest here is that wild grapes and wine grapes have more resveratrol than supermarket eating grapes; the speculation is that the table grapes are so coddled in their raising that they fail to produce the substance, which guards the wild grapes and wine grapes from disease.

GRAPE JUICE

Remove wild grapes from their stems, throwing out any grapes that are rotten. For 5 pounds grapes, add about 1 cup water. Heat slowly to a boil but do not crush the grapes. Make a cheesecloth lining (two layers) in a colander or sieve, and pour the boiled grapes into the sieve. Let the grapes drip for I hour. You can gently move the cheesecloth to facilitate the dripping, but don't squeeze or the juice will be cloudy. Add sugar to sweeten and drink fresh or refrigerate for up to I week, or use the grape juice for jelly.

DOLMADES (STUFFED GRAPE LEAVES)

In the spring, when the leaves are full grown but still tender, choose 24 large, perfect grape leaves. Wash them if need be, and lay them one on top of the other in a pan. Add I cup water, I cup vinegar, and I cup salt. Bring them to a boil, and boil them gently for 5 minutes. Remove from heat and leave overnight in the brine. Next day, they are ready to use.

Assemble I cup cooked rice; I tablespoon olive oil; I pound ground beef or lamb; I onion, finely chopped; I clove garlic, finely chopped; ½ teaspoon dried dill weed; salt; pepper; I tablespoon catsup or tomato paste; ⅛ teaspoon each cinnamon, nutmeg, and allspice; and ¼ cup chopped parsley. Reserve the rice. Heat the olive oil, and add the meat, onion, garlic, and spices to it. Cook, stirring, until the meat has lost any red color. Add the cooked rice, mix well, and there is your stuffing. In the center of each grape leaf, place 2 tablespoons of the mixture. Fold the sides in first, then roll the grape leaf into a neat, fat envelope, entirely covering the stuffing. Place them seam side down, tightly nestled side by side, in a pan, add I cup water, cover tightly, and bake I hour at about 350°F. When taking them out of the pan, handle them carefully so as not to unwrap or pierce the envelopes.

SPICED WILD GRAPE JELLY FOR VENISON

Assemble I quart ripe wild grapes, plus about I cup unripe grapes, I cup cider vinegar, I tablespoon whole cloves, I stick cinnamon, broken, and I pound sugar. Put everything but the sugar together, let set overnight, then bring slowly to a boil, cooking until the grapes are soft. Strain. Bring the liquid gently to a boil. Add the sugar all at once to the boiling liquid, reheat to a boil, and boil about 5 more minutes, or until the jelly tests. (To test jelly, dip a cold spoon into the simmering mixture, and then hold it over a saucer for a few seconds. When a double bead forms on the spoon's edge, the jelly is done.)

Fox or Wild Grape Jelly

Follow the direction on a box of pectin for Concord grape jelly, using any fragrant wild grape. The wild grapes have a wilder, tangier taste than tamed ones and make a wonderful jelly.

Grape-Stuffed Chicken

(Serves 2 to 4)

This delicious, easy recipe is adapted from a Native American dish.

Wash a whole frying chicken, and salt it inside and out. Heat the oven to 350°F. Stuff the bird with grapes removed from the stems and seeded if they have objectionable seeds. The grapes may be salted a little first and tossed with 1 or 2 minced cloves of garlic. Let the grapes spill out and surround the chicken. Bake for 1½ hours, uncovered. You can baste it with its own juices a couple of times if you like. Wiggle a leg to see if it is loose, which lets you know the chicken is done. Serve the chicken with rice, and spoon grapes and their juice over the rice.

Grape Juice for Weight Loss

The sleeping prophet Edgar Cayce often prescribed grape juice for weight loss: 2 parts of water, 1 part grape juice, taken half an hour before meals. I add it here because it is so benign—and it seems sensible that a bit of sugar before meals—just a bit—might curb the appetite much more safely than the shipload of unsafe and expensive suppressant drugs on the market today. Just an idea!

MULBERRIES

Description, Habitat, and Season

Mulberry trees, genus *Morus*, are variable in size and foliage and are long-lived. They are 30 feet tall on average, though red mulberries grow as high as 75 feet in the South. The large (2 to 8 inches long) leaves of mulberry trees are thick, dull, and dark green. They are toothed, often lobed, and the trees have a milky sap. The multiple compound fruit, each bead fertilized independently, is ovate, compressed, and covered by the succulent calyx. Mulberry trees have spread from early cultivation in Virginia and other eastern states. The hardier black or red varieties

of mulberry grow along city streets and back alleys, in meadows, along roadsides, and in backyards from New York to the Carolinas and west to at least Missouri.

The aggregate fruits ripen in early to late summer. Because red mulberries are acidic, they are tastier than the black or white varieties. Southerners have long made a popular cheap wine from red mulberries, but *Morus rubra* is now primarily considered important as a food for wildlife. It has been noted that the taste of mulberries varies enormously from species to species, and even from plant to plant. Some are flat—sweet without any tang. Most often the ground beneath a tree of ripe mulberries will be red with trampled berries and their juice. Nobody picks up the soft, juicy berries or climbs to pick them. With the addition of lemon juice, however, they might be turned into marvelous jellies, jams, and pies. Sometimes it seems that we're not hungry enough these days.

History and Lore
A charming Greek legend says that the berries of the white mulberry turned red when its roots were bathed in the blood of Pyramus and Thisbe, lovers who committed suicide because each mistakenly thought the other was dead. (Shakespeare, as you may recall, revived and parodied the legend in *A Midsummer Night's Dream*.) The Romans, who wanted everything the Greeks had, also wanted silk. In AD 220, Heliogabalus, Emperor of Rome, obtained and proudly wore a silk robe. So did Aure-

lian, a generation later. The Romans, again copying the Greeks, imported from Persia and cultivated the black mulberry (*M. nigra*), the food of silkworms and a host for their own silkworm cultures. It was worthy of documentation that in AD 780 in Britain, Charlemagne presented a silken robe to Offa, King of Mercia. From about 1500 on, English clergy wore silk vestments. Henry VIII, quite an iconoclast, owned several pairs of Spanish silk stockings, initiating a fashion craze that lasted for two and a half centuries.

In the New World in 1623, the Virginia House of Burgesses required that each free man must cultivate one-quarter acre of "vines, herbs, and roots." A year later, the law became more specific: Four mulberry trees and twenty (grape) vines had to be planted by every male over the age of twenty. The Virginia Company, failing after only one generation, determined to recoup its losses through the wine and silk industries. Neither thrived, though the law stayed on the books for many years. No matter how much silk was made, better could be purchased cheaper from Asia, where labor was almost free. Those original mulberry trees (*M. alba*) have spread far and wide. When I sought to learn why the silkworms, out of work and with nothing but leisure time on their hands, have not overtaken us, I learned that they face many natural predators, feed chiefly these days on an Asian weed tree of the genus *Ailanthus*, and transform themselves quietly into beautiful silk moths. They are presently fairly rare, exclusively inhabiting the east coast of the mid-Atlantic states. No source I have found answers the obvious question: Why have they changed their diet from mulberry leaves to *Ailanthus*?

Hexander of Athens wrote in 340 BC of a blight of mulberry trees in his time so great that for twenty years there were no mulberries. Gout raged, he reported, so that men, women, children, and eunuchs all got the disease. Obviously, he considered mulberries an effective cure for gout. On this continent, Native Americans and early settlers used the native red mulberry as a mild laxative, and a drink from the fruit has been used to allay fever. Syrup of red or white mulberry is employed in Appalachian folk medicine to soothe coughs. Red mulberry root bark has been used as a vermifuge—that is, to rid the body of tapeworms and other intestinal parasites. It is shaved, pounded, then boiled as a tea and drunk. The tree's sap, applied directly to the affected area, was used by Native Americans and white folks alike in treating fungal skin ailments such as jock itch and ringworm. Like blackberries, mulberries are still used in Appalachia to treat gout. When my grandfather suffered from gout, a local doctor told him, "Hogmeat done it," and advised mulberry juice. I can't remember if it helped, but whenever one of us had an upset stomach, someone was bound to say, "Hogmeat done it."

Mulberries can be used in any recipe calling for any other berries. If they taste flat, add a bit of lemon juice.

PEARS

Pears, many species and even more varieties of the *Pyrus* genus (from the Latin *pirum*, "pear"), are easily recognizable even to small children. Pears and apples are of the same species; botanists disagree on where to place many of them. Some apples contain the grit cells we associate with the texture of pears; some pears are subglobose, the shape of apples. Some apples are elongated like pears.

Pear trees, originally introduced to Europe from Eurasia, are spread by cultivation, as well as by tossed-away pear cores. Often pear trees are found on abandoned homesites, for they are long-lived trees. I have found them near decaying cabins and on abandoned farms, as well as occasionally in the uninhabited parts of the woods.

Description, Habitat, and Season

Pear trees are small to medium, with spinelets on the branches; slender, smooth, sharply serrated or roundly serrated leaves; and a beautiful white 5-petaled spring blossom. The fruits of the many trees of this large genus range in color from yellow to green to red to brown, and vary enormously in size, flavor, and texture. In the wild, they sometimes cross with *Sorbus* (mountain ash). In short, there are seemingly endless varieties, many of which have not been identified.

Look for ripe fruit from midsummer to early fall. Pears ripen more quickly on the tree and ground than any other large fruit I know, so they bear watching and picking at just the right moment.

History and Lore

The Romans first introduced pears to Britain, where the Christian monks later tended to them. A legend has it that evil King John I of England was killed in 1216 by the monks of Swinsted, who were clever enough to put poison into a dish of pears so delicious as to overpower the taste of the poison.

{RECIPES}

In 1846, a Boston naturalist wrote that there were over 200 American varieties of pears, but that only about 20 of them were edible. That's about my experience with pears, but a friend tells me it's because I don't pick them right. So here is the right way: Pick pears while they are still hard, noting where you found the tree. Wrap them in a paper bag or cotton cloths and set them in the dark for up to two weeks, checking them daily so that when they are ripe, you will know. If you can find one abandoned pear tree with good pears, that's all you need: You can return to it year after year.

Lizzie's Pear and Ginger Preserves

Gather about half a gallon of ripe pears; chop enough to make 1 quart of fruit; half a lemon, sliced thin, the seeds removed; about 2 cups sugar; 1 cup water; and ½ cup chopped candied ginger. You can add half a vanilla bean also. Bring to a boil, then simmer this mixture on low heat until the pears are transparent and the syrup somewhat thickened. Stir it every few minutes. This makes a gorgeous, dark gold condiment that is fine on pound cake or ice cream.

PLUMS

Prunus is the name of the genus that includes plums. The word *prunus* in Latin means "plum tree," though today we know prunes (dried plums) better than the fresh variety. Plums are small trees or shrubs of temperate North America and South America that bear fruit in late summer.

Description, Habitat, and Season

Plums are deciduous trees, the leaves serrated and alternate, oval to rounded, and smooth, with 5-petaled flowers that bloom white or pink in spring. Many wild varieties of plums grow in the temperate parts of this country, with fruits green, golden, purple, blue, or red, sometimes sweet, sometimes sour, sometimes clingstone, sometimes freestone, ripening in the fall. All are smooth skinned, some have a dusty "bloom" to the skin, and they usually have the characteristic of tasting sweet near the skin and sour near the stone. The fruits of all plums have a single flat stone, are usually over an inch in diameter, and are oval, with the faint or deep suggestion of a long indentation (called a suture) on one side. The fruits of wild plums are smaller than commercial plums, often not more than an inch or so in diameter.

Pomological Magazine in 1835 reported that a plum tree, purchased sometime in the 1790s, would not bear, though it appeared healthy. Seven years after it was planted, during a violent thunderstorm, the tree was struck by lightning and destroyed. But afterward, the root put up a number of vigorous shoots, which grew into trees and subsequently produced much fine fruit. (In contemplating this story, I wonder if the tree needed male and female both to bear, and had no companions until the small trees came up.)

Among the best plums are several varieties of a beach plum, *Prunus maritima*, typical in shape, but variable in size and color, from lemon yellow through red to deep purple, from ½ inch to 2 inches, that grow many places along the Atlantic coast from Maine to North Carolina. They are tart and make a distinctive jam.

History and Lore

Plums entered Britain from Asia originally and are popular around the Mediterranean.

Plum bark is astringent, and it has been used as a substitute for quinine in the treatment of malaria. The Native Americans used plums as laxatives and claimed that in years when the plums were plentiful, dysentery abounded.

The fruit has been used for generations in Appalachia to make a sweet wine, as well as damson preserves. (The name damson indicates that the plum originated in Damascus.) One kind of wild American plum, the sloe, was used as a flavoring for homemade gin during the Depression, and sloe gin is still popular in some rural areas of the South. Its name comes from an Old English word for plum, *slah*.

{RECIPES}

One word of warning: The pits of all *Prunus* and *Malus* species (apples, peaches, plums, cherries) contain cyanide (cyanogenic glycosides) in such quantities that 12 pits or ½ cup of apple seeds contains a sufficient amount to kill an adult. So be careful about not letting seeds into the final food.

PLUM JAM

Use any damson, greengage, Mirabelle, Italian, or tasty wild plums. Wash, halve (but don't peel), and remove the pits from the wild plums, up to 1 quart; add an equal amount of sugar; and let the mix stand several hours before cooking. Then, bring the pot to a boil and turn it down to a simmer. Stir often, cooking slowly until the syrup and fruit are thick and fragrant. Be careful not to scorch the jam. This usually takes under 1 hour, but does need constant attention.

QUINCES

Quince trees are various species of the *Cydonia* genus. Modern shrub books sometimes call the genus *Chaenomeles* or *Pseudocydonia*. Common species include *C. oblonga*, *C. maliformis* (also known as *C. vulgaris*), and *C. sinensis*. Some botanists place the quince in the *Malus* genus along with apples. Both quinces and apples are in the Rosaceae family, and quinces have the same internal aspect as apples; that is, a cartilage protects the seeds, carried in the center. *Cydonia* is the Latin name for the fruit and

Ripe quince

Quince bloom in spring, 4 to 5 months before the fruit.

tree. *Oblonga* describes an oblong fruit shape, *maliformis* indicates a lop-sided apple-like fruit, and *sinensis* points to a Chinese origin. The genus is probably named for the ancient city of Cydon, on Crete. But another possibility is that the name, from cy, meaning "circular," and *donia*, a "gift," kin to our word *donate*, implies that quinces are "circular gifts." The Portuguese word for quince, *marmelo*, gives us our word *marmalade*. Most quinces found in America originated in Asia. My grandparents called their quince hedge *japonica*, which might confirm its origins.

Description, Habitat, and Season
Quinces grow on hardy, deciduous, small, thorny trees or shrubs with crooked branches. They have oval leaves similar to apple tree leaves and beautiful red, pink, or rose flowers in early spring. They are found in the wild and cultivated in gardens and hedges. The fruit turns from pale green to pale yellow as it ripens, often has rosy cheeks, and is speckled with small dots that are actually glands. It looks like a little apple, 1 to 2½ inches in diameter, or an oblong up to 5 inches long. Many of the fruits will be lopsided. Quinces ripen in late fall, giving off an intense fruity perfume. Quinces grow well throughout the South and the mid-Atlantic states, and can tolerate winters as far north as Michigan. As the tree has dense growth and fairly nasty thorns, it forms quite an effective barrier. The sour quince makes wonderful jelly or marmalade. The Portuguese quince turns wine red when cooked.

Today, the quince is out of fashion, but even fifty years ago, it was popular. My grandparents, and many other Lexingtonians, marked their property with quince hedges, thorny and difficult to go though, and productive at the same time. My grandparents had a vigorous quince hedge between their long cinder driveway and their deep front yard. In the spring, the intense rosy blossoms were a joy, and in the early fall, we always made quince marmalade out of the yellow-green fruit to give neighbors at Christmas. As soon as the buds swelled in early spring, quince branches were brought into the house and forced (watered until they opened in the indoor heat), and that meant spring was under way.

History and Lore

Quinces were known in ancient times as golden apples. The ancients loved the quince, believing it to be the fruit of happiness and love. In Paphos and Cyprus, temples to Venus were decorated with quinces. The ancient writer Goropius declared that the quince was the Golden Apple of the Hesperides. Pliny advised the quince as a remedy for swollen spleen and dropsy and wrote that it alleviated pulmonary difficulties and allayed nausea. Quince flowers were made into a decoction for tired or sore eyes, and the fruit was a remedy for asthma. It was introduced by the Romans into Britain, where it was grown for a wine that was also supposed to cure asthma. It is still a popular fruit in Italy, often hybridized. Though some modern "designer" quinces have orange or red fruit, Sardinian quince trees have fruits weighing up to three pounds each, and Mulvian quinces are sweet enough to eat raw, these are rarities; wild American quinces for the most part are yellow, small, and sour.

Hildegard von Bingen, who reviled peaches and strawberries, adored the quince and claimed that it cured rheumatism in an hour, and purged and decontaminated the body so that no healthy person who ate it would ever be plagued by arthritis or rheumatism.

Early American settlers also believed that quince juice overcame nausea. The juice of raw quinces, which is quite styptic—that is, it makes the mouth pucker—was used to subdue hemorrhage, staunch nosebleed, and stop runaway bleeding. The Native Americans also used the quince in conjunction with tobacco as an asthma cure. In the nineteenth century, quince marmalade was much prized. Quince blossom honey is a beekeepers' specialty today in some parts of the South.

{RECIPES}

Wild quinces are sour and unpleasant raw, not fit for eating, but after their autumn ripening, they smell wonderful and can be used to make a delicious tart jelly. Quinces can also be stewed into a sauce resembling applesauce or used as pie filling.

QUINCE MARMALADE

Slice, but do not peel, ripe quinces—which will have paled to yellow and perhaps become tinged with red, but will remain hard. Measure them. Put the quinces in a steel or enamel pot, and barely cover them with water. For every quart of quinces, add the juice and thinly sliced rind of 1 lemon. Bring to a boil, add a weight of sugar equal to that of the quinces, and boil for 15 minutes, stirring gently but continuously. After that, raise the heat, and cook another 15 minutes, stirring constantly to prevent scorching. Put 3 or 4 saucers briefly in the freezer. When a blob of the marmalade holds a shape on a cold plate, it is ready. Jar and seal it. Feeling that the pale yellow-gray color of the marmalade was not very attractive, we'd add at the end 1 drop red food coloring. But do so carefully, only a tiny drop at a time, until the marmalade is a blushing pink. You could, instead, add a little bit of purple grape juice or a little red wine, toward the end of the cooking process, to achieve the same blush.

RHUBARB

There are many species of wild rhubarb (*Rheum* genus), and they are all fine to eat. Just one caution: When you find the plants, with their pink to pinkish-green celery-like stalks and big bright-green leaves with flamboyant triangle shapes, remove the leaves before chopping the stems into 1-inch pieces. The stems are actually full of so much oxalic acid that they are poisonous. The stalks are quite sour, and our ancestors recognized the plant as a strong laxative. Uncooked rhubarb is astringent. In the temperate zones of this country, rhubarb is ready to be harvested in April or May and lasts until frost. In warmer places, it grows year-round. To make rhubarb sauce, simply stew equal parts sugar and chopped stalks together with a little water until tender, just a few minutes. The sauce can be made into jelly or jam, or put into a piecrust for a favorite American dessert, rhubarb pie.

Rhubarb

STRAWBERRIES

The strawberye is the wonder of all the Fruites growing naturally in these partes.
—SIR WALTER RALEIGH

Strawberries are probably America's favorite berry. The name of the American wild strawberry is *Fragaria virginiana*, apparently suggesting its fragrance and the fact that it was first identified in Virginia. (There are others in Europe and England, including a white one in the Alps.) Wild strawberries are found everywhere in the temperate United States, and they are grown commercially from North Carolina to Florida, and on the West Coast. Their common name is shrouded in mystery: Maybe they were called stray-berries after their meandering habit; perhaps straw-berries because straw was often laid beneath the heavy, ripening berries to prevent their sinking into the mud underneath them; some even think the habit of selling them strung on straws in medieval markets gave them their name.

Description, Habitat, and Season
Strawberries grow low to the ground beneath their bright green foliage. They have white blossoms and mother plants that put out runners to

form new plants. They sport three leaflets on a divided leaf, and the berries (accessory fruits, really) are born singly and terminally. You will find the ripe fruit a month after the roselike blossoms appear in mid-May, though blossom and fruit may be found together. Although wild strawberries grow potentially everywhere, they prefer full sun and sandy roadsides, hilltops, pastures, and upland meadows. Early summer is the time to begin looking for the tiny wild strawberries that were, according to the account of an early Virginia settler, so thick in some places that the white feet of cows were stained red as they grazed.

Wild strawberries are so tiny that collecting them seems nearly futile, but they are wonderful. The best patch I ever found was by accident when I was cutting across an open field at the top of a hill, in search of a horse. I came back later and gathered a quart of wild strawberries, which for me was surely a record.

There is one strawberry imitator, the *Duchesnea indica*, or Indian strawberry. It is harmless but not good to eat. People are often fooled by this Indian strawberry, or snakeberry, which looks like the wild strawberry, leaves, fruits, and all, and has made its way around the world. Its flowers are yellow instead of white, but by the time of fruiting, the flowers have vanished, leaving behind only the clever impostors. One taste and you will know this plant with white insides is not a strawberry.

History and Lore
In medieval art, strawberries are associated with the Virgin Mary. Early American chroniclers described "Indian strawberry" bread, a mixture of cornmeal and the mashed fruit baked in flat cakes in the coals of a fire. In colonial times, strawberries were eaten in great quantity as a cure for consumption (tuberculosis). Some recorded and believed that actual cures occurred. The famous eighteenth-century American diarist William Byrd II, who recorded his daily food intake for years, ate asparagus and strawberries every day that he could obtain them.

Strawberry shortcake has long been the dessert associated with Independence Day in the United States, for early July is generally when strawberries are ripe throughout the mid-Atlantic states. Strawberry ice cream still runs a close third after vanilla and chocolate in the hearts of Americans, even with such beguiling competitive flavors as Ben & Jerry's Coffee Toffee Bar Crunch.

{RECIPES}

Wild strawberries are by any economic measure a waste of time, for they are tiny and hard to pick. But they are worth a great deal in superior flavor and pleasure. Gathering these tiny fruits, most of the time no larger than the end of your little finger, is a labor of patient love, as you sit on the ground staining your jeans beyond recovery in an aura of strawberry essence. Ideally, they should be gathered in a flat, wide-bottomed basket, so they don't crush each other. But the reward is a flavor so intense it seems fair to say that each tiny wild berry concentrates more flavor than is found in five of the giant modern hybrids. When you get home, red fingered and sunburned, you would be wise to scrub with coarse soap, rinse, scrub again, and rinse, to exorcise possible chiggers and poison ivy. Then spend a few more hours picking out stems and caps. You really can't wash wild strawberries, they're so tiny. Just pick them carefully.

WILD STRAWBERRY JAM

(This works well with commercial strawberries, blueberries, and blackberries, too. It makes a wonderful, fresh-tasting, runny jam.)
Take a quantity of wild strawberries and add ¾ as much sugar. Boil them gently together for 17 minutes without stirring, squeeze the juice of half a lemon over them, stir briefly, and seal them at once in sterilized jelly jars.

FRESH BERRIES FOR WINTER

This method saves fresh fruit for out-of-season treats. The disadvantage is the amount of sugar needed. Mix fresh, cleaned, slightly crushed berries with twice as much sugar (that is, 2 cups sugar to every 1 cup berries), stirring hourly until the sugar is dissolved. (If you don't, it may recrystallize in the jar.) Then store in tightly closed sterilized jars for up to seven months. The sugar preserves the fruit in its uncooked state. I've used it with mixed success, best with strawberries, but with freezers I'd choose another method of saving fresh fruit; that is, light sugaring and freezing.

STRAWBERRY SOUFFLÉ

(This is adapted from a famous Swiss hotel's [Walliser-Kahn] recipe.
Serves 4 and can be doubled. Have all ingredients at room temperature.)
I use 4 individual casseroles and a large (10 × 13-inch or larger) 2-inch-deep baking dish half full of boiling water. Assemble 2 cups fresh wild strawberries, 1 lemon, ¾ cup powdered sugar, 4 large eggs, an 8-ounce block cream cheese, ½ cup granulated sugar, 4 tablespoons of either rum, brandy, kirsch, or a mix, and 2 teaspoons vanilla. First, clean and mash the 2 cups berries. Grate 1 tablespoon lemon peel and set aside, then squeeze and strain the juice of the lemon. Add ½ cup powdered sugar and the lemon juice to the berries, stir well, and set aside. Separate the 4 large eggs; soften the 8-ounce block of cream cheese; and measure the ½ cup granulated sugar into one cup and the liquor into another.

Preheat oven to 425°F. Butter 4 individual baking dishes or 1 large baking casserole, and dust with some of the granulated sugar. Save the rest. Beat egg yolks and cream cheese with the remaining 4 tablespoons powdered sugar and the 2 teaspoons vanilla for 5 minutes, then beat in the liquor and the lemon peel.

Beat egg whites with the granulated sugar until they hold soft peaks. Fold a blob of the whites into the yolk mixture, then pour the lightened yolks into the whites and fold. Divide the mixture among the casseroles, and set casseroles into the baking pan half full of boiling water. Bake about 20 minutes for the small soufflés, 40 minutes if using a large casserole. When the hot soufflés are ready, pour the crushed berries over them and serve at once.

Strawberry Shortcake

(Serves 4)

I make this all the time, but it is especially good with wild strawberries. It can also be made with raspberries and blueberries. I think the oil is the secret. Or maybe it's the vanilla. Heat the oven to 400°F. Mix 1 package (2 cups) biscuit mix with 3 tablespoons sugar and 3 tablespoons cooking oil, then add ½ cup milk and ½ teaspoon vanilla. Mix lightly. Handling as little as possible, pat the mixture out evenly on the bottom of an 8- or 9-inch cake pan that has been sprayed or oiled. Prick all over with a fork, score it lightly into 4 equal sections, and bake until golden, about 10 to 15 minutes. Cool. Split as you would a big biscuit. When you are nearly ready to serve dessert, whip 1 cup heavy cream with 2 tablespoons sugar, a few grains salt, and 1 teaspoon or so vanilla. Withholding 1 perfect berry for the top, crush 1 quart ripe berries and spoon most over the bottom half of the shortbread, letting some fall to the sides. Put the top half back on. Top the whole with the whipped cream, and put the single beautiful berry in the middle. Let it sit 5 minutes before serving it. Cut into quarters.

PERSIMMONS

The scientific name possibly implies where these fruits were first found. Persimmons (*Diospyros virginiana*) grow all over the South, the East, and into Texas. In the fall, in Virginia, they grow on a generally small spindly tree with very dark gray bark that looks almost like tiling—small squares of bark. The tree is usually no more than 30 feet tall. The fruits are small, about 1½ inches across, and in the reddish-range of color when ripe. They are unpleasantly astringent when they aren't ripe, but when they are ripe, they are sweet and very pleasing to the palate. They must be squishy to be ripe, so don't bite into hard persimmons. If you know where a persimmon tree is, keep a hawk eye on it, for bears and raccoons and possums love to eat the ripe fruit before their winter hibernations. Around here, in the Virginia mountains, their ripening must come naturally, and seems to demand a freeze the night before (but I have also read that may not necessarily be true). I, in an attempt to trick nature, picked green persimmons once and stored them for a week in my freezer. It didn't help at all; they must ripen on the tree. When you perceive that they are ripe, spread out a blanket and shake the tree to get at the orange to red fruits. Discard any hard fruits. Then, you can remove the six flat seeds and use the persimmon flesh for bread, jellies, jams, or just messy sweet fruit flesh.

PAWPAWS

Pawpaws (*Asimina triloba*) seems to me a similar tree. Also small and spindly as trees go, pawpaw leaves on the other hand are large and floppy, and larger at the top than at the stem end. The spring flowers are purple, but you need to hunt for the fruit as autumn comes on. Pawpaws remind one of short fat bananas, stubby at the ends. They can be gathered green and ripened; they, too, are not ripe until they look over-ripe, like persimmons. They get black spots and turn soft and squishy, but the custardy flesh is fun to eat cooked or out of hand. It can also be made into breads or sweet jams. I confess to not liking pawpaws very much; nor do I care for papaya, their tropical cousins.

[5]
FLOWERS AND HERBS

What are all the oranges imported into England to the hips and haws in her hedges?
—HENRY DAVID THOREAU

Lest you think herb lore merely a quaint and primitive Appalachian pastime, it was estimated by the World Health Organization as late as 1985 that over 75 percent of the world's population depended upon plants (which are called herbs if they are used medicinally) as their only medicine. Herbing is not considered a dignified profession any longer, but medicinal herbs are still big business. And late in the eighties, the journal *Economic Botany* reported that "America exports around 600 million dollars' worth of herbs annually, and imports ten to twenty million dollars' worth." Of this huge quantity of American medical plants, 90 percent or more are from the wild. These days, Elderhostels, or Road Scholars, abound to teach over-fifties people about herb lore. The Deep South is rife with schools that teach identification and use of herbs. As there is no profit in herbs for pharmaceutical companies (herbs cannot be patented), most of what is known about herb use is still relegated to the "folklore" category.

When you set out to pick herbs or flowers, you need scissors, a basket for gathering, and a field guide or two for identification of plants. Know what you're doing before you add anything to your salad. You don't want to get a mouthful of poison ivy leaves or buttercups—they are poisonous—by mistake. By the way, an infusion is a tea. A decoction is a reduction, or a boiling down of an herb in water to increase its intensity.

ROSE HIPS

Roses, members of the *Rosa* genus, come in thousands of varieties that include tea roses, bush roses, climbing roses, and wild roses. They are prized for their fragrance and symbolize love in many cultures. Everyone knows what roses look like and how wonderful they smell, but few have been intrepid enough to eat roses.

Description, Habitat, and Season
Roses are, of course, various members of the family Rosaceae and borne terminally on the stems of the thorny shrubs. Roses can be from 1 foot tall to 10 feet or so for climbers. All roses have dark green, smooth, serrated, opposite leaves, with a terminal leaf, usually five to seven leaflets on each stem.

Rose hips are the fruits of rosebushes, all rosebushes wild and tame have them, and they ripen in autumn and are used after the first frost. Hips are a nickname of the hypanthia, or enlarged tori, the flower receptacles below the flower calyx, or seed container. The hips, also sometimes called haws, vary greatly in size and color, from the size of a huckleberry to the size of a small plum, and from light orange to deep scarlet. Few people know the great health secret of rose fruits. Rose hips have a high vitamin C content, about forty times as much as oranges, which I take to mean that there is probably a full day's requirement in one large rose hip.

History and Lore

Rose hips appear in all sorts of herbal medicines and teas, touted for their excellent antiscorbutic quality. In the lean years of World War II, when citrus fruits were unobtainable, most people in northern Europe and Great Britain ate rose hips as an acceptable substitute for fresh fruits and vegetables. The darker the rose, the more potent the hip, goes one old saw. Naturally, the flowers have value beyond their odor and lovely appearance. Crushed rose petals infused in water have long been a remedy for sore eyes.

{RECIPES}

Hips can be gathered from any rosebush, wild or cultivated. Collect them after the first frost, which softens their texture and their sour taste. (In England in the fall, I have eaten hips that actually tasted sweet, but generally they are quite sour.) They have a high pectin content and make nice sunset-colored jellies and syrups. These berrylike fruits are easy to see on a tramp across freeze-dried monotone autumn fields, or in some winter garden where almost everything else is asleep. *Rosa rugosa*, the "rugged rose," has an especially large, succulent hip, as does *R. canina* ("dog rose"), but all rose hips are usable. Many are sour, and all are seedy, so you probably wouldn't want to toss them in a salad.

ROSE HIP JELLY

Assemble 4 cups rose hips, 6 green apples chopped coarsely, 1 lemon, 6 cloves, half a cinnamon stick, 1 cup water, 1 box dried pectin, and 4 cups sugar. Cook everything but the pectin and sugar until tender. Mash the fruit mixture slightly. Cool, and strain the mixture through several layers of cheesecloth. If the liquid does not measure 4 cups, pour a little water through the dregs to make 4 cups. Mix liquid and pectin and bring to a boil, stirring all the while. When it boils vigorously, add the sugar all at once, and, stirring constantly, bring it to a boil again and boil 60 seconds. Remove from the stove, skim, and jar. This makes a pretty pink to red jelly that makes great Christmas presents and is good for you.

ROSE HIPS FOR WINTER

Collect some rose hips, at least 2 cups. Use an enamel or stainless steel pan. Add half as much water as you have rose hips. Cook the hips until they are tender. Mash them, and force them through a fine strainer. To this puree, add an equal amount of sugar, and boil the mixture gently only until the sugar is dissolved. Store in the refrigerator or freezer, and eat a spoonful a day for vitamin C, or enjoy the tasty conserve on your toast or pancakes.

CANDIED ROSEBUDS

Choose perfect, tiny buds of wild rose, fairy rose, or others, in the spring and summer. Tight, tiny buds hold together best, and you can also use larger buds, up to ¾ inch across. Boil them gently in a half-water, half-sugar mixture for about ½ hour, or until they begin to look china-like, or semitransparent. Lift them carefully out of the syrup, and drain them on a screen or even on waxed paper. When they are well drained, roll them in granulated sugar, dry them thoroughly for one or two days in a dry, warm place, lay them carefully in a box, and seal them against moisture. Decorate cakes, cookies, or candies with them.

VIOLETS

Viola species are numerous, the name meaning "violets" in Latin. They include pansies as well as violets.

Description, Habitat, and Season

Most people are familiar with the shy-nodding, small white, lavender, or purple long-stemmed violets that grow in lawns and gardens from early until late spring. In the continental United States, they can be found in profusion in damp areas in the Temperate Zone east of the desert. They have large, dark green, heart-shaped leaves and are ubiquitous to shady areas and the edges of streams, as well as lawns, woods, and less well-kept yards. They have the reputation for sweetness, and bloom early in spring. We all know them, but few know that they are edible and pleasant. The leaves add deep color to a spring salad, but personally I find them uninteresting and flavorless.

History and Lore

Ever since the goddess Diana changed the nymph Ia into a violet, to hide her from Apollo's unwanted ardors, violets have been the emblem of modesty and the model of shyness. There are two interesting facts about violets. One: They are nature's litmus and turn red in the presence of acid and yellow in the presence of alkali. Two: Some violets smell divine, while others have little or no odor. This is apparently because the English violet (*Viola odorata*), grown by early settlers for perfume and medicine and still popular as a scent, escaped from colonial gardens and intermingled with scentless native violets, thus causing a mixed population, in which some of the natives exude perfume, while identical others, untouched by the fragrant foreigner, don't have any odor at all.

{RECIPES}

It is still fashionable in France to decorate fancy cakes with candied violets. These delicate flowers tend to lose their shape with cooking, though they are preserved by the syrup. Violet leaves, as well as flowers, are nice in a green spring salad, for looks as well as for a shot of vitamin C.

CANDIED VIOLETS

Violets may be prepared the same way as rosebuds, only cooked for less time (around 10 minutes) and handled carefully. However, there is another way to "candy" rosebuds and violets. Wash and drain dry violets or the buds of wild roses. Dip into a "wash" (1 egg white beaten thoroughly with 1 tablespoon water), then shake gently in a bowl of sugar to cover each flower with sugar completely. Lay the flowers, not touching each other, on a cookie sheet, and dry in the oven at about 200°F, or the lowest possible heat setting, until each flower is completely dry. Handling the flowers carefully, store them in an airtight container, and use them to decorate cakes.

VIOLET BLOSSOM JELLY

I have to tell you, I've not had success with this, but I think I have mostly or all odorless violets in my yard. If you are lucky enough to have sweet violets, this would probably be good. I had a violet-flavored truffle somewhere recently, and it was delicious and delicate, and definitely perfumy.

Collect enough fragrant violet blossom with stems removed to make 2 loose cups or 1 cup of pressed down flowers. Add 1½ cups water, the juice of 1 large lemon (strained), 2½ cups sugar, and 1 package of pectin. Follow directions for mint jelly.

MINT

Some kind of wild mint (*Mentha* spp.) grows near you. These plants are identifiable from their square stems and pungent odors. We find the plant's name in our word *menthol*. There are several dozen mints that grow wild in this country, as well as many cultivars that combine flavors nicely but unfortunately will not persist in the wild. Some of the harsher mints, like menthol, would not be appealing for food, but all are safe to try, and many are delicious. As you know, mint lends its scent to many medicines in the modern world. It is most calming for nausea.

Description, Habitat, and Season
Peppermint (*Mentha piperita*, "peppery mint," from the hot flavor) and spearmint (*M. spicata*, from the plant's spiky shape) are two favorites, and wherever one is found usually the other is also. All mints have square stems.

Spearmint grows to about 2 feet, sometimes higher, each unbranching spear a solid emerald green color. The leaves are opposite, 1 to 2 inches long, serrated. The midsummer flowers are whitish to purple. Peppermint is similar but has wider and shorter leaves, is a slightly darker green, and the stalks have a purplish tinge. Both grow in early to midsummer, usually in huge patches. They are most obvious because of their sharp perfumes; the slightest disturbance, even brushing a leaf, causes it to give off its peppermint or spearmint aroma. The plants have disappeared by late August. Spearmint, peppermint, and other mints grow in damp places, such as alongside creeks and rivers, in ditches by roadsides, and in low-lying pastures. If a mint smells good to you, it's fine to use it.

A BRIEF HISTORY OF THE MINT JULEP

In colonial times, liquor was considered safer than water to drink. After all, back in Europe, water was the most dangerous drink of all, carrying many diseases. Alcoholic beverages, as has already been pointed out, insulated pioneers from cold, slaked the thirst brought on by salted meats, and anesthetized folks against the numerous miseries of colonial living.

The happy early discovery that excellent whiskey could be made from maize (corn) created a nation of bourbon devotees. When George Washington ran for the legislature in 1758, he doled out a quart and a half of liquor for every voter. When we won independence and Washington's brand-new government tried to raise money by imposing a tax on whiskey, they were faced with the famous Whiskey Rebellion, resulting in our first civil bloodshed as a nation. Although the insurrection was quickly quelled, many farmer-distillers, deciding that facing Native Americans was preferable to facing revenuers, moved westward specifically to be able to continue making untaxed whiskey.

A common breakfast item throughout the colonies north and south was a julap, a drink made of rum, brandy, or whiskey, mixed with sugar and water. Mint was soon added, probably functioning as a sort of night-breath cleanser. And thus the mint julep was born.

History and Lore

Mint is the plant of virtue, named for a Greek nymph who had the bad luck to fall in love with Pluto, god of the underworld. When Persephone, the wife of Pluto, discovered that the brazen nymph Mentha had chosen to seduce her husband, she in a fit of jealousy turned the poor girl into a lowly mint plant.

Mint is said to have cured more than forty illnesses among early settlers here, from halitosis to high blood pressure. Today, 95 percent of its use is as flavoring for candy or toothpaste or medicines, like ointments for joint or bone pain.

{RECIPES}

MINT TEA

I dry both spearmint and peppermint in my kitchen in summer in huge bunches, which makes the kitchen smell good, then strip the crisp leaves off into jars when they're dry, and use them all winter for a hot tea that is comforting, head clearing, and harmless, perhaps even salubrious. A handful of the dried leaves steeped 3 to 5 minutes in a teapot of water is all that's needed. Pour it out through a strainer for a delicate, pale tea.

MINT JELLY

The exact proportions of water and sugar are necessary to make this product jell. Use 4½ cups water; 1 large bunch of spearmint, peppermint, or, better, mixed mints; 1 box pectin; 4½ cups sugar; 1 tablespoon cider vinegar; and 1 drop blue food color (optional). Simmer the water with the bruised, cleaned mint leaves and stems for 15 minutes in a covered pot. Allow to cool entirely. Strain to remove stems and leaves. Mix pectin and mint water thoroughly, bring it to a boil, and add sugar all at once. Return to boil, boil 1 minute hard, remove from heat, skim. The resulting jelly is an unattractive pale greenish yellow. Add vinegar, and food color if desired, and pour immediately into small jars. If you wish, you can add a perfect leaf or two of mint to each jar. When cool, pour melted paraffin over the tops to seal. This jelly is the accompaniment for roast lamb.

Possibly the finest use to which bourbon whiskey can be put is in the mint julep. If you have the intent to get drunk, or only slightly loopy, this in my estimation is the way to do it. You can only do it in summer, when you've a great thirst and the mint is fresh. There is a sterling silver 8-ounce container known as a julep cup, but any glass will do. Pick 2 stems of good mint about 8 inches long each. I personally prefer a curly English variety, mild and somewhere between peppermint and spearmint in flavor, but any will do. Wash the mint well. From 1 stalk, strip the leaves into your cup. Add 2 teaspoons confectioners' sugar, and, with a wooden knife handle, bruise the leaves with the sugar, grinding them together until the sugar is stained with mint and the leaves are mashed and shredded. Next, fill the glass with crushed ice, and pack it down. Now fill it to the top with bourbon whiskey, stir it well, "plant" the other stem down into the glass, and serve. (Some say add pineapple or cherries or orange slices or lemon, but Virginians and Kentuckians consider anything but mint a desecration.)

CATNIP

Catnip's botanic name is *Nepeta cataria*. *Nepeta* comes from a Tuscan town, Nepet, but that word in Latin means "cat nip."

Description, Habitat, and Season
Catnip is a grayish green, slightly fuzzy-stemmed, erect mint (look for the square stem), 1 to 4 feet tall. It has white to pale lilac flowers that bloom in late summer to early fall, and the leaves are pointed. Though the odor is minty, it is distinctive.

Catnip grows all summer long, throughout the Temperate Zone, at the edges of woods, in fields and pastures, in roadside ditches, and at the edges of country vegetable gardens, and can be gathered anytime during the summer months, given to your cats fresh, or hung in bunches from a rafter and dried for winter use.

History and Lore
Catnip, widely distributed throughout this country, has a long history as a soothing tea useful for comforting, and even curing, winter colds and summer heat stress. It has been found useful for stimulating sluggish appetites and for lulling people into sound sleep. It also has a long history of inducing ecstasy and aggression in cats. They appear to love it and be made drunk by it. Herbologist James Duke believes it can help prevent cataracts in humans.

It is at least as much fun to watch cats playing with catnip as it must be for the cats to do it. Our cats rub their cheeks in it; they gnaw on it, they roll over in it, toss it into the air, and let it fall on top of them, and then they get into drunken-but-desultory battles with the other cats. Eventually, they go and sleep it off, and ignore catnip for a week or so. Interestingly, a small percentage of cats (10 percent, says my vet, Dr. Sheryl Carls) don't care a thing about catnip. Of the nearly forty cats I've shared my life with, some of them living into their early twenties, only two have been unaffected by catnip.

Catnip is reputed, as it does to cats, to make timid people bold, and I've even read that hangmen years ago would fortify themselves with catnip before doing business.

{RECIPES}

CATNIP MICE

(For cats)
You can stuff little scrap-cotton bags to make dried catnip toys for your favorite cats, who will love them for the smell, so the shape isn't impor-

tant, though adding some sort of tail seems to enhance the cats' enjoyment. You can also give catnip to your cats fresh and watch their ecstatic drunkenness. Our vet assures us it won't hurt the cats, and some people use it as a training device by putting it on the places where they prefer that the kitties sleep or play.

Catnip Tea

(For people)

Crush a handful of catnip in your hand, and steep it in a pot of boiling water for 3 minutes, to yield a soothing and refreshing tea, said to calm the stomach and the nerves. Catnip can also be dried (hung upside down in bunches), the dried leaves stripped off the stem and stored in jars, for year-round tea. Many other fragrant herbs, like sage, basil, savory, rosemary, or thyme, may also be made into tea that is soothing and harmless. Either the fresh or the dried herbs can be used.

BAYBERRY

Bayberries (*Myrica cerifera, M. pennsylvanica,* or *M. californica*) are a group of evergreen shrubs native to different sections of the country, but all put to the same uses. They are distant cousins of the more highly scented Turkish bay leaves.

Description, Habitat, and Season

In the South, *M. cerifera* is a small shrub in coastal areas and dunes. Bays have gray, stiff, waxy branches; erect, narrow, dry, aromatic leaves; and terminal fruiting branches that produce rough, crowded, dull grayish-green, waxy, aromatic berries. The berries (often called spiceberries), leaves, and twigs can be gathered from fall into winter.

History and Lore

This useful plant's leaves are fine seasoning for soups or stews, but its perfume more often appears in candles and potpourris. Because of the fatty composition of the berries, they are a valuable food for birds and other wildlife in the winter months, but they are not palatable to humans.

The genus name *Myrica* is from the Greek *myrizein*, "to perfume." *Cerifera* means "wax bearing," *cera* being Latin for "wax." (Sincerely means, literally, "without wax" and originally referred to the sly custom in Roman times of repairing chipped or broken statuary with wax and selling it to unsuspecting buyers as perfect.) Bayberry's folk names of candleberry, waxberry, and wax myrtle point to the common practice of boiling off the wax to make candles.

In this country, bayberry's first use was in making fragrant candles, possibly the only good-smelling thing in a colonial home without refrigeration, running water, or a habit of bathing. Bayberry leaves were handy replacements for Turkish or tropical bay leaves in cooking. The Native Americans had many medical uses for bayberry, and the colonists followed suit, finding in the plant a valuable tonic, a powerful astringent, and a stimulant. A mouthwash decoction of bayberry leaf was said to help the spongy gums of scurvy, as well as canker sores in the mouth, and drinking the leaf tea quickly helped cure scurvy because of the vitamin C in the leaves. In New England, bayberry bark tea was used to stanch uterine hemorrhage, reduce jaundice, stop dysentery, and clean out the digestive system, among other uses. The dried berry was ground up and used for snuff, which may be why tobacco snuff today tends to be flavored with aromatics like bay and wintergreen.

Bayberry root bark and plant bark contain several powerful substances, chief among them being myricadiol, which influences sodium and potassium metabolism in the body. But the plant also contains a lot of tannin, a carcinogen. Therefore, it is probably best used only for candles or for a subtle grayish-green dye.

{RECIPES}

Bayberry Wax

The berries are boiled in water for several hours until the wax floats to the top, and when all is cooled, the perfumed gray-green wax solidifies and is easily separated from the berries and the water beneath. The berries may be profitably boiled up to 4 times before all the wax is boiled out.

NASTURTIUMS

Nasturtiums ("nose-twisters," from *nasus*, Latin for "nose," and *torquo*, Latin for "twist") are in the same family as watercress. Nasturtium is the common name. Its folk name is Indian cress; its scientific name is *Tropaeolum majus*. *Tropaeolum* derives from the Latin word *tropaeum*, or "trophy"; it describes how the leaves are shield shaped and the flowers helmet shaped. White men first saw nasturtiums on the shores of South America.

Description, Habitat, and Season

The nasturtium, whose leaves are the same round shape as watercress leaves, is a native of Peru and Chile, where many colorful varieties thrive. Many varieties have escaped civilization and are found in the wild, in ditches, along roads, and at the edges of pastures. They are lowly 5-petaled, 2-inch flowers with round leaves. Both the leaves (round and light green) and the many-colored scarlet, red, orange, or yellow flowers grow on spindly, wavy stalks or stems. They have a peppery taste (a cross between watercress and horseradish) and are wonderful additions to spring or summer salads.

History and Lore

Elizabeth Christina, Linnaeus's daughter, observed that nasturtiums emitted a tiny spark from time to time, visible only in the dark. I knew of this from childhood, and used to sit in the yard at night and watch my mother's nasturtiums, hoping to catch sight of one. I never did. Nor have I ever seen a ghost, a UFO, or the green flash as the sun goes down, though I have spent many an hour looking for them all.

These flowers are easy to find and grow, and they add a cheerful and pleasant note to any flower garden. This pretty, long-blooming flower (spring to frost) has an antibiotic and antibacterial principle, and thus found use as a mild medicine among the South American native people. It has been eaten since in Europe to treat genital and urinary infections. The flower buds and the mature seedpods make an exceptional substitute for capers.

{RECIPES}

Faux Capers

Bring to a boil a mix of one-quarter water and three-quarters cider vinegar, with a dash of salt. In a jar, place a garlic clove and a handful of tight nasturtium buds, or, after the flowering, the seedpods, and pour the boiling pickling water over them. Seal and wait two weeks to use.

MARIGOLDS

The marigold (*Calendula officinalis*) is a bright yellow flower with a pungent fragrance that makes a nice bright yellow tea and is otherwise a useful plant medicinally. The name, kin to the word *calendar*, means "of the months," and probably indicates its long growing season. It is used to color cheese, as a tea, in salads, as a wool dye, as a hair dye, and as an ingredient in other cosmetic preparations.

Description, Habitat, and Season
The marigold is not native to this continent but escaped from colonial gardens. It is found mostly in cultivated fields, in full sun, and is an all-summer bloomer with oval, pale green leaves and round, radiant, many-petaled flowers of bright yellow or gold.

History and Lore
Medicinally, marigold is an anti-inflammatory and an antiseptic, and as such is used in soothing eye drops and for treatment of external ulcers on the skin.

{RECIPES}

In a Japanese restaurant, I once ordered marigold tea and got three yellow marigold flower heads floating in scalding water. To my surprise, it tasted really good. Marigold tea, I later learned, is said to promote menstruation and to be sedative in an infusion.

FLOWER TEAS

Gather the full-blooming flower heads of jasmine, violets, lavender, marigolds, or honeysuckle, or the petals of fragrant roses, and steep them 3–5 minutes in boiling water, or dry them carefully for later use and store them loosely in jars. I have in the attic a screen door on two sawhorses, which makes a nearly perfect place for drying herbs and flowers.

HIBISCUS

Hibiscus comprises a large genus of flowering plants that grow in warm, subtropical and tropical areas all over the world. It's a member of the Mallow family, a large group of plants that includes okra.

Usually (though not always), they have five petals and are shrubby. I know hibiscus from gorgeous hedges in Mexico, and from pots on my terrace that I have to replace every year, here in the mountains of Virginia. They grow in every color, beautiful, big flashy flowers with stamens like long tongues. If you are lucky enough to live near some, these flowers make a useful and tasty tea. In Mexico, it's called Jamaica (pronounced hah-my-ka). It's made by boiling petals of hibiscus for a few minutes, letting them steep, then straining the petals out. Use a teapot, glass or enameled pot, say the locals, as a metal pot will destroy the useful components of the tea. It's widely used in Mexico to lower blood pressure, and it's a pleasant, slightly sourish, very light drink. It tastes, with the addition of honey or sugar, like a sort of grown-up Kool-Aid (but you can drink it without sweetening, too). Mexican markets all have bins of the dried petals. Three cups a day is the prescription to lower blood pressure. Hibiscus leaves, a common ingredient in African soups, were recently discovered to contain antioxidant polyphenols that may eliminate melanoma cells from the body without harming healthy cells at the same time.

DAYLILIES

Description, Habitat, and Season

The name of daylilies means beautiful day. Daylilies (*Hemerocallis fulva*) were originally from Asia, but you wouldn't know it, they are so ubiquitous throughout America. They originally spread from gardens, and all my life, they have been on the loose everywhere I've lived. They have long leafless stalks and flat long leaves, whereas florist's lilies, which may look like daylilies, all have short spiky leaves to the tops of the stalk. The reason you need to pay attention is that only the original orange daylilies are sure to be edible; the hundreds of recent species of various-colored lilies (*lilium* species) growing all over the place may be edible, and they may not be, so you don't want to mistakenly try a poisonous one. Stick to the orange flat-leaved ones that bloom in early summer, with many flowers atop each 2- to 3-foot stalk, each blossoming only for one day in May or June, hence their folk name, daylily.

Up until the 1930s, when botanists began manipulating plants, there was only one species of *Hemerocallis*, the orange daylilies, "outhouse lilies" or "jailhouse lilies." They are not lilies, but are so-called because they look to the untrained eye like lilies. They are jubilant perennials so familiar to most of us we hardly see them. They're edible, from top to root, and really delicious. You know them, too—they're those orange beauties that line our driveways, our country roads, mark homesteads and cabins that have long since gone to ruin. The daylilies don't care—they just keep on going. But they're very welcome, because they don't spread or take over; they stay in the same places year after year, putting out edible tubers, tasting slightly like faintly sweet parsnips. The flowers can be stuffed like squash blossoms; Chinese dishes often feature the dried flowers reconstituted as a part of the vegetable of a dish. I like the fresh blossoms best when battered and deep-fried. The taste is green bean–like. They've been used in Asia for at least two thousand years. The young white roots are delicious, and taking them will not harm the plant. The fresh but newly—um—retired blossoms are a pretty and tasty addition to any salad; the dried blossoms can be used wherever you need a vegetable. The Chinese call the dried blossoms "golden needles," in the way Chinese have of naming people and things. I know a Chinese girl whose name means "most precious jade."

CHRYSANTHEMUMS

Chrysanthemums, species of the genus *Chrysanthemum*, are found worldwide. Not a wild plant, yet they have "wilded" all over the world and, with a few warnings to be heeded, are edible, useful, and medically beneficial.

Description, Habitat, and Season
"Mums" grow in all seasons except for winter. The many-petaled, sharp-smelling blooms come in all colors except blue. The sharp-tasting leaves can be added to salads.

History and Lore
For at least fifteen centuries, chrysanthemums have been used in Asia to treat respiratory problems, high blood pressure, and hyperthyroidism. The tea, made of fresh or dried flowers, is thought to calm nervousness and reduce inflammation. It is also claimed to help alleviate cold symp-

toms and osteoporosis. Maybe all these claims are true, but what I know is that a tea made of the dried flowers and added to boiling water, then cooled for five minutes, is delicious and a pleasant and worthy addition to one's diet. However, be careful and watch for allergic reactions, and, of course, stop at once if you experience any. Pyrethrum, the active principle in mums, which is an effective ingredient in many pesticides, can in rare instances irritate skin, mucus membranes, or eyes. You can buy the dried mum flowers for tea in Chinese groceries, which is how I got to know it, and enjoy it at odd times. I add a bit of honey and have headed off many a cold with chrysanthemum tea. That's my story, and I'm not backing down!

[6]
NUTS

The bitter-sweet of a white-oak acorn which you nibble in a bleak November walk over the tawny earth is more to me than a slice of imported pine-apple.
—HENRY DAVID THOREAU

When you focus on wild foods, you discover a lot that other people just don't notice. For instance, one day you'll stumble on the fact that a lot of people have black walnut trees in their yards and rake up and throw away bushels of the intense, oil-flavored nuts. You might want to try some.

There are many varieties of hickory nuts in this country, widely scattered throughout the temperate parts of the United States, and some are excellent. I've gathered wild pecans in Georgia, smaller than the ones you can buy at Christmas in the stores, but just as good. I've found beechnuts in Missouri.

I truly love those times, during brisk autumn, for that is when the nuts fall, when I can walk through the speckled or washed woods, freed from the annoyance of insects and reptile-wariness, tramping on and through the incredible colors that nature paints itself with in autumn, feeling the heat of the waning sun on my head when the wind is still, feeling the chill of coming winter when the wind takes up—and nutting. I look forward, too, to coming home and making a fresh pot of tea or coffee, and sitting down with a friend. I'll assemble the equipment for our surgery: a couple of industrial-strength hammers, an old brick to hit the nuts on, a heavy plastic bag to put the nuts in for the first shattering (to keep the pieces of shell from flying into the far corners of the kitchen or into anyone's eyes), crackers, and picks. It is then that we can get into real philosophy: Where did a word come from? What do you think about UFO abductions? Cap-

SIT A SPELL

You know the term "a spell" in southern dialect? "Sit a spell," they used to say to me, those old ladies on our street, the men in country stores, my friends' grandfathers, and my grandfather's friends. Part of it was that I made them nervous with my tireless energy, but part of it was they wanted to talk while they shelled peas, unstrung beans, or shattered and picked walnuts. "Sit a spell" promised a discourse on the ways of the lightning blinking up a storm, and why thunderstorms occurred either in the late afternoon or at night, hardly ever in the morning, or what it meant when the cows on a hill all stood facing the same way: Maybe rain was coming, maybe fish were biting. "Here, honey," one might say, handing me a rare walnut meat that was entire. "Don't say I never gave you anything," the giver would warn.

Sometimes they'd bring the War into the discussion, usually concerning the picture in a local paper of one of the hometown boys in England or Germany or on one of those islands, sometimes even Daddy.

"Here, honey," someone would say. "Snap these beans for me." They speculated on whether they'd ever find gold, or tin, or iron, or cassiterite in the nearby mountains, or if it was all mined out. Was it true that you had to near kill a walnut tree for it to bear good nuts? Andaddy would nod sagely: The one in our drive had been hit many times by his confounded machine, the Model T he was so proud of. Got hit by lightning a lot too. He'd thought it was dead. Then it started giving the biggest and best black walnuts in town. So you never could tell.

More cracking. More hammering. More tasting. The cost of walnuts if you were to find them in the store.

The cost of everything!

Well, if I had money, reckon I'd just drink it away, someone would say. Laughter all around.

ital punishment? What really causes cancer? And it is then that the memories of my grandfather Andaddy come back to me. If I'd been born into this generation, I'd surely have been labeled with ADHD.

BLACK WALNUTS AND BUTTERNUTS

Black walnuts and butternuts are two species of the *Juglans* genus, and the nuts of both taste similar. The name of the walnut family explains how highly regarded it was once: In Latin, *Juglans* means the penis head of Jupiter—which one assumes implies fairly high praise for this nut.

Description, Habitat, and Season
The leaves of both kinds of walnuts are alternate, once-compounded, with seven to seventeen pairs of light green, serrated, fragrant leaves (and no tip leaflet), so that the visual effect from a distance is lacy or ferny.

Black walnut trees grow all over our town, and all over our woods, as do, to a lesser extent, a related species called butternuts. The black walnut trees have long been prized for their elegant purplish wood and their solidity, regal shapes, and pretty light foliage. They grow to 150 feet, have an aromatic odor that most find pleasant, and a deeply furrowed, dark gray or blackish bark.

Butternut trees, sometimes called white walnuts, are similar trees, but the fruits are more elongated than the green fruits of the walnut, and the trees have lighter gray bark that is not as tightly furrowed. The nuts taste the same to me. Walnuts are the strongest flavored of our wild nuts.

In recent years, however, when gardening has become a national obsession, folks sometimes want to be rid of their walnut trees, for the *Juglans* species exude an unfriendly substance called juglone (after the plant) into the soil that keeps a lot of things from growing near it. It's actually an adaptive mechanism of the tree, which naturally is trying to get all the nearby soil nutrients for itself.

History and Lore

I have read that walnut trees can be tapped for a sap that makes a syrup similar to maple, but I have not tried it. It must be made in the early spring, when the sap rises in all trees. (See "Maple Syrup," pages 186–190.)

Despite vegetable gardeners' dislike for walnut trees, they are beautiful and formidable plants, and a lot of them still reign high over backyards, casting light shade on the ground below. In autumn, they drop fragrant green fruits that are ripened nuts encased in protective coverings. Left around the yard, the fruits turn black and mushy. The best way to shuck the walnuts down to the shell is to dump a bushel of the nuts into the street or driveway and drive over them for a week or so, which will remove the husks. Wear gloves when you handle walnuts of any sort, or your hands will get stained yellow brown, and the stain will remain literally until you grow entirely new skin. Even Clorox has no effect on walnut stain. It's been used as a brown dye.

{RECIPES}

The nuts of either the walnut or the butternut, when ripe and unhusked, are hard, and they have to be broken open with a vise or hammer and the heavenly oily nut meats removed with little picks. It's a job to be done while drinking tea and passing time with people you love talking to when you haven't anything pressing to do. Be careful not to let any pieces of shell into the nut meats, or you will have a broken tooth somewhere around the table: They are that hard.

And when you're done, here is how to use the nut meats.

WALNUT OR BUTTERNUT TORTE

Heat the oven to 350°F, and assemble 10 eggs, 1⅓ cups sugar, 1 tablespoon vanilla, 1 to 2 cups black walnut or butternut meats, salt, cinnamon, allspice, ¼ cup sifted flour, 2 cups cream, 6 tablespoons powdered sugar, and 1 tablespoon instant coffee dissolved in 2 tablespoons rum or brandy with ½ teaspoon vanilla added.

Separate the 10 eggs carefully. Beat the sugar with the yolks, and add 1 tablespoon pure vanilla, the nut meats finely ground in the blender, and a pinch each of salt, cinnamon, and allspice, and mix thoroughly. Beat the egg whites until stiff, sprinkle with sifted flour, and gently fold in the flour and the yolk mixture. Bake in three well-oiled cake pans until done, about 20 to 30 minutes. Turn out the cooled cakes onto waxed paper. Whip the cream with the powdered sugar and the coffee-rum-vanilla mixture. Ice between the layers and on top. If desired, you can sprinkle the top with more walnut meats. I don't know anyone with the strength to do this more than once a year, but it's ambrosial.

PICKLED GREEN WALNUTS

Pick 50 small green walnuts (black or butternut) off the tree around the first of June, when they are hard, green, and small. They must be used before the shell develops inside. Don't shell them or husk them. Run a hatpin or fork through them, and don't use any that the pin won't pierce. (They expel a sap or liquid at the first prick, sometimes shooting it 2 feet or more.) Prick each walnut several times. Scald them in boiling water, drain them, then stir enough salt into water that an egg will float on it. Immerse the walnuts in the brine for three days, change the brine, leave three more days, change the brine, and leave one week, keeping them weighted and covered. After the two weeks is over, drain, rinse, and pat dry the walnuts. Let them sit in the sun for a day to dry entirely. They will become jet black. Pierce again several times with a needle. Make the pickling mixture: 2 thumbs of gingerroot, sliced, a handful of whole peppercorns, a handful of whole allspice, a handful of whole cloves (one method says to remove the clove heads), a handful of mustard seed, and 1 or 2 grated nutmegs. Bring to a boil the spices and enough vinegar to cover the walnuts, and boil for 5 minutes. Pour the boiling vinegar over the walnuts, cover tightly, and let them age for one month or more. They will last five years. Note: These were considered a great delicacy a century ago; I have made them only once and did not find them very good. They were spicy, but also very salty and styptic. The method is the same in all three old cookbooks where I have found a recipe for them. It occurs to me that green English walnuts would make a much better product, but they don't grow wild in America.

Pickled walnuts (which can also be purchased at specialty food shops) are an ingredient in the best sauce I ever tasted, alleged to have been invented at the Pendennis Club in Louisville, Kentucky, by a chef named Henry Bain, for whom the sauce is named. It is a hot, spicy concoction of a lumpy consistency, dark blackish brown in color. It contains many ingredients—most of them already themselves prepared—including Worcestershire sauce, steak sauce, catsup, anchovies, Tabasco sauce, and pickled walnuts. Henry Bain Sauce is absolutely delicious on steak or beef or with a cheese sandwich or nearly anything else I could name.

HICKORY NUTS AND PECANS

There are many species of wild hickory nuts that grow throughout the Temperate Zone of the United States. Their genus is *Carya* (named for their characteristic opposite serrated leaves).

Description, Habitat, and Season
From a distance, it is not easy to distinguish between hickory and walnut trees. Of course up close, the nuts tell you. Hickories have four-sectioned husks, nowhere near as thick as walnuts. Hickory trees can grow over 100 feet tall. These trees have leaves similar to walnut trees, once-compounded, alternate, nine to seventeen leaflets. They grow in warmer parts of the Temperate Zone, and the nuts fall in autumn. Hickory nuts are pale tan, two opposite sides flattened

and two convex. They are about an inch long and across and much milder flavored than either butternuts or black walnuts. The pecan, darker tan and somewhat elongated, is a thin-shelled hickory nut of the Deep South, especially Georgia and Mississippi. Some of the new, thin-shelled varieties of pecans have escaped into the wild, as have the smaller, harder-shelled, older varieties. The best of the hickories come from the shagbark hickory tree, recognizable by its long, loose, gray scaly bark. Some hickories are bitter, and one is called a mock nut because the shell is so hard and the meat so nearly nonexistent that it mocks the forager. So crack and taste one before you go to the trouble of collecting and shelling a bunch. But a good hickory is a delicious nut: mild and sweet, just like a pecan.

BEECHNUTS

Fagus is Latin for "beech tree" and the name of the genus; the word *fagus* (from the Greek *phegos*, "edible") notifies us that the fruit of the tree is good food. Beech trees, *Fagus grandifolia* or *F. sylvatica*, grow anywhere in rich soil and sheltered locales east of the Mississippi River and from Canada to southern Georgia.

Description, Habitat, and Season
The beech is a beautiful, tall (over 100 feet) tree with smooth, roundish but triangular, tan nuts and a rich golden-red fall color to the leaves at the time the nuts are ripe. The tree has a smooth, pale, grayish bark and long, coarsely serrated, oblong-ovate leaves that are blue green on top and lighter green underneath. It is often planted by farsighted landowners for future shade. The tannish nuts, which mature in autumn, often fall out of the papery husks, which tend to stay on the tree, and you have to beat the squirrels to them. Beechnuts are darker in color and stronger flavored than hickories, but not as strong flavored as walnuts, and some are downright bitter. They contain a high amount of oxalic acid, so it's not advisable to eat too many at one time.

Nut Pie

Preheat the oven to 350°F. Assemble 1 stick butter, 2 tablespoons flour, 1 cup brown sugar, 1 cup white sugar, 2 teaspoons vanilla extract, 2 eggs, and 1 cup shelled pecans, black or white walnuts, beechnuts, or hickory nuts. In a food processor, blend the butter, flour, sugars, vanilla, and eggs until light and smooth. Pour into an uncooked piecrust (see recipe, pages 207–208), sprinkle the nuts on top, and bake for 40 minutes or until puffed and browned and a knife in the middle comes out nearly clean.

COCONUTS

Coconut palms (*Cocos* spp.), among the oldest plants on earth, grow along tropical and subtropical beaches, bearing coconuts free for the taking. Their name comes from a Spanish word, *coco*, which means "frown" or "grimace," because the inner hairy shell looks like an angry, scrunched-up face.

Description, Habitat, and Season

Coconut palms have the typical flat, evergreen leaf and rough, overlapped bark of palm trees everywhere, and they are frost sensitive. Of the many species, some coconut palms fruit year-round, some at specific times of the year. Their large green fruits—roughly a foot or more in diameter when ripe—are highly visible to anyone on the lookout. To tell if a coconut is ripe, shake it; if you can hear water sloshing around inside, it's ready.

In this country, coconuts can be found in Florida, and sometimes in states as far north as South Carolina, all along the Gulf of Mexico coast, on the California coast, and throughout Hawaii.

Coconuts propagate by floating from place to place, taking root where they land, which is why they are found on all tropical coasts.

History and Lore

Like the kernel of most nuts, the coconut meat is fatty and nutritious. It has found uses in cosmetics and in cooking, particularly in confections like cookies, where crispness is necessary. It is used in medicine and in industry. Copra, sun-dried coconut meat, was once the greatest export of the Hawaiian Islands or so I learned in fifth grade.

{RECIPES}

If you find a coconut on the beach, shake it near your ear and listen for sloshing (to determine if it is good to eat). Strip off the green outer husk (you need a heavy, sharp knife or machete), remove the fibrous inner layer, and crack the hard inside shell (which also calls for a serious hammer or machete). Inside that shell is the shell lining, or the meat, and in the center of it is a pearly, drinkable substance called coconut milk, which is sterile and fine to drink straight from the coconut.

COCONUT CUSTARD PIE

Make a piecrust as directed on pages 207–208. Heat oven to 450°F. Scald 2 cups whole milk, but do not boil. Into a blender, break 4 large eggs. Add ¾ cup white sugar, a few grains salt, and 1 teaspoon vanilla. Turn on the blender, and gradually pour the hot milk into the other ingredients. In a bowl, mix the custard with 2 cups grated coconut. Pour into pastry, place in oven on a cookie sheet, then reduce heat at once to 350°F and bake for about 45 minutes, or until the top is nicely browned and the center is firm.

Unbelievably Easy Coconut Pie

Preheat oven to 325°F. Grease a heat-resistant glass pie pan. Mix together the following: 1 cup sugar, ¾ cup biscuit mix, ⅓ cup melted margarine, 2 teaspoons vanilla, 6 eggs, and ¾ cup milk. Pour them into the pie pan, top with 1 cup shredded coconut, and bake until done, about 1 hour.

Coconut Bacon

Here is another way to fix coconut that is so delicious you won't believe it isn't meat. Heat the oven to 300°F. Break the outer hairy brown shell of the coconut with a hammer. Discard the milk or save it for another use, and remove the flesh by wedging a knife tip between the shell and flesh, and popping it off in the biggest pieces you can get. Leave on the brown skin of the white meat. Slice the meat into strips with a sharp blade, or on a slicer. Spread the strips on a cookie sheet, salt them lightly, then bake them slowly until they brown slightly. Check them often, and move them around so that they brown evenly.

Cooled, these crisp, toasted coconut strips are fine as a nibble. They are delicious eaten with cold soup. They make a wonderful condiment for a hot curry. They taste remarkably like bacon.

[7]
MISCELLANEOUS FORAGING

We cultivate imported shrubs in our front yards for the beauty of their berries, while at least equally beautiful berries grow unregarded by us in the surrounding fields.
—HENRY DAVID THOREAU

Wild foods are, of course, free for the picking. But so, quite frequently, are cultivated plants that no one else wants. Walking one day, you may discover, as I did, a row of flowering crab apple trees planted along a sub-urban street for the blossom and shade, but not for the fruit, and you'll notice how much good food is wasted. Almost every field has horserad-ish growing in it, and almost nobody digs fresh horseradish anymore. Almost every town has its lanes of maple trees, which nobody outside of New England taps for the expensive, delicious syrup. Modern farmers who raise corn harvest it by machine, which leaves a lot of perfectly good ears just lying on the ground.

As mentioned, I have seen lamb's-quarters in city lots and ripe black-berries growing in Central Park in New York City. At picnics, people gather up garbage bags full of watermelon rind to toss in the nearest Dumpster.

In every case, there is free food nobody seems to want. The point is, if you look in the right places, and are willing put in the labor of prepa-ration, you will be rewarded with good things to eat.

CORN

Corn (*Zea mays*), a grass of unknown origin, though probably native to Central America, was known to the Aztecs and was introduced to Europe first by Christopher Columbus, who called it *mahiz*, or "maize." Corn, purchased or stolen from the Native Americans, sustained both the Jamestown colony in 1607 and the Plymouth colony in 1620, so it is

fitting that *zea* in Greek means "I live." The word *corn* in Old English (Anglo-Saxon) meant a hard nub of something, such as a peppercorn or a "corn" of salt (as in corned beef). Corn came to mean whatever grain had hard "corns." Thus in England, the word *corn* came to mean wheat. From there, it came, through the linguistic process known as generalization, to designate whatever the major grain of an area was: So in the case of the colonies, maize was soon called corn.

Description, Habitat, and Season
Corn is, of course, a tall, large cane grass 6 or more feet high that is cultivated throughout the eastern and middle sections of the continental United States. It has the flat, light green leaves typical of canes. It can be found north of the tropics, from sea to shining sea.

History and Lore
It has been said that without Indian corn, hard corn, and feed corn, America would never have been colonized and civilized. Wheat takes about six months to grow, but a corn crop matures in half that time, and some of it matures in six weeks. Unlike wheat, corn doesn't deteriorate when left in the field but can be left on the stalk until the owner needs corn. Wheat, of course, must be harvested when it is ripe.

CORN, GORGEOUS AND GOLDEN

In 1961, my friends Julia and Jeanne and I made the grand tour of Europe, and by August, we were driving through northern Italy, Liechtenstein, and Austria, when we noticed that we could never find corn on the menus of the places where we ate, though in the car we passed mile after mile of cornfields. Back in Virginia, it was the season for sweet corn on the cob, and as we talked, we got hungrier and hungrier. As a consequence, when we stopped for lunch, after a small amount of soul searching, we helped ourselves to six ears of corn out of some farmer's field, planning to borrow a pot and cook it that night wherever we landed.

We pulled up at a house with a B&B sign, made arrangements to spend the night, and explained that we needed a pot to cook our corn in. Imagine our surprise when the woman said, in German, "You stole that."

Was she psychic? How did she know? We sheepishly confessed, explaining in horrible pidgin-German combined with horrible pidgin-English how homesick we were for corn. She shrugged and gave us a pot and stood, arms crossed, to watch what we would do next. In fact, another farm woman showed up soon after, and stood watching also. And another. None of them smiling. We brought a cup of water to the boil and cheerfully put in the six ears, shucked, gorgeous and golden, and steamed them for the holy seven minutes. We took them out, gilded three with butter, and took a bite each. Well, we tried to take bites. Puzzled, we opined they hadn't cooked long enough, so we returned them to the pot. After we had done that several times and an hour had passed and they still weren't edible, and the farm women had watched the entire operation solemnly (by then, there were four of them in the kitchen leaning up against the wall to observe the insane and thieving Americans), it dawned on us that this wasn't our kind of corn. Europeans don't eat sweet corn, only cornmeal made from fodder corn. Those women kept straight faces the whole time, but every time I think of them, I imagine them telling the story to someone, laughing so hard they are falling on the floor, whooping and slapping their knees at the stupidity of Americans.

Corn's only fault is that it severely depletes the soil it is grown in, so until crop rotation was discovered, wherever corn grew for two or three years, nothing else much would grow from then on. The Native Americans were cleverer than the English settlers at this game: Some planted in each hill of corn a whole fish and a handful of wood ashes, which replenished the soil. Others knew, too, that planting beans in the same hills with corn returned nitrates to the depleted soil and, in addition, allowed the bean vines to use the cornstalks for climbers. The English, impatient with such foolishness, took a while to catch on that the Native Americans knew what they were doing.

Nowadays, corn and other crops, such as soybeans, are rotated, or grown in the fields in alternate years, to replenish the soil. By the time Columbus first "discovered" corn, Native Americans had already developed over three hundred different varieties that included many kinds of colored corn, hard corn (feed corn), popcorn, and sweet corn (corn that can be eaten off the cob).

{RECIPES}

Today, harvesting machines often miss some ears of corn, leaving them still attached to the stalk or lying on the ground still neatly wrapped in their husks. Just a few windfall ears collected on a chilly fall or winter afternoon will yield you a good supply of cornmeal. So collect some ears of hard corn (corn used to feed stock) left by the harvesters. (Soft corn, a marvel of cultivariation, will be readily distinguishable, for the kernels of it when old are soft and shrunken and moldy, whereas hard corn kernels are sturdy and hard as rocks.) Take off the husks, dust the ear, and worry off the hard, dry grains of corn with your fingers (or hit or rub the ear against something to dislodge them). Grind about ½ cup of the kernels at a time in your blender until it becomes cornmeal, and store in small packages of 1 cup or so each in the freezer. (Each large ear averages 1 cup of meal.) This is whole grain cornmeal, and it contains corn germ, corn oil, and corn bran, as well as carbohydrate. It is infinitely superior to any you can buy, but it must be frozen or it goes rancid quickly. It makes wonderful corn bread and spoon bread.

Finally, this corn keeps naturally on the ear. I just ground an ear of red corn that's been hanging in my kitchen for several years, and made hoecakes (see method below), which were perfectly fresh tasting and delicious. Corn is truly an amazing grain.

COUNTRY CORN BREAD

Preheat the oven to 375°F. Put a large iron skillet in the oven to heat. In your blender, put 1 egg, 1 cup and a slosh of milk, 1 teaspoon baking soda, 1½ cups cornmeal, ½ cup biscuit mix or Baking Mix (see recipe, pages 208–210), 1 teaspoon sugar, 1 teaspoon salt, and ¼ cup melted bacon drippings. Mix. Remove the skillet with an oven glove and put 1 tablespoon bacon fat or other oil in it, tilt it around to grease the bottom, and pour in the batter. Return to the oven and bake about 30 minutes, or until it's risen and begun to brown at the edges. Of course, you can use margarine, or butter, or vegetable oil, and you can leave out the sugar (or put more in)—but it really does taste better with bacon fat.

GRAND NATIONAL SPOON BREAD CHAMPION

In 1975, *CommonWealth* magazine and the Virginia State Chamber of Commerce sponsored a national spoon bread contest. My spoon bread won first prize, and I received the title Grand National Spoon Bread Champion. The gala bakeoff was at the famous Homestead resort in western Virginia and judged by their staff.

Preheat the oven to 400°F. Sprinkle 1 cup fine cornmeal into 1 pint vigorously boiling water, stirring continuously to prevent lumps. Add ½ teaspoon salt and 4 tablespoons butter. Stir until the butter is melted, and let sit 10 minutes. Beat together vigorously (or blend) 4 medium eggs and 1 cup cold whole milk. Stir the cornmeal mush and the milk-and-egg mix together. Butter a big round or square baking dish or casserole dish, pour in the batter, pop in the oven, reduce the heat to 375°F, and bake until puffed and golden, between 40 minutes and 1 hour. Serve with more butter.

This is the way Lizzie, my grandparents' cook, born the year the Civil War ended, made it and taught me to make it, and it is sublime enough to have surpassed scores of other recipes in taste.

HOECAKES

This makes a quick and delicious breakfast. Boil 1 pint water with ½ teaspoon salt, and sprinkle in slowly some of your home-ground cornmeal—about ⅔ cup. Stir it 1 or 2 minutes until it thickens to the consistency of batter. Meanwhile, heat a little bacon grease (or vegetable oil or butter) in a skillet, spoon the mush into the hot fat, and fry like hotcakes, turning once. Serve as they are, or with more butter. Try them with maple syrup. These were described to me by the lady who first made them for me as a child as fare for slaves who often had to cook outdoors. They were supposedly cooked over fires on cleaned and greased hoes—hence the name.

CHESS PIE

This is a Virginia favorite using cornmeal as thickener. It probably had an English origin, with the "chess" a misspelling of "cheese," as lemon curd is sometimes called lemon cheese in England. But this method, using cornmeal, is definitely a New World variation.

Make a one-crust piecrust (see recipe, pages 207–208). Preheat oven to 375°F. The filling: Stir together 2 cups white sugar (or 1 cup white and 1 cup brown) and 2 tablespoons cornmeal. Beat together 4 medium or 3 large eggs, 4 tablespoons melted butter, 4 tablespoons milk, 4 tablespoons lemon juice, and 2 tablespoons finely grated lemon rind. Stir the dries and the wets together. Pour the filling into the shell and bake for 35 to 45 minutes.

Modern hint: I peel off the zest of 1 large lemon (or 2 small ones) and put the rind into the food processor with the 2 cups sugar and pulse it until the peel is finely ground. Then I proceed with the cornmeal.

During World War II, the women in our town used to make chess pies with vinegar instead of lemon juice, and they were equally tart and wonderful, though not of course specifically lemony. I recall that they used chicken fat sometimes in the crust, if there was no lard, and, again, that it tasted just fine. I couldn't wait for Saturdays when I could walk the mile uptown to the garage where the farmers' market was held and pay a nickel for a chess tart from the farmer's wife who brought them to town to sell. Other things were made during the war with the same substitution because, I suppose, other fats weren't available. I recall, for instance, delicious chocolate chip cookies made with chicken fat.

ITALIAN POLENTA WITH WILD CORN

Strip the husks off an ear of hard corn and pop the kernels off into a big deep bowl (they tend to bounce and scatter). Grind them in a food processor or a blender until they are ground into a reasonably fine cornmeal. Mix the meal with some salt and boiling water, enough to make a thin gruel. Cook this gruel for one hour, stirring often. Keep it on the edge of boiling. If it gets too thick, add water by the tablespoon to thin it. At the end of an hour, it will be cooked through. Pour this gruel into a loaf pan, and chill overnight or at least 8 hours. Slice it up and fry it in butter, bacon grease, or olive oil until it is heated through, brown, and crisp on both sides. Serve it as the base for your favorite pasta sauce, and sprinkle parmesan on top for extra flavor. This is sophisticated northern Italian cuisine! One ear of ground corn is quite enough for 4 servings.

JERUSALEM ARTICHOKES

The common sunflower, *Helianthus annuus*, has delicious edible seeds, but they are a nuisance to get at. However, the sunflower has many relatives, and among them is a native American plant called *H. tuberosus*, or the "rooted sunflower." (*Helio* is "sun" in Greek, and *anthus* is "flower.") We call this plant the Jerusalem artichoke, though the name is more than misleading. The plant was discovered by early American explorers who took it to Europe, specifically to Italy, where it was called by the Italian name for sunflowers, *girasole* (meaning "turning toward the sun," which was later corrupted to "Jerusalem"), and to France, where it was dubbed *artichaud de Canada*, or "Canadian artichoke." The combined name is what we are left with today. The plant is no kin to artichokes, nor is it from Jerusalem.

Description, Habitat, and Season
This coarse, 8-foot-tall wildflower has broad, rough, serrated alternate leaves on sturdy, hairy, round stems, though at the bottoms of the stems the leaves become opposite. It has in late summer a cheerful yellow daisy-like flower about 2½ inches in diameter, with the central disk, as well as the petals, being yellow. The difficulty in identifying this plant is that many late-summer flowers are similar. Some flowers that look similar

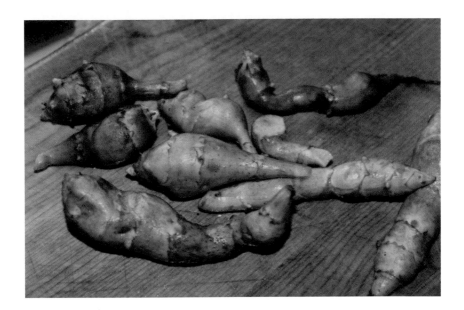

have flanges up the main stem, but Jerusalem artichokes have round, rough, and purplish stems and "fatter" leaves. This is the only plant with yellow-centered yellow flowers that has, when you pull up a main stem, a tuber (or several) at the end. It grows enthusiastically in wastelands, damp woods, roadside ditches, and fields throughout the temperate parts of eastern Canada and the eastern United States.

The flower, which blooms in late summer, identifies the plant for later digging of the tubers. The tubers stay fresh underground until they are dug out, so they can be eaten all winter. Freezing does not affect them adversely. But, of course, there are no flowers to identify the plants when it's time to harvest them.

History and Lore
Jerusalem artichokes are native to America and were widely used by the native people of North America. The taste of the tubers is mild and does resemble artichokes, in that they share a slightly sweetish aftertaste. Truly, they are a treasure for the forager.

To harvest them, dig around the plants any time after the first frost, and the tubers will appear, the way potatoes do. Scrub them thoroughly to avoid any grit or dirt, and peel away parts of them that won't come clean.

{RECIPES}

The irregular 1-inch to 2-inch tubers are more like potatoes than anything else, but unlike potatoes, they get tough if overcooked. Once they have been scrubbed clean, and scraped or partially peeled to make certain no dirt remains, they are fine sliced raw into salads, where they add the same kind of crispness as water chestnuts do. They can be lightly sautéed in oil or butter, salted, and served as a vegetable.

Jerusalem Artichoke Salad

Boil the tubers no longer than 10 minutes in salted water, drain, and chop coarsely. Chill. Add a couple of chopped hard-boiled eggs, a small amount of chopped onion, and a spoonful of sweet pickle relish, and toss with enough mayonnaise to dress all lightly. Chill and serve on lettuce leaves.

Jerusalem Artichokes au Gratin

Parboil the tubers in salted water to which the juice of half a lemon has been added until they are just beginning to be tender (but be careful not to overcook). Drain, and make a medium white sauce or Cream Sauce (see recipe, page 210) seasoned with nutmeg, salt, and pepper. Slice or chop the tubers coarsely, mix with enough cream sauce to coat them, and place them in a buttered casserole dish. Sprinkle them with grated cheddar cheese, and broil them only until the cheese bubbles. They should not be overcooked, as they toughen up again with too much cooking. This dish can be served as a vegetable, a luncheon main dish, or a cocktail party dip or spread for crackers.

WILD RICE

Zizania aquatica is a cereal grain, named by Great Lakes Native Americans, that grows in water; it is misnamed, being no kin to rice. Its name comes from *zizanion*, a wheat field weed. *Aquatica* refers to its growing medium. It is also sometimes called water oats.

Description, Habitat, and Season
Wild rice is the seed of an annual grass, with slender, basally (from the base) branching culms (grass stems) 6 to 10 feet tall. This reedy water

grass has light green, long, flat leaves 1 to 2 inches across, goldish-green seedpods, and a long foxtail cluster at the top. The seeds are long and thin and cylindrical, in papery husks tipped with bristles. The many varieties are naturalized in some places where it grows outside its natural range. Much of its traditional range has now been "civilized," and the wild rice eradicated.

The varieties of wild rice mature in late summer. Euell Gibbons declares that it grows from the Canadian border to the Gulf of Mexico and is sometimes planted by hunters who want to shoot the birds that the wild rice attracts. However, it is most prevalent around the Great Lakes and throughout southern Canada. It grows along shores, in quiet, shallow waters such as farm ponds and swamps, and it can grow in fresh or brackish water. Some varieties have adapted to the Deep South, though in general, wild rice is a cool-climate plant. Its ripe seeds darken a little as they mature.

History and Lore
The Native Americans who lived around the Great Lakes made use of the grain. Their method of harvesting has never been improved upon: Among the mature reeds, pull a handful down over your boat, and whack them sharply with a stick. The grains should then dislodge into your

boat. (If they don't, try again in several days.) You can put a sheet in the bottom of the boat to catch the grains and gather them up more easily. Peterson warns of ergot, which is a deadly fungus that sometimes replaces the grains in corn, rye, wild rice, and other grains. The ergot grains will be a different color from the other tan, brown, or blackish grains, usually purple but sometimes pink or reddish. If they are present, either pick them out carefully or do not use the rice. They will be similar to the rice in shape, but often larger.

{RECIPES}

Once home, the grain must be dried for several days, parched in the sun for a day, or parched in the oven by putting the grains in shallow pans at around 250 to 275°F for about 1 hour, stirring often so they parch evenly. Finally, the rice must be husked by rubbing the cooled grains between the palms. It can then be stored in a glass jar, tightly sealed, or in a glass jar or plastic bag in the freezer. It needs a good washing before it's cooked.

BOILED WILD RICE

When you are ready to use the rice, wash it thoroughly in bowls of cold water, skimming off any husks that rise to the top and re-rinsing until the water is perfectly clear. Actually, it might take 3 or more washings. Then cook it as you would rice; in this case, 1 measure grain to 3 measures water, salted, boiled gently for 30 minutes, or until the water is absorbed. You can also cook it in seasoned broth. I add a bay leaf, and sometimes a packet of dried onion soup. Wild rice is especially good with game of any kind, but I also like it with morels (see chapter 3).

POPPED RICE

I have fried dry rice and wild rice by heating peanut oil to about 375°F and, as it heats, dropping in a grain at a time, until it suddenly puffs up in the hot oil. That tells you the temperature is right. Then you slowly add 1 to 2 tablespoons dry wild rice, dry white rice, or some combination. Almost at once, the grains pop and swell to double their size, and they are wonderful scattered on top of soup or salad, or just salted and eaten as you would popcorn.

I have sometimes tried to do this and found the rice won't pop. After a bit of research, I found that the secret is to wash the wild rice well, then leave it slightly damp in a tightly sealed jar for a day to let it absorb moisture. If you find your rice won't pop, try this trick. The popping is caused by steam in the grain suddenly expanding and bursting open the grain. So if the rice is too dry, it obviously won't work. This works with old popcorn, too: Add a teaspoon of water to the jar and cover it tightly. Shake the jar and wait a day. The corn will pop better.

ORIENTAL SALAD

Gather a bunch of spring greens (see chapter 2), wash and dry them, and toss them with popped rice and the following dressing.

ORIENTAL SALAD DRESSING

This dressing may make enough to use for several salads. Mix in a jar with a tight lid 4 chopped cloves garlic, 1 knob fresh ginger the size of your thumb (grated), 2 tablespoons dark sesame oil (available in grocery stores among Asian food products), ½ cup peanut oil, ¼ cup orange or tangerine juice, 2 tablespoons lemon juice, and 2 tablespoons soy sauce. This dressing has a distinctive and different flavor. Shake well before dressing the greens lightly with it. The leftover dressing will last in the refrigerator at least a couple weeks.

HORSERADISH

While you're gathering spring greens, you can dig your year's supply of horseradish, to be grated with vinegar and cream. Horseradish (*Armoracia lapathifolia*, dock-leafed horseradish, or *A. rusticana*, rustic horseradish) came with the English settlers and escaped into the wild. The name suggests that it was first identified in Armorica, an ancient name for northwest Gaul. *Lapathifolia* is likely from the Latin *labi*, "to fall," kin to our words *lapse*, a falling away, and *lap*, to fold over (*folia* is "leaves"), for the leaves have the appearance of falling away from the plant and have slightly wavy edges.

Description, Habitat, and Season
Horseradish is a perennial with a long, white, irregular root. Its dark, tough, wavy, scalloped, heavily veined leaves about a foot long and 2 to 6 inches across spring from a channeled stalk out from the root. Horseradish has tiny white flowers in early summer (May to July) that grow

higher than the leaves, and out of a central stalk. It grows in fields, in pastures, along roadsides, and especially along riverbanks and creek sides. As it will grow a new plant from only the tiniest portion of a root left in the ground, it is sometimes found in fairly thick clumps. Spring to fall is the time to gather it by digging up the fat, long root.

History and Lore
Horseradish, with its pungency, has a long history as a medical stimulant. Many Native American tribes employed it to stimulate glandular activity, to combat scurvy, and as a diaphoretic (perspiration-inducing) "loosening" treatment for the common cold. It is believed to aid in the digestion of rich, fatty foods; thus, it is most often paired culinarily with roast meats. Euell Gibbons warns against cooking it, for heat destroys the flavor and quality.

{RECIPES}

Horseradish doesn't release its pungent smell until it's grated. One root is probably all you need for a year's supply. In addition, the young leaves of the plant are pungent but make a good potherb when mixed with some milder greens.

Prepared Horseradish

Grate scrubbed, cleaned horseradish root finely into a bowl of salted water, or shred it in the food processor and pour it from there into salted water. Drain it well and pack the horseradish in a jar. Cover it with white vinegar and store it in the refrigerator. To serve, add it to tomato catsup or salsa to taste for cocktail sauce or, best of all, fold it into salted whipped cream or commercial sour cream to accompany beef or venison.

SASSAFRAS

Sassafras is a flavor nearly everyone loves; sassafras root is what root beer was originally made of. *Sassafras albidum*, sometimes called *S. officinale*, grows abundantly everywhere in the East, from Canada to Florida. It was first discovered by early French settlers in Florida, and the name is of unknown origin, though possibly the French learned it from a local Native American name for the plant.

Description, Habitat, and Season

Sassafras is generally a small tree, though it may grow to 100 feet tall. It is readily identified in thickets and woods and wood marges by its four leaf patterns: a left and right mitten, a simple (plain) leaf, and a three-lobed leaf. The leaves are bright green, smooth, smooth-edged, and fragrant.

The twigs, or new branchlets, are pale green. In the spring, it has clusters of fragrant yellow flowers. The entire plant, but especially the root, smells like root beer.

History and Lore

Sassafras has figured in folklore ever since the English colonized North America, and it was known by the English before they settled here. A shipload of sassafras root leaving Virginia for London in 1609 was North America's first export. The plant had already, in the century of Spanish exploration of the Western Hemisphere, gained a nearly magical reputation. Called ague tree and tea tree, sassafras was reputed to cure many ailments, from broken bones to fevers, from worms to baldness. Modern herbalists classify sassafras as a weak antiseptic. The root bark was believed to be the most potent part of the plant.

Today, we know that it should be used with caution, if at all, for the entire plant (part of the laurel family, which contains many poisonous plants) contains a compound, safrole, that is mildly carcinogenic. Yet my grandmother believed this tea "thinned your blood" in springtime in preparation for the coming hot weather, so I drank the pinkish tea with her every spring from 1943 on—and often at other times of the year. The leaves we collected, dried, and crumbled into fragrant powder, called filé by the Cajuns, were used to thicken the gumbos that my grandmother's cook occasionally made.

Unfortunately, today, because of its carcinogenic nature, the root cannot legally be bought or sold; yet the flavor, now artificially formulated, remains popular in soft drinks, medicines, candies, and toothpastes.

{RECIPES}

SASSAFRAS TEA

Dig sassafras roots in late winter or early spring, clean them well, chop them up a bit, and boil a handful in 1 quart water for about 10 or 20 minutes.

FILÉ

Filé is the spring leaves of sassafras dried and pulverized. It is a thickening, seasoning agent added (1 tablespoon for a regular recipe) at the end of the cooking time, just before serving, and lends a smooth, slippery quality to gumbo and other Creole dishes.

GINSENG

Ginseng, *Panax quinquefolius*, is the most interesting plant I know. Its scientific name, from the Greek words *pan* ("all") and *akos* ("cure"), is close kin to the word *panacea*, meaning "cure-all." The word *ginseng* comes from the Chinese *jin-chen*, a word meaning "man-root"; and *quinquefolius* refers to the usual five-leaf arrangement of each prong, emerging from the main stem of the foot-high plant.

Ginseng is mysterious and very exotic, and I believe it deserves inclusion among the best of wild foods. In 1995, good Appalachian ginseng root properly dried brought its diggers $430 a pound. In 2008, the price of a pound of good, aged ginseng was over $1,000. In specialty stores in Asia, it is enormously expensive, sometimes bringing up to ten thousand dollars an ounce. The most lucrative markets for the plant are in the Far East. The mystery is, and always has been: Why? What has ginseng got that has kept it popular for over four thousand years? What does it do?

Description, Habitat, and Season

Ginseng is a common name for several of the plants in the family, including Chinese, American, and Korean ginsengs. The family otherwise includes English ivy, the rice-paper plant of China, and sarsaparilla. This small and unprepossessing plant has a series of long, slender stems, sometimes dark red in color, each with five leaves emerging from the top; a tiny, insignificant whitish or reddish flower in the spring; and come fall, a bright red berry cluster in the middle, from which come the seeds that will eventually, if the plant is left alone, fall and take root in the soil nearby. First-year plants have only three leaves to a branch, and the berries are lighter red, sometimes yellowish. Only in the third year do the plants develop the characteristic five leaves. Ginseng grows far back in dense woods and prefers heavy shade. As it is so valuable, it is sought diligently, and it is near extinction in some places where it used to be common.

Neither seeds nor leaves have any uses. Ginseng's value is all underground. As the plant dies back each year and puts out a new stalk each spring, there remain at the top of the root right at ground level the scars from the previous year's stalks. These bumps or wrinkles at the top of the root, called the coils, where the stem emerges from the ground, can be "read" for age like the rattles of a rattlesnake or the rings on a tree trunk.

Ginseng is undeniably hard to find. As much time as I spend in the woods, I have not seen more than a dozen plants in my life, all of them young. Obstacles, dangerous and tiring, do not daunt the hunters. The harder the going gets, the more the diggers' efforts will meet with success; the more isolated and unattainable the area, the more likely it is (they believe) that they will find the plant. There seems to reside in lifelong hunters the belief that only the virtuous among them can find the plant, and that the dangers only exist to frighten away cowards and weaklings.

History and Lore

The plants are steeped in lore. Oriental ginseng was an article of tribute (demanded by the emperor) as early as the T'ang dynasty in China, which began in AD 618.

This small and ordinary-looking shrub was first recorded in China about four thousand years ago. It grows in the mountains in only the Northern Hemisphere of our planet. The states where it is found most commonly are Virginia, West Virginia, Pennsylvania, North Carolina, Tennessee, and Georgia. These days, however, it is so overpicked as to be rare every place it grows, from Canada to Florida and from Quebec west to Manitoba. Ginseng is now cultivated in the Great Lakes states, primarily in Wisconsin and Michigan.

Panax ginseng, the oriental variety that grows in Korea and northern China, is believed to have many palliative medicinal qualities; but *Panax quinquefolius*, the American variety, is even more valued by Asians. Perversely, Americans overwhelmingly prefer Asian ginseng. I will explain presently.

Some say ginseng glows in the dark and that it moves around—literally uprooting and changing location. It is reputed to shriek if yanked rudely out of the soil. It is said to grow only in tandem with certain other trees—mainly a variety of hardwoods (but no agreement can be had on which ones)—and never in fields, valleys, marshes, river bottoms, or exposed places. One hunter told me that it will not grow for three years on land devastated by a forest fire. Another told me it grew on the shady sides of deep gullies in the mountains. But some believe it grows only on a mountain's cool and duffy north slopes. 'Sang diggers say that the plant occurs only by itself, not gregariously (though in the virgin forests in the early days of European occupation, it reportedly grew in huge colonies and often spread across many acres). It supposedly won't grow anywhere near metal. It is rumored—perhaps to discourage competition—to share its habitat intimately with copperheads and rattlers.

I hold in my hand a fresh root. Sniffing it closely, I smell nothing but earth, dirt. I bite off a piece, and chew. The first impression is bitter,

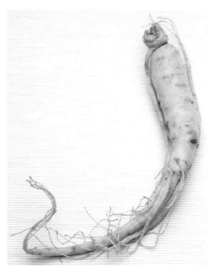

peculiar, and then a mild sweetness and a flavor fleetingly like—maybe ginger?—comes through. Although I chew and chew, the root does not diminish in my mouth. I wait after I've spit it out, wondering if it really banishes hunger and thirst, as it's reputed to do.

What is it that makes this plant so valuable? It seems that the primary reason for such astonishing prices for a wild plant is that ginseng root is, as most folks know, widely believed to be a potent aphrodisiac. In China today, when an elderly relative begins to feel the effects of age upon his sex drive or just in general, a family may go into debt to buy ginseng, sometimes only enough for one dose. Of course, if one's general health gets a boost, it follows that one's sexual vitality may also be reawakened.

Ginseng, whatever clinical trials show or do not show, apparently works often enough to keep up the trade. One Korean physician told me that Chinese ginseng is "hot medicine," while American ginseng is "cool." But Paul Hsu, Taiwanese president of the American Ginseng Association, told me the opposite: that Americans, being of "hot" disposition, should take oriental ginseng, as it is "cooling." Asians, being by nature cooler than Westerners, would profit more from "hot" American ginseng. Thus, ginseng either picks up on or reflects the disposition of the people it grows among. The prices reflect these beliefs.

Have you ever known anyone who was cured by ginseng of a really serious illness? I ask, over and over again. The answers are never definitive.

Asians chew the root or brew tea from the scraped or chopped root. They also make decoctions, boiling the root down to syrupy consistency. Ginseng is one of a large number of Asian herbal remedies, which include some truly alarming ingredients like poisonous sea plants, jellyfish, insects including earthworms, and various kinds of dried lizards and toads, as well as bear gallbladders, sea sponges, and rhinoceros horn (which is nothing but keratin, the same substance your fingernails are made of). There seem to be as many opinions about dosage and frequency of use as there are users. But before you scoff, remember that Chinese medicine has endured for at least four thousand years—so I conclude it must be effective.

Native Americans, notably the Chippewa, treated various illnesses, including heart trouble, with ginseng. Probably the doctrine of signatures is at work here, which, as mentioned earlier, states that any plant's uses to man are suggested by its shape or color. Ginseng, according to this thinking, is believed to have many properties mysteriously relating to man because its shape, occasionally a trunk and four limbs and, rarely, a small rootlet where a penis ought to be, suggests the shape of man. Man-root is another folk name for ginseng.

Some medical studies have concluded that the well-known placebo effect matches the effect of most medicines; it is common in double-blind drug tests to have a high percentage of the placebo users respond to the drug they think they are taking.

Yet pharmaceutical companies have tried in vain to discover what it is that ginseng contains. Controlled studies, literally hundreds of them, have yielded contradictory results. Korean tests report that ginseng "facilitated mating behavior" in rats. Tests in this country remain inconclusive. In Russia, scientists have continually tested ginseng's results. In one study among Russian factory workers, volunteers who took a mere four milligrams of ginseng a day lost significantly fewer days at work due to colds; sinus, bronchial, and tonsil infections; and influenza than their fellow workers who did not take ginseng.

Other studies have suggested that Siberian ginseng users proved able to endure noise, stress, extremes of hot and cold, and long hours of hard labor more readily than nonusers. Additional tests indicate that people hospitalized with problems such as insomnia, neurosis, or anxiety respond more frequently and profoundly to Siberian ginseng than to other drugs. Yet Eastern and Western medicine may not be as far apart as they once were. For the brisk business and high price of ginseng in America are evidence that we are just as willing as the Chinese to believe in its general efficacy. And maybe there is something to ginseng, particularly if, in addition to using it, we guard our health by not smoking, by eating and drinking moderately, and by taking regular exercise!

{RECIPES}

GINSENG TEA

Shave off 1 teaspoon or so ginseng root, fresh or dried, and steep it for 3 to 10 minutes in a small pot of boiling water. Then drink it. How often?

Three times a day. Once a day. Every day for a week. You can reuse the root up to a dozen times.

Or not.

GINSENG CORDIAL

Into 1 gallon of excellent bourbon or brandy, place 1 large ginseng root at least 5 inches long. Close the bottle and let it sit for 3 months before drinking 1 ounce a day. This is said to be a sure palliative for rheumatism and arthritis. When the whiskey is gone, the root can be used again in whiskey at least 2 more times.

MAPLE SYRUP

The author taps a huge old maple tree in the 1970s in her yard.

Acer saccharum is the sugar maple. Its name is kin to our "acre" and "agriculture," and *saccharum* means "sweet."

Description, Habitat, and Season
We have over 150 species of maple trees in the North Temperate Zone. Many of them are planted along streets as shade trees or along coun-

try lanes or roads. Most of them have leaves that turn brilliant reds, oranges, and yellows in autumn. The leaves are generally opposite and simple, with three or five lobes. It takes some expertise to tell one from another. But all of them have sap that rises in early spring, when the nights are below freezing and the days above. Among these is *Acer saccharum*, the sugar maple. That one is supposed to be the best, but you couldn't prove it by me. I've tried syrup from many, and they all taste about the same, including syrup from the box elder, which is the only maple with compound leaves. Maples are so common in our cities and countryside that you needn't go far to find one.

The US Forest Service says the tapping won't hurt the trees if it is done right, and proof of that is the maple syrup industry in New England, which taps the same trees year after year for the sap. It is easy to tap the tree for the watery sap that, boiled down, makes maple syrup and maple sugar. Even if all you get from your own attempt at sugaring is a cup of the lovely dark syrup, do it once so you'll know how, and then you'll probably want to do it again, year after year.

Just a wet stain on the side of a maple tree on a sunny February afternoon may be your signal. Look for sap dripping from a cut branch, and you'll know the time is right.

When it first comes from the tree, the sap is so diluted that you generally can't taste any sweetness at all. So to obtain syrup, you must boil it down to about one-fortieth of its original amount. That translates to about forty gallons of sap to make one gallon of maple syrup. It sounds daunting, but your buckets or cans fill rapidly, and the water boils away rapidly, especially if you start the syrup outdoors on a windy day.

All you need do is drill a hole with a half-inch drill, about 2 inches into a maple tree, 3 to 6 feet above ground, aimed slightly upward into the tree. When you hit the layer where the sap is, the tree will immediately begin to drip. So go slowly and stop when you hit the sap layer.

Then you insert a spile, an inexpensive, graduated metal spout with a hook on top to hold a bucket, to channel the sap out of the tree and into your container. You can also use half-inch plastic tubing, which can lead to a container sitting on the ground, a fat plastic straw, or a small metal pipe. For the truly intrepid, a half-inch hollow tube can be made from an elderberry stem with the center pulp bored out. A very large, very old tree may sustain as many as four or even more taps, on different sides and at slightly different heights. The size of the tree should be your guide. (We have one wonderful old maple that measures 16 feet around, and I put four taps into it most years.) Open wounds and sawed-off branches will yield sap, so a container can be placed to catch any drips. You can find spiles of various designs on the Internet.

{RECIPES}

Strain or filter the collected sap into a pan with a large open surface, such as a speckleware canning pot. I used to use a flat baking pan but lost a lot of syrup from sloshing. We do the first boiling outdoors, where the fire smells sweet and the wind drives off the water vapor more quickly, but you can do this in your kitchen too.

Then you simply boil the sap down, adding more as your sap containers fill. You don't stir it, but you can skim off the dirty foam as it forms. Keep the pan simmering. Obviously, the sap is getting denser all the time. As it boils down and begins to form a blanket of tiny bubbles, it is nearly done. If you are working outside, remove the pan from the fire, and finish it on a stove indoors where you can watch it carefully and adjust the heat to keep the syrup from scorching. You will know when it's ready by the profusion of tiny little bubbles all over, as well as from the color and taste of pure maple syrup. I always pour it through a fine sieve at the end, just in case any bark or soot has fallen in while it cooked.

MAPLE SUGAR CANDY

(This is not my favorite way to use maple syrup. The blocks it makes are hard and dense, albeit pure, and don't melt in the mouth the way the second recipe for Maple Fondant does. If you want to make pure maple sugar, though, follow these directions carefully.)

I recently discovered an easier way to test candy than the cold-water method, my own "cold plate" method. Place three or four little saucers in the freezer before you start your candy. Instead of having to fish around in ice water for the ball of candy, drop a few drops onto one of the cold plates fresh out of the freezer, then see if it forms a soft ball, or a hard thread, or whatever.

To turn maple syrup into sugar, start with 2 to 3 cups cooled, strained syrup. The amount doesn't particularly matter, as you don't add anything else. Heat it with a candy thermometer in an open pan slowly, without stirring, until it reaches hard-thread consistency, 233°F. Check by both methods, candy thermometer (which may vary with altitude) and the cold-water test. (Test by dropping a few drops into a cup of cold water, then reaching in with a fork and tugging at the syrup. Does it pull out into a thread? If not, it isn't ready.) When it makes a stiff thread and has reached 233°F, take it off the heat and leave it alone with the thermometer still in it until it has cooled to 110°F. At that point, add a little vanilla, about 1 teaspoon, and beat it until it turns a pale color and is stiff enough to hold a shape. I use a handheld electric beater, but you can use a wooden spoon. Pour or scrape it into a buttered square pan, or press the sugar into maple leaf molds sprayed lightly with vegetable spray, and put it into airtight containers. I like it with the vanilla, but if you are a purist, you can leave that out.

SUBLIME MAPLE FONDANT

Follow this exactly for best results.

Stir together over low heat 1 cup maple syrup, 2 cups sugar, ¾ cup half-and-half, 2 tablespoons butter, and ¼ teaspoon cream of tartar. Cook until they come to a gentle boil. Put a candy thermometer into the pot, and cook this mixture slowly and without stirring or disturbing until it reaches the soft-ball stage, or 238°F. This may take about 45 minutes.

Test the mixture with the thermometer and with the cup of cold water. When it has reached about 238°F and when a drop of the syrup makes a nice flat, soft ball on the bottom of a chilled saucer, slide it off the heat, leave the thermometer in it, and let it cool undisturbed to 110°F. This may take 1 hour or so. Add a little vanilla, and beat until it turns creamy—or pull it with buttered hands into silvery taffy.

Cut or shape this into individual candies, and in a short time, it will transform itself into smooth, creamy fondant, arguably the best melt-in-your-mouth candy in the world.

MAPLE NUT MERINGUE GOODIES

(Makes one dozen delightful light, chewy confections)
Heat oven to 275°F or 280°F. Beat 2 egg whites with a pinch of salt and a pinch of cream of tartar until stiff. Gradually fold in ⅓ cup maple syrup, stir in ⅛ to ⅓ cup chopped wild nut meats, and drop by spoonfuls onto a vegetable oil–sprayed cookie sheet. Slow-bake until browned, possibly as long as 2 hours, then let cool in the oven. Store in an airtight container or eat at once.

Maple Custard

Preheat oven to 350°F. Beat or blend together 4 eggs, about ¾ cup maple syrup, 1 teaspoon vanilla, a few grains salt, and 2 cups of either milk or half-and-half, or even heavy cream. (I use some combination of the above.) Pour into a soufflé dish, and bake in a larger pan of hot water until the middle is set. Note: In custard, the more yolks, the more tender and creamy the custard will be, and the more whites, the firmer. Of course, the more yolks, the richer in calories and cholesterol. So, using the basic ingredients here, try omitting the whites, which will give you a creamier custard; doubling the number of yolks, which will give you a richer custard; cutting down to 2 yolks and using 4 whites, to reduce calories. Any way you make it, it's a delicious dessert or a gift that will tempt an invalid to eat.

AVOCADOS (AKA ALLIGATOR PEARS)

A native of the West Indies, the avocado (*Persea americana*) is a member of the Laurel family. The name is from an Aztec word, *ahuacatl*. The Latin name, intended to convey exoticism, suggests wrongly that the fruit is an "American Persian." The folk name, alligator pear, comes about because of the scaliness of the rind, though it might possibly indicate a propinquity between the localities of fruit and animal.

In the continental United States, there are technically no wild avocados; yet Floridians tell me that some trees have escaped from cultivation to grow wild wherever it is warm enough. Some varieties grow in California and Hawaii, and others in Florida, but frosts farther north regularly kill them.

Description, Habitat, and Season
Though we nearly always treat it as a vegetable, the avocado is in fact a fruit. The tree upon which it grows is fairly small, about the size of an apple tree, or no taller than about 20 feet. The leaves are large and oblong, with prominent veins, and the fruit pulp is about the size and shape of a pear, but dark green with a leathery rind. From the outside, it looks the same green or ripe. When it's ready to eat, it falls to the ground. But when you buy one in the supermarket, it is ripe when it loses its rock hardness and yields just a little to the touch. Then the mellow nutty fruit will be creamy, mild, and yellow or yellow green, surrounding a large round seed. All it needs is salt and pepper and a drop or two of lemon juice for a wonderful snack, for lunch, or tossed in a salad. In some parts of South America, avocados are treated as fruit: That is, they are sugared and served with whipped cream or ice cream or in a mélange with other fruits.

Once when I was in Florida in November to swim with dolphins, the motel where I stayed backed up to what seemed to be a wild avocado grove in full ripeness. When I asked the motel owner about whose it was, and whether I might poach, he hitched up his tattered Bermudas and shrugged. It was like being in King Croesus's garden to be able to go across the little sandy path and pick up a ripe avocado off the ground whenever I wanted. I was told that animals eat them in the wild, but this was right along Highway 1, and there were few wild animals about.

{RECIPES}

GUACAMOLE

Cut the flesh out of 2 avocados. Sprinkle with the strained juice of 1 lemon. Add a light sprinkle of salt and some chili powder (start with 1 teaspoon, and add until you get the taste right), and add 2 to 4 crushed cloves of garlic. Add black or red pepper if you want. Mix well with a fork, and serve with corn tortillas, cut into quarters and fried quickly in hot vegetable oil. This makes a wonderful light lunch. I've recently learned that if you leave the avocado pit in the bowl of guacamole, the flesh won't brown. Of course, lemon juice helps with that also.

CREAM OF AVOCADO SOUP

(Makes over 1 quart)

Cut 1 avocado's meat into little cubes, sprinkle with lemon juice, and set aside. Mash 2 or 3 ripe avocados (seeded and peeled) with 1 tablespoon Worcestershire sauce, a little lemon juice, and a little minced fresh onion (and a small crushed garlic clove if you like) in a bowl. Add to it 2 cups good chicken broth, and mix well. If you want it perfectly smooth, blend it or force it through a ricer at this point, but I don't. Transfer to a saucepan, heat it slowly to not quite boiling, and add 1 cup whipping cream. Mix well, cover, and bring to a near-boil again. Taste, correct seasoning, and serve immediately, with the cubes on top for garnish.

PASSION FRUIT

Passion fruit (*Passiflora edulis*) is a South American native, with edible subspecies worldwide in tropical countries. If you live in Florida, California, or Hawaii, you can find wild passion fruit to eat. Elsewhere, probably not. It's a wild vine, with three leaves, exotic flowers, and big smooth green fruits the shape of eggs. We have a gorgeous passion fruit in Virginia, with an exquisite purple flower and a promising egg-sized green fruit, which never ripens no matter how long you wait. I eat ripe passion fruit in Mexico in the winter, where it's called *granada* for its delicate fragrance and sweet flavor. The Virginia fruit, which grows wild in meadows, along paths, and in sunny late-summer hedgerows, smells like the Mexican one, but alas, never ripens. I've transplanted seeds to sunny spots in my garden, where it goes limp and dies.

The outside of the passion fruit is hard and leathery and eggshell-like; inside are the sweet seeds and pulp. It's a wonderful wild food if it grows where you live and will ripen. Its flavor is perfumy and delicate, and it may have the most wonderful flower in the world: complicated and many-leveled, in white, purple, pink, or yellow. It is named for Christ's passion, as the top stigmas look vaguely like a cross.

PRICKLY PEAR

Throughout not only the desert regions of this country, but also dry fields nearly everywhere, can be found four or five similar species of the native American genus *Opuntia*. Prickly pear, also called Indian fig and tuna, is easily recognized by its flat, round pads (stems, really) called nopales. It is well protected by dangerous spines and by its pear-shaped spiny fruits, which develop from the yellow flowers and are green at first, then either yellow, dark red, or reddish purple.

Both pads and fruit are not only edible but delicious, though both must be gathered carefully with leather gloves or by burning or cutting off the spines before picking. The fruit may ripen at any time throughout the summer and fall, and the pads are good to eat whenever you find them. Their taste is rather green beanish.

{RECIPES}

PRICKLY PEAR PADS (NOPALES)

Handle carefully! Rid the pads of spines by cutting them off, burning them off, or knocking them off. Then rinse the pads, slice into string bean–size lengths, and use as you would a string bean, cooking them about the same length of time. They may be chilled and added to salads. I had a wonderful dish in Mexico once that I have replicated satisfactorily: Cubes of lean pork are stir-fried in olive oil with sliced onion, minced garlic, chili powder, and sliced prickly pear pads. When done, season to taste and serve on rice. The pads add an okra-like mucilaginous quality that is smooth and pleasant.

PRICKLY PEAR JAM

The fruit of prickly pear can be eaten as is, like any other fresh fruit, but it also makes a lovely red jam. It is not very tart, so it needs lemon juice. After removing the spines of ripe fruit, chop or pulverize the fruit, add 2 tablespoons lemon juice to 1 cup fruit, and add an equal amount of sugar. Cook slowly until thickened, stirring frequently.

WATERMELON RIND

Citrullus vulgaris ("citrus-like gourd") is the Latin name for watermelons. They do not grow wild in America (though many other members of the family, such as crookneck squash and pumpkin, do), so if I were to describe where to forage them, I'd be advocating stealing. Instead, I'm advocating a different kind of foraging, the kind that can be done at picnics and church suppers. All you have to do is to surreptitiously (or obviously) gather up the leftover rinds of the watermelon after folks are finished devouring its sweet pink flesh. Any variety will do. Put them in a plastic bag and take them home. The only other way to make watermelon

rind pickles is to actually go out and buy a watermelon and eat it yourself, saving the rind. These pickles are definitely the best in the world, and in my growing-up years, there were few midday dinners that didn't have watermelon rind pickles to accompany whatever else there was: chicken, beef, lamb, venison. Jars of these more-or-less free pickles make great presents, and everyone loves them!

{RECIPES}

WATERMELON RIND PICKLES

This process requires five days.

Day 1: Take the rind of 1 large watermelon, wash it in several waters, and trim off the hard green rind and the soft, crisp red fruit, keeping only the white. Cut the rind into 1 inch squares (smaller is also fine). Put the cubes in a large bowl or a small plastic enamel dishpan, add 1 cup pickling lime (available in the canning section of grocery stores), fill it to the top of the rind with water, and stir it well. Weigh it down to keep the rind submerged, and keep in it the lime for 24 hours.

Because the lime settles more or less at once, you must stir it up and turn the pieces every time you think of it, for a day, to redistribute the lime in the water and move the rind around.

Day 2: After a day, feel a piece of the rind for crispness or firmness. If it isn't crisp yet, let it sit longer, stirring very often to distribute the lime. When it's crisp, wash the rind in several waters until the water is clear, to wash away the excess lime.

Make a syrup of 5 pounds sugar, 3 pints cider vinegar, and a handful of each of the following whole spices: cloves, ginger root, allspice, celery seed, cracked nutmeg or mace, and cinnamon sticks. Boil the mixture and stir until the sugar is dissolved. Pour the fruit into the boiling syrup, cut the heat off, and let it stand (covered) for 24 more hours.

Day 3: Bring the pickles in the syrup to a boil. At once, give them a stir, cut the heat off, and let them sit for another day.

Day 4: Repeat Day 3.

Day 5: Bring the pickles in syrup to a boil, and boil them gently for 1 hour. Pick out the rind squares, and pack them in sterilized jars. Strain the syrup, and fill each jar of pickles to the top. Wipe the edges and screw down the clean lids carefully. No sealing is necessary if the jars and lids are clean and the pickles are used within the year. My grandmother's maid, Lizzie, called these Seven-Day Pickles, and stretched the process out by adding two more boils. But five days is plenty.

Finally, this method will also work beautifully with any number of vegetables and fruits. I've used zucchini, overlarge cucumbers, yellow squash, and other melon rinds through the years. Once there was a frost warning when we still had unripe tomatoes on the vines, so I made green tomato pickles using this method. I've never failed to get good pickles.

ALOE VERA

Aloe Vera is a wild succulent plant of the tropics, but many American households grow it, as a first aid treatment for burns and stings. It grows indoors or out—in your garden in summer and on your sunniest windowsill in winter. Though it doesn't taste good, it's useful for many minor injuries and is certainly qualified to be called an edible wild plant. I've recently polled friends about its uses and can recommend it as a useful and harmless aid (externally) for burns, stings, bruises, sunburns, infected bites, herpes sores (genital and oral), and even warts! I couldn't find any friends who use it internally, but grocery stores sell quarts of the juice, so I have to assume someone is drinking it. A bit of research on the Internet claims it is curative for an astonishing number of internal illnesses, from alleviating constipation to shortening the time of colds to easing arthritis!

[8]
ANNUAL FORAGERS' CALENDAR

Human beings like clear boundaries. Nature is continuous, but we want divisions. Thus, this calendar—less calendar really than reminder so that you won't forget to go looking for something wild that you really intended to look for. Calendars of things that grow must necessarily be vague, for they are subject not only to specific latitudes but also to early or late frosts, much or little rain, mountainous or flat locales, hot or cold seasons, and other variables. An example is that this year, because of record late frosts that nipped them in the bud, we got no crab apples. And because our spring this year was very late as well as wetter than usual, the morels were later than usual. So this is a general and approximate reminder. The Shenandoah Valley of Virginia is my territory; yours may be different.

In the late winter, rest and dream, take a month off. As bears know, everyone needs to hibernate for a while.

Early spring, when the nights are still frozen, but the days bring thaws, begin checking maples for sap to gather and boil.

When the ground is thawed, and green things begin to appear, look for dandelion greens. Begin your search for fiddleheads. Collect sassafras root in the woods. Dig Jerusalem artichokes.

Soon after, when the ground is unlikely to frost again, a million spring greens appear. Begin to look for lamb's-quarters, watercress, poke, and sorrel now. Morels start growing, and fruit for at least a month, especially if the winter has saturated the ground. I've noticed recently that folks report finding morels in the Virginia mountains earlier—sometimes as early as March 1. I'd attribute that change to global warming.

Among the first things to bloom is elderberry, with its flat white bounty. On the ground, you will find violets to candy and their tender leaves to add to salads.

As the green plants leap into light, begin to look for wild asparagus, chicory, greens, and ramps. All these are a week to two weeks earlier than they used to be, or at least that seems to me to be true.

When there are no more morels, when the days begin to warm and feel like summer but the nights are still cold, in that between-spring-and-summer time, begin to look for wild strawberries. Rhubarb has sprung up in the woodland ditches by now. Lamb's-quarters ought to be prolific by now. Look for milkweed and nettles. Sorrel will continue to grow all summer. This is the prime of the watercress harvest. Look for spring coprinus mushrooms. Dig horseradish. This is the time of year that rewards foragers most richly.

As summer begins, if it rains, look for puffballs. June apples are ripening. Now, while they are still as small as Ping-Pong balls, pick walnuts for pickling. Lamb's-quarters are thriving. Keep an eye out for oyster mushrooms on tree trunks; look for purslane, upland cress, and various mustards. All the mustards are edible year-round but most tender in the late spring and early summer.

As the sun reaches its northernmost point, black raspberries begin. Gather June apples. Make mint jelly, and keep some mint to dry for tea. Pick catnip for drying. Add nasturtiums and their leaves to salads.

In midsummer, pickle the brined walnuts. Wineberries fruit in the mid-Atlantic states beginning around July 1, raspberries elsewhere. Begin looking in wet woods for chanterelles and sulfur shelf mushrooms. Some crab apples ripen. At a Fourth of July party, collect up watermelon rinds at a picnic and make pickles. Two or three weeks after, wineberries and raspberries (black and red) and, a week or so later, blackberries begin to be ripe. Candy some roses.

In late summer, look for blueberries and huckleberries. Land cress is wonderful from now into cold weather. Figs ripen. After rain, look for puffballs and field mushrooms. In the woods, search for boletes. Coprini are likely to be around again. Oyster mushrooms often fruit again about now, and nasturtiums continue to bloom cheerfully. Elderberries ripen. Wild rice is ready to harvest. This is the time to make jellies and pickles. Some apples ripen now.

In very late summer, plums and cherries ripen. From now on, field mushrooms and puffballs will fruit overnight in warm, wet weather. Land cress is bursting.

As summer turns to fall, look for wild cherries and crisp apples. Pears begin to ripen about now. As the days grow longer, grapes ripen. So do figs, and you can still harvest rhubarb. The corn is also ready to harvest.

When the weather begins to turn chilly at night, cornel cherries and pecans fall. Ginseng season begins, continuing to frost. (The legal window for gathering ginseng is generally from September 1 to December 1, although states have different laws governing the digging of ginseng. Most states require seeds to be planted on the sites dug, and most states forbid digging any plant with fewer than three prongs. States differ on whether licenses are required and whether harvest is allowed on state lands. Check your own state laws before digging.) After frost, dig the first Jerusalem artichokes. This is the time for boletes.

In the late fall, after some frosty nights, gather black walnuts, hickories, and beechnuts. Pick wild mustard, steam it, and freeze it for winter. Gather fall apples and have a cider party. Look for rose hips. Collect abandoned ears of corn. Quinces ripen and can be made into marmalade.

In early winter, begin to look for cranberries. Take a trip to Florida and gather some coconuts and avocados. You can still gather wild mustard. Now is the time to draw a chair close to the fire and pick nuts.

And in December, give as gifts marmalade or apple butter, dried mint, flavored vinegars, maple syrup, catnip mice, a ginseng root in a bottle of whiskey, some pickled watermelon rind, or fruit jelly redolent of summer. Buy yourself a new pair of comfy walking shoes for Christmas!

[9]
THE LAST WORD

An interest in wild foods is a healthy hobby, and it's a hobby that gets us out and going, that makes us move. And of course, there's some brain exercise going on as we attempt to distinguish between one hickory and another, or to remember a location, or keep separate the identifications of many plants. Knowing the outside world around us reestablishes the links we have broken with nature and the seasons. I take seriously the idea of hunting and eating wild foods. It's what we all started out doing, eons ago. Cultivating an interest in gathering and cooking at the very least means more respect for the world that sustains us, as well as healthier diets. I keep books in my car trunk to identify trees and plants.

There may be a real health benefit in using wild foods in our diets. Despite miraculous medical advances, the evidence is that we are not very well nourished in our modern civilizations. We know some of the reasons, of course: smoking, too much fat, too little exercise. But optimum health continues to evade most of us.

Everything we eat that is grown commercially is grown in depleted soils or soils artificially and often only periodically fertilized. Of course, there are some nutrients in such foods, but I believe a food can only be as good as the soil in which it is grown. Only wild foods found in pastures, woodlands, on the edges of streams and rivers, in wild places, are grown in real, mineral-rich soil that has not been tampered with. Perhaps the tiny amounts of trace minerals in such foods can make a real difference in our health. In fact, a physician friend of mine has suggested that perhaps it is the tiny traces of minerals we never ordinarily ingest (maybe even things like arsenic, or tin, or iridium—who knows?) that make wild ginseng the healer it is reputed to be.

Sharing wild foods is one of life's joys. I love serving morels to guests and listening to them rave, or having for a dinner party a salad I have gathered of wild greens, dark and tasty, perhaps dotted with violet blossoms. Wild foods make wonderful presents and great hostess gifts. It means a lot to have someone drop off a bunch of fresh asparagus, bound in cheery ribbon, in May, or bring by a jar of homemade apple butter as thanks for having been included in a party. A basket of several kinds of jelly makes a lovely birthday gift. You'll find your own ways to share your bounty.

One wonderful old mountain man whom I interviewed several years ago on the subject of folk medicine said to me, "If it works, it's good. If it don't, it's worthless. Sometimes you can't tell if it's the medicine or the person's own body that done the healing. But that's true of them fancy medicines and doctors and hospitals, now ain't it?"

Either nature heals the body, or the body heals itself. Foraging is a wonderful inexpensive path to wellness.

I wish for all of you who have this book in hand happy foraging, delicious cooking, and vibrant good health!

Appendix: Basic Recipes

ABOUT JELLIES AND TEAS

A few definitions: *Jelly* refers to the consistency of the product we call jelly, which is stiffish and clear or semitransparent. The word comes from the Middle English *gelee*, meaning "frost," which in turn derives from the Latin *gelare*, "to freeze." Jellies made of fruit and sugar have no gelatin in them. Gelatin, which is made by boiling animal skin, ligaments, and bones (formerly it was known as calf's foot jelly), yields foods of the same consistency as jellies, as well as explosives and (still!) photographic plates. Fruit sugar jellies are jelled with a vegetable product called pectin, made from green grapes and apples, whereas jelled desserts and salads are made from gelatin. Tea is an herb soaked in boiling water. An infusion means tea, and a decoction is a reduction—an herb boiled in water until some, or even most, of the water has evaporated.

BEEF BROTH

(This is a substitute for canned consommé or beef broth or bouillon.
It's cheaper, very good, and you can control the salt.)
Brown in a 350°F oven 2 pounds marrow bones, those rings of bone with the soft interiors sometimes labeled "soup bones." Ask your butcher for some if none are on display. When they begin to sizzle, add a couple of onions, stir them into the fat that the meat has already rendered, return to the oven, and keep browning until the bones are dark. Remove from the oven, place in a large kettle, add ½ teaspoon peppercorns, 6 cloves, 2 bay leaves, 2 carrots, 2 stalks celery (and some leaves), a cup of cider vinegar, some parsley and thyme if you wish, and 1 gallon water. No salt. Bring this to a boil, reduce the heat, and cook slowly for 2 to 3 hours, or until it's reduced by about half. Be sure to dig out all the marrow and dump it into the soup. Strain it, cool it, and refrigerate it. When the fat on top is solid, remove it all. Then freeze the broth in small portions for easy future use. Add salt when you thaw and use it.

Chicken Broth

Do everything the same way, only use leftover chicken parts, such as necks, backs, gizzards, and hearts, and 1 tablespoon oil.

Vegetable Broth

If you are a vegetarian, melt a little butter (or use oil), and stir into it several coarsely chopped stalks celery, 6 cloves, 2 bay leaves, 1 sprig thyme, 2 crushed garlic cloves, 1 turnip (optional), 1 chopped pepper (optional), and 1 big chopped onion. Bake the vegetables uncovered in the oven at 350°F for 30 minutes. Boil 6 cups water, add the veggies, and keep boiling. Reduce it by boiling to about 1 quart, and that, strained, is your broth.

Mayonnaise

In a food processor or blender, put the following: 2 tablespoons fresh lemon juice or 2 tablespoons cider vinegar, 1 egg, 1 teaspoon salt, 1 clove garlic, peeled (can be omitted), 1 teaspoon Dijon mustard. Measure 1 cup peanut, corn, or olive oil. Turn the food processor on high. After 15 seconds, slowly pour in the cup of oil, over the course of 1 minute. The final product will look like store-bought mayonnaise but taste better. Keep it in the refrigerator, and use it within two weeks. Mayonnaise is better made on a sunny clear day than on a rainy day, when it sometimes fails to homogenize.

Vinaigrette Salad Dressing

(Makes 1 cup or so)

Mix ½ cup olive oil with ¼ cup good vinegar (cider, wine, flavored, balsamic, etc.), 2 tablespoons fresh lemon juice, ½ teaspoon salt, ½ teaspoon coarse ground pepper, and ½ teaspoon sugar. (I always add 1 or 2 cloves crushed garlic, because I love garlic, but you can omit it.) That's what gives the palate joy: zing, salt, piquancy. Shake it up well. That's the basic mix, and it is just fine by itself. I make it in a pint jar with a tight-fitting screw-on lid. It keeps in the fridge for as long as a month. I use sparing amounts on salads and cold vegetables.

For variety, add anything else you fancy, such as 1 teaspoon dry or prepared mustard; honey or more sugar; some herbs or capers, or both; a dash of Worcestershire sauce, soy sauce, paprika, or tomato paste; 1 teaspoon poppy seeds; 1 inch to 2 inches anchovy paste; or any combination of the above.

SOUFFLÉ

Soufflés are elegant, and very versatile. I made my first for some boy when I was fifteen. It was a colossal failure. To make it worse, the boy commented that his mother had told him never to marry a girl who couldn't make a soufflé. I was not planning to marry anyone at that time, but the blow fell hard.

Always break eggs one at a time into a container like a teacup. That way, if a tiny piece of the shell falls in, you can remove it fairly easily. You can also separate eggs more easily if you break them one by one in a cup. If one yolk breaks, that egg can be discarded without ruining the whites for an entire soufflé.

In the years since, I have read the pros and cons of greasing the pan, of low versus high versus high-then-low temperatures for baking, and many other practical fine points of the art of soufflé making.

Nobody has to fail at matrimony because of a sunken soufflé. Here are the rules that work, at least for me.

Use a standard porcelain 8-cup soufflé dish with straight sides. Butter both sides and bottom, and then dust lightly with flour, or sugar if it's a dessert soufflé. Confectioners' sugar works better than granulated.

Use 5 egg yolks and 6 egg whites: That extra white will make a difference. They should be at room temperature. Separate them carefully; you know that if you get even the tiniest bit of yolk in the whites, they won't whip up, so be very careful. The yolks must be well beaten, and the whites beaten not too stiff: just swoopy and glossy, but never dry.

Preheat your oven. Set it halfway between 325°F and 350°F. Be sure it is thoroughly heated before the soufflé goes in.

Begin with a hot heavy cream sauce: 3 tablespoons butter and 3 tablespoons flour, stirred until smooth over low heat. Add 1 cup milk or half-and-half (or other liquid if it seems appropriate, like chicken broth for a mushroom soufflé); stir it continuously until it is thick and smooth.

To finish the cream sauce, pour a small amount into the yolks and beat furiously. Pour the yolks into the hot cream sauce and beat until thickened and smooth. A whisk is good for this. Set aside to cool.

Whatever else you add should not exceed I cup. Grated cheese melted then cooled, grated semisweet chocolate or chocolate chips, chopped asparagus tips, chopped ham or other meat, coarsely ground peanuts, I cup seasoned chopped broccoli, I cup prepared morels. Remember: It can't be too heavy for the egg whites to hold up.

The last step is folding in the egg whites. First, put a big spoonful of them on top of the cooled cream sauce with the other ingredients already in it. Fold it in to lighten the sauce. Then, pour the whole thing over the rest of the whites, and gently fold everything together. Bake in the preheated oven for 40 minutes to I hour, until the center is firm.

BY HAND

The best way to separate eggs, really and truly, is in your hand. Get out a little bowl for the yolks and a bigger one for the whites. Crack the egg on a heavy bowl or the counter rim, hold it over the top of the big bowl, and break it gingerly into your palm. Spread your fingers just enough to let the white run through until only the yolk remains. Gently dump the yolk into the small bowl.

PIZZA

First, preheat the oven to 450°F. Assemble your food processor, I envelope rapid-rise dry yeast, ½ teaspoon sugar, ½ teaspoon salt, and about 3 cups unbleached all-purpose flour or bread flour. (You can substitute about ½ cup semolina flour or ¾ cup whole wheat flour. You can put up to ¾ cup whole wheat flour in the dough, but more than that destroys the glutinous quality that bread and semolina flour give and makes the crust brittle, heavy, and hard instead of flexible and chewy.) Mix yeast, sugar, salt, and I cup of the flour in the processor. With the machine running, add I cup hot (120–130°F) water, and mix. Stop the machine, add another cup of the flour, and run it again. Then, begin adding flour a little at a time with the machine running, until the dough balls up into a single lump. After that, run the processor for 2 whole minutes, adding I teaspoon flour each time the dough ball starts to stick to the sides. This replaces kneading.

I bought my pizza tile at a carpet store. It's a 14 × 14-inch bathroom tile that had been discontinued, and it cost a dollar. I reasoned that any glazed tile wouldn't crack at a mere 500°F, and I was right. So I preheat it in the oven. I use a pizza peel, a thin wooden paddle with a longish handle on which you make the pizza (flour it first), then gently shuffle the pizza off onto the hot tile when you're ready to cook it.

Turn the dough into a warm, dry bowl that's been oiled with a few drops of olive oil, cover with a cloth, and let rise 10 minutes or so. Punch the dough down and roll it again into a ball.

Sprinkle the counter with 1 tablespoon flour or cornmeal, and pat the ball out into a flat circle. Sprinkle a little flour over it, and roll dough out from the center with a rolling pin or a straight-sided wine bottle. When it gets to about 14 inches across, move it to a baking sheet that you've sprayed ahead of time with vegetable spray or to a floured wooden pizza peel. (Some folks sprinkle the pizza pan or tile with cornmeal, but I don't.) Straighten it up if it has gotten lopsided. Now, with the heel of your hand, nudge the dough from the middle out toward the edges to form the "lip" of the pizza. Bake it 3 minutes in the center of the oven before putting the toppings on. This keeps it crisp.

Now you're ready to decorate and bake it. Top the pizza lightly. Bake until the cheese melts and the edges turn brown. Watch it carefully so that it doesn't burn. I find scissors cut hot pizza more easily than a pizza roller-cutter.

QUICHE

For a basic quiche process, you need a raw pie shell (see below), about 1 cup cheese on the bottom to keep that lower crust from getting soggy, other ingredients layered on next, a custard of 1 egg for every ½ cup milk or half-and-half poured in next, and cheese on top. Skim milk can be used, with 1 tablespoon flour for thickening, but the result is not as creamy. Evaporated skim milk used without dilution is a good compromise. Bake 1 hour or so in the middle of a medium-heat oven (350–375°F). Quiches can be made with wild greens gently steamed, crisp bacon or fat-free ham, milkweed blooms, and many other things. You are limited only by your imagination.

PIECRUST

The best method I know for making piecrust is in a food processor. This makes two crusts, for a two-crust pie or two one-crust pies. In the processor, put 3 cups all-purpose flour and ½ teaspoon salt, and whiz it around to mix the salt in. With the machine running, add 1 cup cold shortening (like Crisco) or, best of all, lard (not butter or oil or margarine) in chunks. (By the way, do this by putting 1 cup ice water in a 2-cup measure, then adding shortening until the water rises to the 2-cup mark. Drain off the water. You will then have exactly 1 cup shortening. This is far easier than laboriously pushing cold shortening down into a cup and making sure there are no air holes or spaces.) When it is grainy and well mixed, beat together in a small bowl ½ cup ice water with 1 egg yolk, and add it with the processor running. At once, the crust will bunch up into a ball. Stop the processor, divide the dough in half, and roll out each half on a floured board with a floured roller or empty wine bottle with the label removed, turning it to keep it roughly round. Roll the circle out gently until it's 1 inch wider all around than your pie pan. Fold it lightly in half, then again in half, and gently lift the resulting triangle into the pie pan where you will then unfold it. Prick it all over with a fork, trim the edges, and press in fork tines, if you want, to make a pretty edge. Or you can mold the edges by pinching them up into a nice design. Fold the second one the same way before placing it on top of the filling.

This is the only piecrust you will ever need. Once you learn the process, you'll never again have to look it up. For some reason, this crust is foolproof. It's the only one I know that won't get soggy or tough, and I'm not deft at pastry.

Baking Mix

My years of scouting and camping taught me a lot, from swimming to square dancing, from camp songs to camp cooking. I remember that there was circulated one year a recipe for a baking mix to speed up cooking, especially useful for Girl Scouts (and others) on cookouts. The idea is to make it ahead of time, then use it as you need it.

Mix 8 cups flour, 3 cups nonfat dry milk, 5 tablespoons sugar, 5 tablespoons baking powder, 1 tablespoon salt, and 1 pound (2 cups) shortening or 1¾ cups vegetable oil. Blend it together well with 2 knives of any sort or a pastry blender until it's the consistency of cornmeal. Store it in the freezer. Now here are some things you can do with it:

Biscuits: 2 cups mix, with around ⅓ cup water to just dampen it enough to hold together. Knead only a few strokes, pat to ½ inch, and cut out biscuits. Bake at 400°F for 10 minutes. (For sweet Stick Biscuits, add enough water to make it sticky, then mold some of the batter around a green, safe branchlet, and cook it on all sides over a fire, remove the stick, then fill the hole where the stick was with homemade Wild Strawberry Jam or Quince Marmalade.)

Far easier and more efficient than a glass dipped in flour to cut round biscuits is square biscuits: Pat the dough gently into a ½-inch-high square, and slice across it quickly with a floured knife to make 2-inch strips, then slice across it the other direction to make 2-inch squares. Just as delicious, and saves time.

Indian Fry Bread: Fry those biscuits in ½ inch vegetable oil, turning once to fry the other side. Serve with homemade maple syrup (see pages 187–188).

Wild Onion Biscuits: 2 cups mix, ½ cup chopped wild onions, and about ⅓ cup water. Mix together, pat out, cut, and bake at 400°F for about 10 minutes.

Wild Berry Muffins: 2 cups mix, 1 egg beaten in ½ cup water, a little additional sugar if you like them sweet, 1 cup berries. Add 1 or 2 drops of vanilla, if you like. Mix lightly until just blended, and bake in greased muffin tins at 400°F for about 20 minutes.

Blueberry Pancakes: 2 cups mix, 1 egg, and about ¾ cup water, or enough to make batter the consistency you like. Mix, pour on a hot griddle greased with oil, butter, margarine, or bacon grease, and scatter blueberries thickly onto the batter. Turn once when the bottom side is brown.

Wild Fruit Pudding: 2 cups mix, 1 cup sugar, 2 eggs, ¼ cup water, and 2 cups fruit (canned, fresh, or frozen). Preheat oven to 375°F. Grease a baking pan or casserole. Pour the fruit on the bottom, and top with the other ingredients, mixed. Dot with butter (up to 1 stick) Bake for 35 to 40 minutes, until done.

Corn Bread: 2 cups mix, 1 cup cornmeal, 2 eggs, and about 1 cup water. Mix thoroughly, and bake in a greased skillet (bacon grease is best) or baking pan for about 45 minutes at 375°F.

Coffee Cake: 2 cups mix, ⅓ cup sugar, 1 egg, ½ cup water. Beat egg and water together, then quickly stir in mix plus sugar. Don't over-stir. Pour into buttered square baking pan, and add a topping before cooking for about 45 minutes at 350°F.

Here are some suggestions for toppings. Wild nut topping: 1 cup coarsely chopped nuts tossed with 1 cup brown sugar, ½ stick butter melted, and maybe a dusting of spice like cinnamon or nutmeg, allspice or ginger, or a combination. Crumb topping: 4 tablespoons butter, 6 tablespoons flour, 6 tablespoons sugar, then a little spice. Mix with fork until crumbly. Fruit topping: 1 or 2 cups fruit tossed with half as much sugar and melted butter.

Forager's Don't-Throw-Out-Those-Bananas Bread: 2 cups mix, ⅓ cup sugar, 1 egg, 1 or 2 bananas past prime, mashed, vanilla, and enough water to make a smooth batter. Beat thoroughly, and bake in a loaf pan about 1 hour at 375°F.

Wild Apple Beer Bread: 2 cups mix, 2 tablespoons sugar, 1 cup chopped apple or applesauce, and enough beer to make a medium batter. Bake in a loaf pan about 1 hour at 375°F.

Nut Sugar Cookies: 2 cups mix, 1 cup sugar, 2 small eggs or 1 large, ⅓ cup water, ½ cup wild nuts, and 1 teaspoon vanilla. Mix, drop by teaspoon onto a greased cookie sheet, and bake about 10 minutes at 375°F. Sprinkle with sugar (and cinnamon, if you like) or gelatin dessert right out of the package when they come out of the oven.

Huckleberry Cookies: 2 cups mix and 1 cup or more huckleberries, stirred together. Add the following, mixed: 1 egg, ½ stick butter or margarine, melted, ½ cup each white and brown sugar, 2 tablespoons water, 2 teaspoons vanilla. Drop by spoonful onto a greased baking sheet, and bake for 10 to 12 minutes, until brown, at 375°F.

Brownies: 1 cup mix, 1 cup light brown sugar, ½ cup cocoa, 1 cup chopped wild nuts, mixed. Add ¼ cup vegetable oil, 1 teaspoon vanilla, and 2 eggs, all beaten together. Stir briefly to mix, and bake at 350°F for 25 minutes.

Come on now—your turn! Fig nut bread? You can wing it with this basic helper.

CREAM SAUCE

Cream sauce can be made thin, medium, or thick. It can be light, medium, or very rich. Cream sauce involves butter or margarine, flour, and a liquid. The process is to melt the butter, stir in the flour for at least 1 minute to overcome a "floury" taste, and slowly stir in the liquid. Never stop stirring until the sauce is smooth and thickened. The list below shows you the options. Add salt and pepper to taste.

For thick sauce: 3 tablespoons fat, 3 tablespoons flour, 1 cup liquid.
For thin sauce: 1-2 tablespoons fat, 1-2 tablespoons flour, 1 cup liquid.
For fat-free sauce: 2 tablespoons flour stirred in the dry pan, 1 cup liquid.
For rich sauce: fat, flour, and cream.
For medium sauce: fat, flour, and whole milk or evaporated skim milk.
For light sauce: fat, flour, and skim milk or broth.
For rich but fat-free sauce: flour and evaporated skim milk.

KATIE'S MULLIGATAWNY

(Really just a fancy foreign-tasting vegetable soup)
The name of this soup means "pepper water." As far as I can tell from the many, many recipes for it, all of them have in common sourness, meat, heat (usually from cayenne), and curry powder. It uses greens, rice, apples, bay leaves, and other ingredients you can forage, which is why it ends this book. It also invites you to be creative: Invent your own soup and name it for yourself! This is really just a diving board recipe.

Heat 2 tablespoons vegetable oil and add 2 cups chopped onions, 6 chopped garlic cloves, I cup chopped celery, 2–4 tablespoons curry powder, and ½ teaspoon cayenne to start, then 3 or 4 whole cloves or a dash of ground cloves, I teaspoon powdered ginger, and 3 bay leaves. When this is all brown and fragrant, add about 2 cups diced cooked or raw chicken, and stir that around for a bit. Add I cup chopped apples and 2 cups chopped wild greens. Add I quart beef or poultry broth and ¼ cup lemon juice. Simmer for 15 to 20 minutes. Remove bay leaves (and cloves if you used them whole), blend to near-smoothness, correct seasoning (which means just taste the soup, add salt and pepper, or more curry, or more cayenne, or whatever), and return to pot with I can coconut milk (which gives it richness) and I quart plain yogurt. Reheat and serve without boiling. You can cook lentils in it or add rice or wild rice. The meat can also be leftover lamb or beef. As Julia Child would say, "Bon appétit!"

Bibliography

Agricultural Research Service of the United States Department of Agriculture. *Common Weeds of the United States*. New York: Dover, 1971.

Allaby, Michael, *The Concise Oxford Dictionary of Botany*. New York: Oxford University Press, 1992.

Allegro, John. *The Sacred Mushroom and the Cross*. New York: Doubleday, 1970.

Baikov, Apollonovich. *In the Wilds of Manchuria*. Harbin, China: private printing, 1934.

Buist, Robert. *The Family Kitchen Gardener*. New York: C. M. Saxton and Company, 1857.

Bumgarner, Marline Anne. *The Book of Whole Grains*. New York: St. Martin's Press, 1976.

Burries, E. E., and Lionel Casson. *Latin and Greek in Current Use*. New York: Prentice-Hall, Inc., 1939.

Burt, Alison. *Preserves & Pickles*. London: Octopus Books, Ltd., 1973.

Duke, James. *Field Guide to Medicinal Plants*. New York: Houghton Mifflin Co., n.d.

———, *The Green Pharmacy*. New York: St. Martin's Paperbacks, 1998.

Emboden, William. *Bizarre Plants*. New York: Macmillan, 1974.

Embury, Emma C. *American Wild Flowers in Their Native Haunts*. New York: D. Appleton & Co., 1845.

Farmer, Fannie Merritt. *The Boston Cooking School Cookbook*. Boston: Little, Brown, and Co., 1936.

Fernald, M. L. *Gray's Manual of Botany*, Eighth Edition. New York: American Book Company, 1950.

Foster, F. Gordon. *Ferns to Know and Grow*. New York: Hawthorn Books, 1971.

Fuller, Andrew S. *The Small Fruit Culturist*. New York: Orange Judd & Co., 1874.

Gibbons, Euell. *Stalking the Faraway Places*. New York: David McKay, 1973.

———. *Stalking the Healthful Herbs*. New York: David McKay, 1966.

———. *Stalking the Wild Asparagus*. New York: David McKay, 1962.

The Gourmet Cookbook, Vol. I. New York: Gourmet Distributing Corporation, 1950.

Gupton, Oscar, and Fred Swope. *Trees and Shrubs of Virginia*. Charlottesville: University Press of Virginia, 1981.

Hamerstrom, Frances. *Wild Food Cookbook*. Ames: Iowa State University Press, 1989.

Harding, A. R. *Ginseng and Other Medicinal Plants*. Columbus, OH: private printing, n.d.

Harris, Ben Charles. *Better Health with Culinary Herbs*. New York: Weathervane Books, 1971.

———. *Eat the Weeds*. Barre, MA: Barre Publishers, 1971.

Hatfield, Audrey Wynne. *How to Enjoy Your Weeds*. New York: Collier Books, 1971.

Hitchcock, Susan Tyler. *Gather Ye Wild Things*. Charlottesville: University Press of Virginia, 1980.

Kimmens, Andrew C. *Tales of the Ginseng*. New York: William Morrow and Company, 1975.

Kluger, Marilyn. *The Wild Flavor*. New York: Coward McCann & Geoghegan, Inc., 1970.

Kumin, Maxine. *Up Country*. New York: Harper & Row, 1972.

Leach, Peter, and Anne Mikkelsen. *Malfred Ferndock's Morel Cookbook*. Dennison, MN: Ferndock Publishing, 1986.

Levy, Juliette de Bairacli. *Common Herbs for Natural Health*. New York: Schocken Books, 1966.

Logden, Gene. *Small-Scale Grain Raising*. Emmaus, PA: Rodale Press, 1977.

Lord, William G. *Blue Ridge Parkway Guide*. Conshohocken, PA: Eastern Acorn Press, 1982.

Lyle, Katie Letcher. *The Foraging Gourmet*. New York: Lyons and Burford, 1997.

———. *The Wild Berry Book*. Minocqua, WI: North Word Press, 1994.

Mabey, Richard. *The New Age Herbalist*. New York: Collier, 1988.

Mann, Rink. *Backyard Sugarin'*. Taftsville, VT: The Countryman Press, 1976.

Martin, Alexander. *A Golden Guide to Weeds*. New York: Golden Press, 1972.

McIntosh, Charles. *Greenhouse*. London: Wm. S. Orr & Co., 1838.

McPhail, Mrs. C. C. *FFV Receipt Book*. Richmond, VA: West, Johnston & Co., 1894.

Miller, Orson K., Jr. *Mushrooms of North America*. New York: Dutton, n.d.

Morse, Sidney. *Household Discoveries*. Petersburg, NY: Success Company's Branch Offices, 1908.

Nagel, Werner O. *Cy Littlebee's Guide to Cooking Fish and Game*. Jefferson City: Missouri Department of Conservation, 1968.

Neal, Bill. *Gardeners' Latin*. Chapel Hill, NC: Algonquin Books of Chapel Hill, 1992.

Nearing, Helen, and Scott Nearing. *The Maple Sugar Book*. New York: Schocken Books, 1950.

Newman, John B. *The Illustrated Botany*. New York: J. K. Wellman, 1846.

O'Brien, Jim. *Herbal Cures for Common Ailments*. Boca Raton, FL: Globe Communications CORP, 1997.

Parsons, Frances Theodora. *How to Know the Ferns*. New York: Dover, 1961.

Perl, Lila. *The Delights of Apple Cookery*. New York: Bonanza Books, 1963.

Peterson, Lee Allen. *Edible Wild Plants*. Boston: Houghton Mifflin, 1977.

Pond, Barbara. *A Sampler of Wayside Herbs*. New York: Crown Publishers, 1974.

Rombauer, Irma, and Marion Becker. *The Joy of Cooking*. New York: Bobbs-Merrill, 1951.

Rorer, Sarah T. *Mrs. Rorer's Cook Book*. Philadelphia: Arnold and Company, 1895.

Schwabe, Calvin W. *Unmentionable Cuisine*. Charlottesville: University Press of Virginia, 1979.

Smith, Alexander H. *The Mushroom Hunter's Field Guide*, Revised and Enlarged. Ann Arbor: University of Michigan Press, 1966.

Smith, William J. "Morels." From *The Hollins Poets*, edited by Louis D. Rubin Jr. Charlottesville: University Press of Virginia, 1967.

Strong, A. B. *The American Flora*. New York: Green & Spencer, 1851.

Stuart, Malcolm, ed. *The Encyclopedia of Herbs and Herbalism*. New York: Crescent Books, 1979.

Taylor's Guide to Trees. Boston: Houghton Mifflin, 1988.

Thomas, William Sturgis. *Field Book of Common Mushrooms*. New York: G. P. Putnam's Sons, 1928.

Torrey, John. *Natural History of New York*. Albany: Carol and Cook, Printers to the Assembly, 1843.

Vegetable Substances Used for Food of Man. New York: Harper & Brothers, 1844.

Weiss, Gaea, and Shandor Weiss. *Growing and Using the Healing Herbs*. Emmaus, PA: Rodale Press, 1985.

Wilcox, Estelle W. *The New Dixie Cook-book*. Atlanta: Dixie Cook-book Publishing Co., L. A. Clarkson and Co., 1895.

Wilen, Joan, and Lydia Wilen. *Bottom Line's Healing Remedies*. Des Moines, IA: Bottom Line Books, 2006.

Williamson, Darcy. *How to Prepare Common Wild Foods*. McCall, ID: Darcy Williamson Publisher, 1978.

Index

About the Author

Katie Letcher Lyle is the author of more than twenty books and many articles. Her short fiction has appeared in a variety of magazines, including *Viva*, *Shenandoah*, and the *Virginia Quarterly Review*. A writer, teacher, folk singer, and speaker, she is also a mother of two and lives in Lexington, Virginia. For more information, please visit katieletcherlyle.com. Her blog is K-k-k-katie.